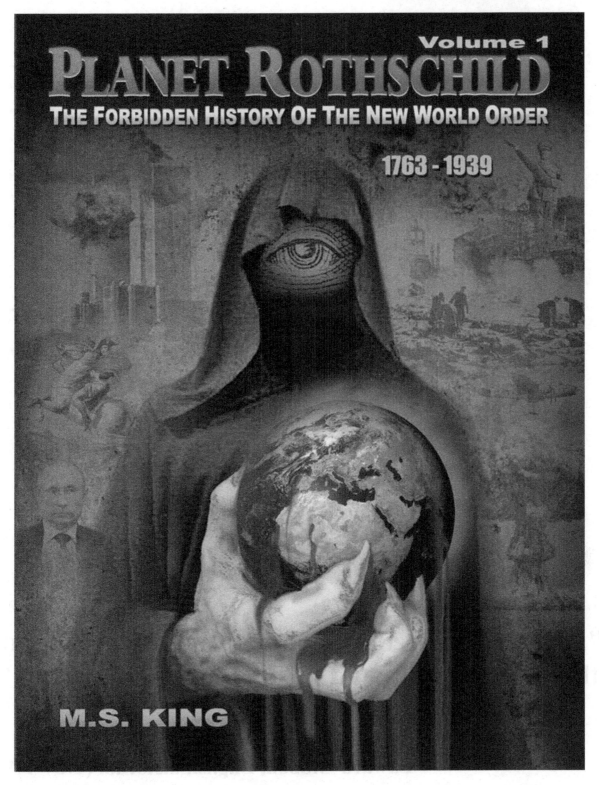

Volume 1

PLANET ROTHSCHILD

THE FORBIDDEN HISTORY OF THE NEW WORLD ORDER

1763 - 1939

M.S. KING

"History is indeed little more than the register of the crimes, follies and misfortunes of mankind."

Edward Gibbon, English historian (1737-1794)

From: *"The Decline and Fall of the Roman Empire"*

About the Author

M. S. King is a private investigative journalist and researcher based in the New York City area. A 1987 graduate of Rutgers University, King's subsequent 30 year career in Marketing & Advertising has equipped him with a unique perspective when it comes to understanding how "public opinion" is indeed scientifically manufactured.

Madison Ave marketing acumen combines with 'City Boy' instincts to make M.S. King one of the most tenacious detectors of "things that don't add up" in the world today. Says King of his admitted quirks, irreverent disdain for "conventional wisdom", and uncanny ability to ferret out and weave together important data points that others miss: *"Had Sherlock Holmes been an actual historical personage, I would have been his reincarnation."*

King is also the author of *The War Against Putin: What the Government-Media Complex Isn't Telling You About Russia.* King's other interests include: the animal kingdom, philosophy, chess, cooking, literature and history *(with emphasis on events of the late 19th through the 20th centuries).*

Be sure to bookmark and follow King's popular website: **TomatoBubble.com**

The Mind-Altering Internet Classics of Alternative History, Economics, Philosophy and Current Events

FOREWORD – PLANET ROTHSCHILD

By Jeff Rense

For over the past 30 years, I've worked in many key positions in broadcast journalism, as a TV news reporter, news director, anchorman, and, for the past 20 years, the producer and host of my own talk radio program. It has been quite a journey and all during that times I really never stop wanting to know the realities of news stories, large and small. Who?, What?, Where?, How?, When?... and, most importantly, Why? When applying those timeless questions towards the crucial subject of History, I have seldom been satisfied with the 'official explanations' for my inquiries and questions. The 'truth' is just not 'out there' nor is it accessible. There is too much sleight-of-hand and structural criminality.

That's one reason I am so gratified that one of the most remarkable, insightful, truthful historians of today, M S King, has tackled the murky, imponderable subject of revisionist history, *(realistic history that is)* with his stunning epic, **"Planet Rothschild"**. Though I am generally cautious in bestowing blessings upon the work of others, 'NWO Forbidden History' caught my attention for a number of reasons. Through his writings submitted to Rense.com, and also from his *'tour d' force'* guest appearance on my show, King's mastery of the subject, formidable writing talent, and unique ability to break down the complex into simple bites - were already known to me. I was pleased when I learned of his project to reformat his Internet Classic into a hard copy version.

As my regular listeners and readers are by now well aware, the world situation becomes gloomier by the day. It is only through a clear understanding of the past, that we can truly understand the present, and the dark future that is being planned for us. By distilling conspiratorial history into easy-to-understand, illustrated mini essays, **"Planet Rothschild"** serves as the perfect reference guide to help you navigate through the sea of lies which have been fed to us since childhood, and continue to be fed to us each day. **"Planet Rothschild"** makes an utterly unique and important contribution to the fields of economics and history - a contribution which we can all appreciate, and all understand.

TABLE OF CONTENTS

PLANET ROTHSCHILD: The Forbidden History of the New World Order (1763-2015)

VOLUME 1 of 2 / (1763 - 1820)

INTRODUCTION

From the days of the American Revolution, to the Jacobin French Revolution, to the coalition wars against Napoleon Bonaparte, to Andrew Jackson's war on the Central Bankers, to Karl Marx's war on sanity, to the American Civil War, to the Reds' shocking wave of 19th century assassinations, to the conspiratorial founding of the U.S. Federal Reserve, to the horrific First World War to enslave Germany, to the Rothschild-Communist subversion of Russia's Czar, to the horrible World War against Hitler and Japan, to the Cold War, to the JFK assassination, to the "women's movement" to the Global Warming Hoax, to the "fall of communism", to the 9/11 attacks & the "War On Terror", and finally, to the looming confrontation with Russia and China - the common thread of the **New World Order** crime gang links all of these events together.

At the heart of this self-perpetuating network sits the legendary **House of Rothschild** – the true owners of **'Planet Rothschild'**. Through an alliance with other billionaire families, universities, corporations, think tanks and media moguls worldwide; the cabal has, for 250 years, manipulated world events and political players like so many pawns on a global chessboard.

If it's true that "all the world is a stage", then the House of Rothschild and its international partners are the writers, directors and producers of the exciting play called, 'History". The politicians are the actors and the TV talking heads are the narrators. The audience is humanity itself – most of which, unfortunately, have no idea that a rigged show has been, and still is, playing out before their eyes. It is a global monster-scam of unimaginable dimensions in which humanity is the target.

Now, you can earn your 'Phd' in New World Order studies by reading this epic two-volume timeline thriller entitled PLANET ROTHSCHILD. It is a unique "blurb by blurb" chronological and photographical review that will enrich your depth of historical and economic knowledge like no other work of its kind. Travel through time in just under 600 easy-to-digest pages loaded with over 1200 images. This life-changing work is ideal as a permanent reference & study guide. You may not like what you find in its pages. Truth is not always easy to swallow. But you won't be able to refute any of it; and nor will you ever look at world events in the same light ever again.

1763 – 1820

Be sure to bookmark and follow King's popular website:
TomatoBubble.com

**The Mind-Altering Internet Classics of
Alternative History, Economics,
Philosophy and Current Events**

In 1743 a goldsmith named **Amschel Moses Bauer** opens a coin shop in Frankfurt, Germany. Above his door he hangs a sign depicting a Roman eagle on a red shield. The shop became known as the Red Shield *(German: Rothschild)*.

Amschel Bauer had a very intelligent son, **Meyer Amschel Bauer**. His father spent much of his time teaching him everything he could about the money lending business and the dynamics of finance. After his father's death in 1755, Mayer went to work at a bank in Hannover, owned by the **Oppenheimer Family**. Meyer's immense ability was quickly recognized and he quickly advanced within the firm. He was awarded a junior partnership.

His success allowed him to return to Frankfurt and purchase the business his father had established in 1743. The Red Shield was still displayed over the door. Recognizing the significance of the Red Shield *(his father had adopted it as his emblem from the Red Flag which was the emblem of the revolutionary minded Jews in Eastern Europe)*, Mayer Amschel Bauer changed the family name to **Rothschild**. It was at this point that the House of Rothschild came into being.

The Rothschild home in Frankfurt / Family Coat of Arms

Through his experience with the Oppenheimers, Rothschild learns that loaning money to governments is much more profitable than loaning to individuals. The loans are not only much bigger, but they are secured by the nation's taxes.

The Rothschild Banking Dynasty becomes the richest family business in world history. **(1)** Forbes Magazine refers to **Mayer Amschel Rothschild** as *"a founding father of international finance"*. **(2)** Rothschild's five sons will later branch out to head banking dynasties in Austria, Italy, France, and England, becoming lenders to the Kings of Europe, often financing both sides of the European wars that will so enrich them.

To this very day, the House of Rothschild and its allies remain the dominant force behind world finance, Globalism, "environmentalism", and 'liberalism'. The Jewish-Zionist Rothschild Family will also play a major role in establishing Israel in the 1900's *(Zionism)*. There can be no doubt; **Mayer Amschel Rothschild** was the original "Godfather" of the **New World Order**.

1 - 1934 Hollywood Film: The House of Rothschild / 1940 German Film: The Rothschilds

2- 2002: Warren Buffett, Governor Schwarzenegger marvel at one of Lord Jacob Rothschild's palatial European estates.

Just a few of the Rothschild Family palaces / England – Austria – France

1764
THE BRITISH CURRENCY ACTS FORBID THE ISSUE OF DEBT-FREE CURRENCY IN THE AMERICAN COLONIES

The Currency Act of 1764 is a British law that imposes a monetary policy on its American colonies. The Act extends the provisions of the 1751 Currency Act and forbids the colonies from issuing debt-free paper currency as legal tender. This creates financial difficulty for the colonies. Benjamin Franklin, the colonial representative, urges the British to reject the Currency Act.

The Currency Act creates tension between the colonies and Britain. When the First Continental Congress meets in 1774, it strongly objects to The Act as *"subversive of American rights."* It is a little known fact of the American Revolution, that the right of the colonists to issue debt-free currency, and spend it into circulation *(as opposed to a private Central Bank lending debt-currency into circulation),* became one of the main causes of the Revolution.

MARCH 5, 1773
THE "BOSTON MASSACRE" / TENSIONS MOUNT AS FIVE AMERICAN COLONISTS ARE KILLED BY BRITISH TROOPS

Exaggerated images of "the massacre" were used to inflame the colonists.

The increase in British troops stationed in Boston leads to tension with the locals. Fights erupt between soldiers and liberty-minded civilians. British troops are sent to Boston in 1768 to enforce the **Townshend Acts**, a series of laws passed by the British Parliament. The purpose of the Townshend Acts is to make colonial governors and judges independent of colonial control, to enforce compliance with trade regulations, and to tax the colonies without their approval.

When an angry crowd of colonists - most likely led by provocateurs of a secret society known as **The Sons of Liberty (3)** - confronts a group of soldiers with taunts and snowballs, the frightened British soldiers overreact. Shots are fired and five American colonists are killed. The embellished news of the Boston Massacre serves the purpose of spreading the revolutionary spirit throughout the colonies.

DECEMBER 16, 1773
THE BOSTON TEA PARTY / COLONISTS REBEL AGAINST BRITISH TAXES AND MONOPOLIES

The Boston Tea Party is an action by Boston colonists in the British colony of Massachusetts, against the British government and the monopolistic East India Company which controls all of the tea shipments coming into the colonies. After officials in Boston refuse to return three shiploads of taxed tea to Britain, a group of colonists, dressed as American Indians, climb aboard the ships and destroy the tea by throwing it into Boston Harbor.

The Tea Party is the culmination of a resistance movement against the Tea Act, which had been passed by Parliament in 1773. Colonists object to the Tea Act for a variety of reasons, especially because it violates their right to be taxed only by their elected representatives. The Boston Tea Party is a revolt against state sponsored monopolies *(British East India Company)* as much as it is about taxation.

It should be noted that, as was the case with the Boston Massacre, the Sons of Liberty orchestrated the event. Many members of this organization are true liberty-loving patriots *(Sam Adams, John Adams, Paul Revere)*, but others may have had ulterior, NWO-related motives for wanting to weaken the British Empire.

APRIL 19, 1775
LEXINGTON & CONCORD / AMERICAN REVOLUTION BEGINS WITH 'THE SHOT HEARD AROUND THE WORLD'

The Massachusetts Militia is storing guns and ammo in the town of Concord, MA. About 700 British troops are sent to seize the military supplies. Patriot leaders learn of the British plan and begin organizing.

The night before the scheduled British raid, **Paul Revere** takes off on his famous **"Midnight Ride"** to warn the local militiamen *(Minutemen)*. The first shots are fired as the sun begins to rise in Lexington, MA. The militias are outnumbered and fall back as the British advance upon Concord. At Concord, approximately 500 "rag tag" militiamen fight and defeat the King's troops.

The "red coats" retreat after a pitched battle in open territory. More militiamen arrive soon thereafter and inflict heavy damage upon the British, firing at them from behind trees as they march back towards Boston. The war for American independence is on! **The Battle of Lexington and Concord** will go down in history as "the shot heard around the world."

1- Paul Revere's 'Midnight Ride' – part real history / part mythology.

2- The Battle of Lexington & Concord

Jewish Professor **Adam Weishaupt**, forms the secret order of **The Illuminati** in Bavaria *(Germany)*. He is most likely a paid agent of Rothschild, also based in Germany. Weishaupt *(code name Spartacus)* recruits wealthy elites to his society. The Illuminati, or, Enlightened Ones, infiltrate Masonic lodges, which serve as cover for their activities.

They plot the overthrow of governments, the destruction of Christianity, and the future arrival of a world communal state **(New World Order).** Bavarian authorities disband the Illuminati in 1784. But the tactics and goals of the order are clearly evident in the French Revolution of 1789, and future Communist plots. To this day, May 1 *(May Day)* remains a sort of 'Holy Day' to Communists, Anarchists, and "Progressives".

The 'illuminated' all-seeing eye atop a pyramid is the symbol of Weishaupt's Illuminati NWO Mafia – and CBS network.

Written by Thomas Jefferson and signed by 56 patriots, the Declaration of Independence officially breaks the colonies away from Britain, and sets forth the ideal that governments exist to serve the people, not to control them.

America's founders believe that rights come from God, not government. Prosperity follows when the power of the state is limited. Small government, God-given rights, morality, stable currency, respect for private property, and minimal taxes represent the *opposite* of what the Illuminati and latter day 'Red" revolutionaries advocate.

These lines of the Declaration sum up what America, and the '4ᵗʰ of July', are *(or were)* all about:

"We hold these truths to be self-evident, that all men are created equal, that they are endowed by their Creator with certain unalienable Rights that among these are Life, Liberty and the pursuit of Happiness. --That to secure these rights, Governments are instituted among Men, deriving their just powers from the consent of the governed, --That whenever any Form of Government becomes destructive of these ends, it is the Right of the People to alter or to abolish it, and to institute new Government." **(4)**

Jefferson: Rights come from the Creator, not the State

1781-1784
JEWISH MONEY-LENDER IS THE MAIN FINANCIER FOR THE AMERICAN REVOLUTIONARY WAR

During the war, Washington relies *heavily* upon a well-connected Polish-born Jewish money-lender named **Haym Salomon** for financing. Salomon is a member of the Sons of Liberty – the same secret society that had instigated the Boston Massacre and organized the Boston Tea Party. From the period of 1781–84, records show Salomon's outside fundraising and personal lending help provide over $650,000 *(approximately $9 billion in 2015 dollars!)* in financing to Washington in the war effort against Britain. **(5)**

Certainly, Salomon's eagerness to finance the war must have had some profit motive *(though he died in 1785 before he could be repaid),* but it is also in line with Jewish Illuminati objectives to weaken the existing Empires of Europe while keeping them all in a "balance of power" situation in which one can be played off of another. Without Solomon's money and other fundraising efforts, the colonies will have no chance of winning the war.

Commemorative postage stamp, Chicago statue, and Los Angeles statue in honor of Haym Solomon.

1782
THE MYSTERIOUS GREAT SEAL OF THE UNITED STATES

Although the freedom-based, Creator-based ideology of American's Founding Fathers represents the polar opposite of the goals of the New World Order / Illuminati system, it does appear that elements of the early NWO Mafia may have assisted the Revolution for the ulterior purpose of weakening the British Empire and then taking control of the new American nation. George Washington certainly was no Globalist Red, but he was indeed a Freemason. It was through the secretive Masonic lodges that Illuminati plotters operated.

The most ominous sign that conspiratorial influence was at work during the earliest days of the United States can be found in the Great Seal of the United States, first established in 1782. The Seal depicts an eagle with the 6-pointed Jewish Star of David above it. The inscription reads: "E Pluribus Unum" – *(out of many, one).* Is that a reference to the uniting of the colonies, as we have been taught? Or is it really a reference to "the chosen people"?

In 1786, a reverse side was added to the Seal. The all-seeing illuminated eye above the pyramid with the Latin phrase: "Annuit Coeptis" *(He favors our undertaking)* and the Roman numeral 1776 *(Declaration of Independence? ...Or founding of Weishaupt's Illuminati?)*. But the 'dead giveaway' is the inscription at the bottom: "Novus OrdoSeclorum" *(New Order for the Ages)* – **New World Order!**

*NWO Symbols and the Star of David are right under our noses, and in our wallets. There is a legend that during the design of the Great Seal, Washington asked what compensation **Haym Salomon** wanted in return for his financial contributions to the Revolution. He replied that "he wanted nothing for himself but that he wanted something for his people".(6) As a result, the 13 stars representing the colonies were arranged in the shape of the Star of David.*

Degenerate modern celebrities like Kanye West, Jayzee, Rihanna, Beyonce & Lady Gaga have all sold their souls to the powerful geo-political force. Above, they make hand-symbols of the Illuminati pyramid and eye.

1783
WITH FRENCH HELP, AMERICA'S WAR FOR INDEPENDENCE ENDS IN VICTORY FOR THE COLONIES

The American Revolution had begun badly for the 13 colonies. The colonists themselves were divided as to their loyalties with as many as one third wishing to remain British subjects, at least at first. The best that General George Washington's 'Continental Army" can do against the better equipped British is to limit direct combat and harass the British instead.

As American "minutemen" and Washington's Army draw the 'redcoats' into a battle of attrition, Ben Franklin visits Paris to persuade the French to help the colonies. After Washington's surprise Christmas Day 1776 attack against the British & Hessian mercenaries, followed by victory at Saratoga in '77, the French are sold. French military assistance will play a huge role in reversing the course of the war. The British grant the colonies full independence in 1783.

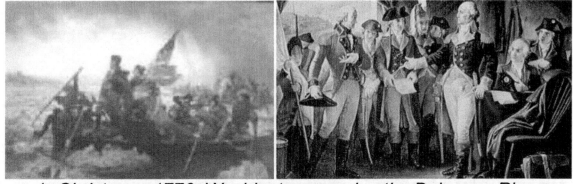

1- Christmas, 1776: Washington crossing the Delaware River

2- 1781: General Cornwallis surrenders to Washington

1781-1788
THE COLONIES ARE UNITED UNDER THE ARTICLES OF CONFEDERATION

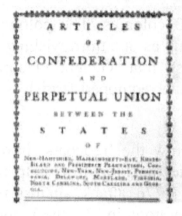

Drafted during the early years of the war, and ratified in 1781, the **"Articles of Confederation and Permanent Union"** establishes a very decentralized government for the colonies. Under the Articles, the colonies *(now referred to as "States")* are sovereign entities. For six years after the end of the war, the colonies are not truly a united nation, but rather a league of allied states living under mutually agreed upon rules.

America's founders are divided. Though all of them believe in freedom and limited government, one camp *(The Federalists)* prefers a stronger central government to help organize the nation's affairs. The other camp *(the anti-Federalists)* fear that *any* centralized American government might become corrupted and dangerous to the people's liberty.

JUNE 21, 1788
THE U.S. CONSTITUTION IS RATIFIED / THE "UNITED STATES IS CREATED"

Some of America's founders believe that the Articles of Confederation are too weak for the government and the new nation to survive. For this reason, the Continental Congress approves the US Constitution in 1787, in Philadelphia. Months of contentious debate follow before the States ratify the Constitution, the framework of the Federal Government.

The checks and balances built into the Constitution establish 3 branches of government, and limit the power of each. George Washington will be chosen as the first US President. **The document also limits the power of the masses of people**. The founders know that "democracy" results in mob rule, in which a "majority" of people can be manipulated into voting themselves the wealth of the productive people. Under the Constitution, taxes and state spending are minimal, and only gold and silver coins are recognized as currency. There is no authorization for income taxes, central banking, and social welfare schemes.

.

The Constitution and its original 10 amendments *(The Bill of Rights)* serve as a leash on government growth and power, and a guarantor of personal liberties, such as rights to free political speech, to own firearms, and to be secure from unlawful searches and seizures.

 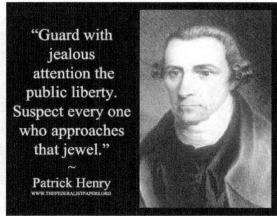

1- Similar to pre-Imperial Rome, the United States is founded as a republic (rule of law) -<u>NOT</u> a socialist "democracy" (rule of the manipulated mob).

2- Even with its strict limits on government power, patriots such as Patrick Henry of Virginia viewed the new Constitution as a potentially dangerous power-grab.

1790
JEFFERSON AND HAMILTON CLASH OVER CENTRAL BANK

The proposed **Bank of the United States** is to be a Central Bank with a 20-year charter. It is the brainchild of New York banker **Alexander Hamilton**. Hamilton, born in the British West Indies and educated in a Jewish school there **(7)**, is an agent of the New York-London moneylenders. Hamilton had previously founded the Bank of New York in 1784.

As President Washington's Treasury Secretary, Hamilton clashes with Secretary of State Thomas Jefferson. Hamilton and the New York bankers believe in strong central government and debt-based central banking and currency issue. Virginians

Jefferson, James Madison *(father of the Constitution)* and the southern agricultural class believe in decentralized government and local banking. The roots of the future American Civil War can be traced, in part, to the Jefferson-Hamilton feud.

Jefferson argues that centralization of power away from private mints and banks is unconstitutional and dangerous. He wrote: ***"...banking establishments are more dangerous than standing armies."*** **(8)** The New Yorker Hamilton argues that if the nation is to grow, it needs a standard coinage supported by a Central Bank and excise tax.

1- Hamilton was London's banker boy.

2- Jefferson wanted no part European Central Banking.

1791
HAMILTON WINS. A U.S. CENTRAL BANK IS ESTABLISHED / WHISKEY FARMERS REBEL

President Washington listens to Jefferson's and Hamilton's position on the Central Bank, but is ultimately taken in by Hamilton. The Father of America has a blind spot when it comes to the smooth talking, foreign- born deceiver. Others are not so easily fooled. In later years, **President John Adams** will describe Hamilton as:

"...the most restless, impatient, artful, indefatigable, and unprincipled intriguer in the United States, if not in the world." **(9)**

Along with establishing an excise tax, Hamilton's Bank is a private company with some foreign shareholders. To cover the government's interest payments to the Bank, Hamilton imposes an excise tax on whiskey.

When Pennsylvania whiskey farmers rebel *(Whiskey Rebellion)*, Hamilton convinces Washington to allow him to personally lead 12,000 troops to enforce compliance. Brute force is used to collect the taxes needed to pay the interest to the foreign shareholders of the Central Bank.

When men were men! Angry whiskey farmers attack, tar & feather Hamilton's tax collectors for the Central Bank.

THE CENTRAL BANKING SCAM EXPLAINED

CENTRAL BANKING AND GOVERNMENT DEBT

When government uses up the money it collects in taxes, it resorts to borrowing. It can borrow by selling bonds to investors, or to foreign governments. **But when governments borrow from a privately owned Central Bank, the Bank is actually creating new money "out of thin air" and then lending it to the government at interest.** The injection of new money into the economy has the effect of reducing the value of existing money (inflation). The government must then tax its citizens to repay the loans (Bonds) to the Central Bank, *plus interest.*

If the government were to simply create its own debt-free currency to cover its bills, there might still be an inflationary effect, but the government would not carry debt, and therefore not need to tax its people to pay principal and interest to the Central Bank.

It makes no sense for a government to pay interest to a Central Bank on new currency when it can simply create the currency itself, *interest free!*

CENTRAL BANKING AND LOCAL BANK / CONSUMER DEBT

The other way in which a Central Bank preys upon people is by lending to the nation's banks. The banks can then increase the number of loans to their customers by borrowing money themselves from the Central Bank *(again, created out of thin air.)* The local bank borrows at a lower rate from the Central Bank, and then re-loans the money to you at a higher rate. Consumer debt is thus maximized as constant inflation erodes the value of existing money.

Consumers do not benefit from debt as they would believe because the new money pumped into the economy artificially drives up the price of whatever they are buying.

In short, behind its academic cover, **Central Banks are legalized counterfeiters and loan sharks.** When a Central Bank, owned by private shareholders, controls the money, every dollar of currency must be loaned into circulation at interest. Therefore, **there will always be more total debt outstanding than there is money in circulation.** Those who control this perpetual debt machine always become powerful enough to control the government.

1789
THE FRENCH REVOLUTION

The French Revolution is a period of radical upheaval in France. Unlike America's Revolution, which put limits on government power, the atheistic radicals of France seek total power. Their rallying cries of "Liberty, Fraternity, and Equality" are empty words that attract gullible mobs.

The revolution leads to the rise of the mad killer Robespierre, and the **Jacobins**. From 1793-1794, the **"Committee of Public Safety"** operates as the dictatorship of France. A "Reign of Terror" is unleashed. King Louis XVI, Queen Marie

Antoinette, and 40,000 others are executed, mostly by public guillotine. The Jacobin mobs single-out priests, nuns, and the wealthy for special brutality.

The Jacobins *(forerunners of the Communists)* are eventually displaced by more sensible elements of the revolution. Robespierre himself is executed. The "Directory" will control France from 1795-1799 as the monarchies of Europe wage a war against Republican France.

Though historians portray The Revolution as a "spontaneous uprising" of the oppressed, the funding of the movement, and the disciplined organization of the radicals, suggest otherwise. Was Rothschild money behind the revolt? Could this be the meaning of the French Revolution's theme color, red? *(Rothschild is German for "Red Shield")*. Many more "spontaneous" red revolts will follow over the centuries to come.

The works of early 20th Century British historian Nesta Webster exposed the genocidal French Revolution as the work of occultists aiming to overthrow civilization and bring about "world revolution".

1795
THE JACOBINS ARE OVERTHROWN; 'THE DIRECTORY'
TAKES CONTROL OF FRANCE

The Jacobins *(forerunners of the Communists)* are eventually displaced by more sensible, Republican elements of the revolution. Robespierre himself is then executed. The **"Directory"** will govern France from 1795-1799 as the worried monarchies of Europe *(led by Great Britain)*, as well as the displaced Jacobin Reds of the NWO, continue to wage war against a divided France.

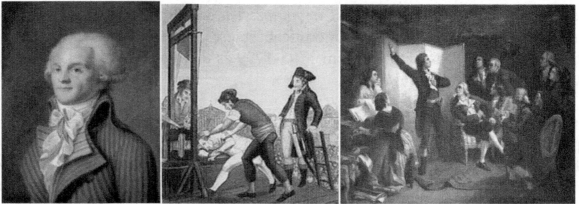

Robespierre gets a taste of his own medicine as the Directory takes control. But the Red Jacobin Clubs are still in operation.

1796
WASHINGTON'S PROPHETIC FAREWELL ADDRESS

In his **Farewell Address to Congress** and an adoring American public, the great General and President George Washington uses the occasion to advise America on how to secure its future happiness and prosperity. Washington's prescient warnings come from his extensive knowledge of history. His wise and prophetic advice includes:

- Maintain religion and morality as supports of a free people.
- Beware of the formation of political parties.
- Avoid alliances & foreign military entanglements.
- Balance the Federal Budget and avoid state debt.
- Keep the government's spending and taxes low.
- Do not weaken the U.S. Constitution with amendments.
- Do not allow sectional differences to divide the Union. **(10)**

In Europe, the early **New World Order/Red** crime gang is already in operation. Eventually, the Globalists will attack America *(and the world)* in each area that Washington warned about.

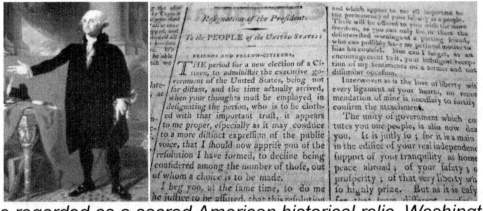

Once regarded as a sacred American historical relic, Washington's prophetic advice has long since been forgotten.

1797
ITALIAN CAMPAIGN – NAPOLEON BONAPARTE CAPTURES ROME / DEFIES DIRECTORY'S ORDER TO DETHRONE POPE

French military hero Napoleon Bonaparte completes his successful Italian campaign, defeating Austrian, Sardinian, and Neapolitan forces before capturing Rome. The French General's stature as a military genius and leader is now such that he can defy the Atheistic Directory's orders to dethrone the Pope and get away with it. Napoleon is by now a legend in the making, soon to be a political force in his own right – a force beyond Illuminati-Rothschild-NWO control.

1- Napoleon crosses the Alps.   2- Napoleon enters Rome.
The NWO gang was behind the French Revolution, but they cannot control Napoleon Bonaparte.

1798
NAPOLEON'S EGYPTIAN EXPEDITION

The **French Campaign in Egypt and Syria** (1798–1801) is Napoleon Bonaparte's campaign to protect French trade, undermine Britain's access to India, and promote scientific enterprise in the region.

Napoleon approaches the Egyptians not as a conqueror, but as a liberator who respects their religion and culture. This position earns him solid support in Egypt and the admiration of Muhammad Ali, who later succeeds in declaring Egypt's independence from the Ottoman Turks.

An unusual aspect of the Egyptian military expedition is the inclusion of a large group of scientists and scholars. This deployment of intellectual resources is an indication of Napoleon's devotion to higher learning. Much of what we know today about ancient Egypt is the result of this mission. The discoveries include the deciphering of ancient Egyptian hieroglyphics by way of "The Rosetta Stone".

1- Napoleon at the pyramids.

2- The Rosetta Stone was etched in hieroglyphics and Greek. The known Greek figures allowed the French to decipher the unknown Egyptian, and translate into modern languages.

1798
JOHN ROBISON WRITES: 'PROOFS OF A CONSPIRACY'

John Robison was a prominent physicist and professor of philosophy at Scotland's Edinburgh University. He worked with James Watt on the early steam car and he later invented the siren. The Illuminati had attempted to recruit him but he declined. In 1798 he writes **"Proofs of a Conspiracy Against the Religions and Governments of Europe"** in which he exposes the secret societies behind the terrorist French revolution.

His warning to Europe is stark:

*"An association has been formed for the express purposes of rooting out all the religious establishments and overturning all existing governments **... the leaders would rule the World with uncontrollable power**, while all the rest would be employed as tools of their unknown superiors."* **(11)**

French priest **Abbe Barruel** independently developed similar views that the *Illuminati* had infiltrated Freemasonry, **(12)** leading to the excesses of the French Revolution. In 1798, the Reverend G. W. Snyder sent Robison's book to George Washington for his thoughts on the subject. Washington replied:

*"It was not my intention to doubt that, the Doctrines of the Illuminati, and principles of Jacobinism had not spread in the United States. On the contrary, **no one is more truly satisfied of this fact than I am.** The idea that I meant to convey, was, that I did not believe that the Lodges of Free Masons in this Country had, as Societies, endeavored to propagate the diabolical tenets of the first, or pernicious principles of the latter (if they are susceptible of separation). That individual of them may have done it, or that the founder, or instrument employed to found, the Democratic Societies in the United States, may have had these objects; and actually had a separation of the People from their Government in view, is too evident to be questioned."* **(13)**

 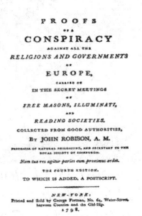 

Robison was a big man of science and letters. George Washington agreed with his observation about Illuminati & Jacobin infiltration of freemasonry.

1798-1815
THE 5 SONS OF ROTHSCHILD SPREAD THEIR MONEY LENDING EMPIRE ACROSS EUROPE

After amassing an enormous fortune from his base in the Hessian city of Frankfurt (Germany) Mayer Amschel Rothschild sends his five sons abroad to expand the Rothschild Family Empire throughout Europe. Each of the brothers will emerge as dominant financial players, and behind-the-scenes political players, in their respective new countries. The five sons and the five sub-dynasties they will operate are as follows:

Anselm: Stays in Frankfurt to run the German operation.
Salomon: Vienna, Austria
Nathan: Manchester, and then London, England
Carl: Naples, Italy
Jacob: Paris, France

Of the five, Nathan in London *("The City of London")* will become the wealthiest and most powerful of the brothers. His power surpasses even that of the other existing Jewish family dynasties that own The Bank of England   (**Montefiores, Goldsmids, Mocattas**).

The London Rothschilds are the beating heart of the centuries old movement to tear down European civilization and erect **The New World Order** in its place.

1 & 2 - The Jewish-produced 1934 Hollywood film, The House of Rothschild made no effort to hide the historical power of the 5 sons, especially Nathan of London (played by George Arliss - brother in center).

3 – Today, young Nat (Nathan) Rothschild, great-great-great-great grandson of Nathan is being groomed as the next Family Patriarch.

Then and now: the immense wealth of the Rothschild Family STILL commands obedience. (Above: Sir Evelyn de Rothschild with gold bars, and commenting on BBC TV)

1799
NAPOLEON STAGES A COUP IN PARIS - OVERTHROWS THE DIRECTORY

Napoleon the war hero returns to a deeply-divided and chaotic Paris. With the help of allies in the French Senate, Napoleon stages a bloodless coup and is named First Consul. A plebiscite *(popular vote)* is held soon afterwards. Napoleon's ascension to First Consul is overwhelmingly approved by the French public.

The New World Order gang created the Revolution in order to overthrow the Monarchy. Now, with the rise of Napoleon, the NWO has lost control of France.

Move over Directory. Napoleon Bonaparte is now the Boss!

The Communistic Jacobins *(working for their secret New World Order Rothschild bosses in London)* want their bloody dictatorship back. They openly call for the death of Napoleon. One leftist agitator, named Metge, publishes a pamphlet comparing Napoleon to Roman ruler Julius Caesar, who was killed by daggers wielded by Brutus and others. Metge openly calls for *"the birth of thousands of Bruti to stab the tyrant Bonaparte."*

Indeed, one of the Jacobin plots which is foiled is the "Conspiration des poignards" *(Conspiracy of the Daggers)* in October 1800. The Jacobins plan to stab Napoleon, as Julius Caesar had been, as he arrives at the Paris Opera House. Informants are able to foil the assassination plot, but the Jacobins will again try to kill Napoleon.

Jacobins plotted to stab Napoleon, as Caesar had been by Brutus & others.

OCTOBER 1800
JACOBIN BOMB NEARLY KILLS NAPOLEON & HIS WIFE

Two months after the Dagger Plot is foiled, the Jacobins nearly succeed in blowing up Napoleon's carriage with a bomb (Plot of the Rue Saint-Nicaise or "The Infernal Machine"). Napoleon and Josephine *(who faints)* both survive the massive blast, but 10-12 innocent bystanders are killed, and dozens more injured or maimed.

Napoleon uses public outrage over the bombing to annihilate the remnants of the violent and conspiratorial Red Jacobins.

The Jacobins never stop plotting. The mighty bomb that nearly killed Napoleon was known as "The Infernal Machine".

1801
NAPOLEON MAKES PEACE WITH THE CATHOLIC CHURCH

After years of persecution at the hands of atheistic Jacobin radicals and also the Directory, Napoleon moves to protect and preserve the Roman Catholic Church that he had spared from extinction during his Italian campaign. Raised Catholic, Napoleon is himself a Deist **(14)** *(belief in a Creative force)* who retains a special fondness for the moral principles and ceremonies of the Church. Napoleon is also impressed by Islam, and believes that people of all faiths should have freedom of conscience.

The Concordat of 1801 between Napoleon Bonaparte and Pope Pius VII reaffirms the Roman Catholic Church as the majority church of France and restores its civil status. While the Concordat restores ties to the Papacy, the balance of church-state relations tilts in Napoleon's favor.

The Concordat reassured French Catholics, angered Red Atheists, and improved relations with the Vatican.

MARCH, 1802
THE TREATY OF AMIENS: PEACE WITH BRITAIN

The Treaty of Amiens ends hostilities between the French Republic and the United Kingdom. It is signed in the city of Amiens on March 25, 1802 and celebrated as the "Definitive Treaty of Peace" between Napoleon and Britain. In retrospect, it appears to have been a British ploy more than a sincere desire to make peace with France.

The Peace Treaty of Amiens. Was it just a British trick to buy time?

MAY, 1803
BRITAIN BREAKS THE PEACE / NAPOLEONIC WARS FOLLOW

The Peace of Amiens lasts only one year and was the only period of extended peace during the 'Great French War' between 1793 and 1815. Britain does not evacuate Malta as promised. Instead, the British protest against Bonaparte's annexation of Piedmont and his Act of Mediation, which establishes a new Swiss Confederation, ***though neither of these territories are covered by the treaty***.

These phony pretexts for starting a new war against Napoleon culminate in a declaration of war by Britain, and the reassembly of another coalition against France. Having failed to kill Napoleon from within France itself, the NWO Mafia and the Royal Families of Europe will continue to wage a series of on and off "coalition wars" on post-revolutionary France. At varying times, Great Britain *(the chief instigator)*, Russia, Austria, Prussia, Spain and other minor Kingdoms unite in opposition to Napoleonic France. The ensuing wars that follow are known as the **Napoleonic Wars**, although Napoleon didn't start these wars with Britain and friends.

It is important to note that without Rothschild funding, these wars would not have been possible, at least not in the long term. The Old World Order *(Monarchies)* and the New World Order *(Rothschilds-Illuminati)* **both** seek the demise of Napoleon Bonaparte.

The Napoleonic Wars were a series of wars declared against Napoleon's French Empire by opposing coalitions, led by Britain and funded by Rothschild.

1803
THE LOUISIANA PURCHASE: RATHER THAN BORROW FROM THE BANKERS, NAPOLEON SELLS LAND TO THE U.S.

Napoleon needs money to finance France's war effort against the European powers, but he is unwilling to borrow from big bankers. Napoleon once wrote:

"When a government is dependent upon bankers for money, they and not the leaders of the government control the situation, since the hand that gives is above the hand that takes. Money has no motherland; financiers are without patriotism and without decency; their sole object is gain." **(15)**

Instead of crawling to Rothschild, Napoleon raises money by proposing to sell the massive Territory of Louisiana to the United States. President Jefferson jumps at the offer. Napoleon's move also closes a possible front in the western hemisphere from which Britain could wage war against French territory.

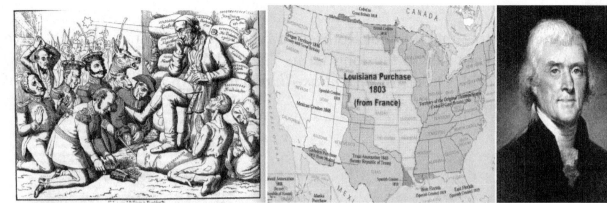

Cartoon above depicts nobles and peasants crawling to Rothschild. Napoleon did borrow money, but he also utilized other means for finance. The Jefferson-Napoleon deal DOUBLED America's territory.

1795 - 1804
THE FALL OF ALEXANDER HAMILTON

Meanwhile, back in the fledgling U.S.A., in 1795, London's banker-tool Alexander Hamilton is forced to resign his Treasury position in disgrace when it was discovered that he is sleeping with another man's wife *(Maria Reynolds Affair)*.

On July 11, 1804, Hamilton is killed in a duel with Thomas Jefferson's Vice President, **Aaron Burr**; a political rival whom the arrogant Hamilton had insulted and defamed. Though dueling was illegal in New Jersey, Burr returned to Washington and finished out the remaining 8 months of his term as Jefferson's first Vice President.

Hamilton had many enemies. He finally messed with the wrong guy.

Napoleon's lasting reforms include higher education, a tax code, road systems and sewer systems. His set of civil laws, the *Code Civil*—now known as the **Napoleonic Code**—is prepared by committees of legal experts. Napoleon participates actively in the sessions of the Council of State that revises the drafts. The Code forbids privileges based on birth, allows freedom of religion, and specifies that government jobs must go to the most qualified. Other codes are commissioned by Napoleon to codify criminal and commerce law. A Code of Criminal Instruction is also published, which enacts rules of due process.

The Code will be accepted throughout much of Europe and remain in force even after Napoleon's eventual defeat. It is a revolutionary idea that spurs the development of the middle class by extending the right to own property. Napoleon also reorganizes what had been the Holy Roman Empire, made up of more than a thousand entities, into a streamlined 40-state Confederation of the Rhine. This confederation will provide the basis for the German Confederation and the unification of Germany in 1871.

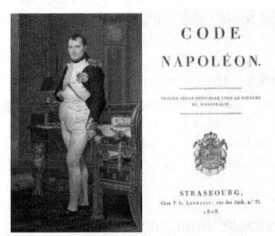

The Napoleonic Code sought to eliminate undeserved privileges and establish true justice.

1804
GENOCIDE IN HAITI: 'BLACK JACOBINS' MASSACRE ALL REMAINING FRENCH WHITES

In 1791, the French Revolution in Europe had also inspired a Revolution in the French Caribbean colony of Haiti. The after-effect of the 13 year conflict will ruin Haiti, which remains an unhappy land to this day. The Revolution begins as a slave uprising but eventually degenerates into a genocidal race war targeting French settlers in Haiti – including many who are opposed to slavery and friendly toward the Blacks.

Even after slavery had been abolished, radical elements of the Haitian Revolution continue to incite racial hatred toward the innocent Whites who were far outnumbered by the Blacks and Mulattos. In 1802, a notorious killer named **Jean-Jacques Dessalines** takes over Haiti by betraying his more reasonable, and actually pro-French, Black predecessor, **Toussaint L'ouverture.**

Napoleon had previously sent troops to retake Haiti, but as many as 40,000 died of Yellow Fever. Now, pre-occupied with European Wars, there is little he can do to save the Whites of Haiti. The smart Whites get out, but many of the "bleeding heart liberal" types refuse to see the danger of being such a small minority under Black Jacobin rule.

In 1804, Dessalines orders the genocidal massacre of the remaining White population of Haiti. His secretary Boisrong-Tonnere declares:

"For our declaration of independence, we should have the skin of a white man for parchment, his skull for an inkwell, his blood for ink, and a bayonet for a pen!" **(16)**

Squads of Black soldiers move from house to house, killing entire families. The weapons used are silent ones; such as knives and bayonets rather than gunfire. This is so that the killing can be done more quietly, thus giving no loud gunfire warning to other intended victims. Killings take place on the streets. Plundering and rape also occur. White children are beaten and stabbed to death; and white women are raped and pushed into forced marriages under threat of death.

To flush out Whites who went into hiding, the monster Dessalines proclaims an amnesty for all Whites. When the terrified Whites resurface, they too are murdered. One of the most diabolical of the massacre participants is **Jean Zombi,** a mulatto known for his brutality. One account describes how Zombi stops a White man on the street, strips him naked, and takes him to the stairs of the Presidential Palace where he kills him with a dagger as Dessalines watches. In the Haitian 'Voodoo' cult tradition, the figure of Jean Zombi is the prototype for the "zombie".

The massacre results in the deaths of between 4,000 to 5,000 people of all ages and genders. **(17)** But because the victims were White and the perpetrators were Black Jacobins; the historians who serve **The New World Order** have forgotten them.

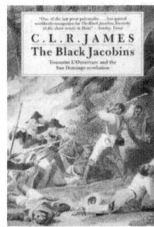

Under orders from Dessalines, the "Black Jacobins" of Haiti carried out the first open manifestation of the New World Order's 'War on Whites'. Because of the Yellow Fever outbreak which had devastated his Caribbean forces, Napoleon is unable to save the French of Haiti.

DECEMBER, 1804
NAPOLEON IS CROWNED EMPEROR BY POPE PIUS VII

Napoleon, by a very wide margin, is elected "Emperor of the French" in a November, 1804 plebiscite. He is crowned by Pope Pius VII as Napoleon I at Notre Dame Cathedral. The story that Napoleon seized the crown out of the hands of the Pope during the ceremony, to avoid subjugating to the Pope's authority, is not accurate, as the coronation procedure had been agreed upon in advance.

After a string of stunning victories, France establishes itself as the leading continental power of Europe and builds alliances of its own. Napoleon is now 'larger than life' – a development which has the British and NWO types seething.

1805
NAPOLEON TRIUMPHS AT THE BATTLE OF AUSTERLITZ

On the first anniversary of his coronation, Napoleon defeats Austria and Russia at Austerlitz. This ends the Third Coalition War against him. To commemorate the victory, Napoleon commissions the 'Arc de Triomphe'.

Austria has to concede territory. The subsequent Peace of Pressburg leads to the dissolution of the Holy Roman Empire and creation of the Confederation of the Rhine with Napoleon named as its *Protector*. Napoleon later states, *"The battle of Austerlitz is the finest of all I have fought."* **(18)**

The famous Arc de Triomphe in Paris commemorates Austerlitz.

1807
RUSSIA'S CZAR AND NAPOLEON MAKE PEACE

In 1805 and 1807 Russia suffers major losses in battles with Napoleon's armies. Napoleon's forces, though victorious, are weary from fighting and unable to pursue the Russian armies further. Finally, Czar Alexander I makes peace with Napoleon with the **Treaty**

of Tilsit *(1807)*. The Russian ruler accepts France's continental position, and vows support of Napoleon. For his part, Napoleon believes Alexander has extended him a hand of friendship.

1800's
NAPOLEON WANTS TO ASSIMILATE THE JEWS

Napoleon is very tolerant in his attitude towards the Jews. As a result, he has won the respect of many of them. But he has his motives. Historian Rabbi Berel Wein reveals that Napoleon was primarily interested in seeing the Jews assimilated, rather than prosper as an alien community:

"Napoleon's outward tolerance and fairness toward Jews was actually based upon his grand plan to have them disappear entirely by means of total assimilation, intermarriage, and conversion." **(19)**

This attitude can be seen from a letter Napoleon wrote in November 1806,

"It is necessary to reduce, if not destroy, the tendency of Jewish people to practice a very great number of activities that are harmful to civilization and to public order in society in all the countries of the world. It is necessary to stop the harm by preventing it; to prevent it, it is necessary to change the Jews. ... Once part of their youth will take its place in our armies, they will cease to have Jewish interests and sentiments; their interests and sentiments will be French." **(20)**

Again, privately, in an 1808 letter to his brother Jerome, Napoleon makes his assimilation plans clear:

"I have undertaken to reform the Jews, but I have not endeavored to draw more of them into my realm. Far from that, I have avoided doing anything which could show any esteem for the most despicable of mankind." **(21)**

Napoleon's outreach to the Jews was intended to eventually assimilate them as Frenchmen. To a hard-core Jew, this is a big 'no-no'!

1808
NAPOLEON'S DECREE CANCELS DEBTS OWED TO JEWISH MONEY-LENDERS

In response to complaints about Jewish money lenders, Napoleon had, in 1806, suspended all debts owed to them. In 1808, he goes a step further and issues a decree that the money lenders refer to as **"The Infamous Decree."**

Napoleon wants the Jews to move away from their traditional money lending practices and become farmers and craftsmen instead. His decree severely restricts the practice of lending, and annuls all debts owed by married women, minors, and soldiers. Any loan that had an interest rate exceeding 10 percent is also annulled.

Napoleon's religious tolerance is admired by many of the Jews. But his efforts to regulate usury upset the Jewish money-lenders and seal his fate. That is why, to this day, they refer to Napoleon's decree as "The *Infamous* Decree." **The Rothschilds of Europe must destroy Napoleon before his anti-debt monetary philosophy can take hold in Europe.**

1808 -1814
THE PENINSULAR WARS, FRANCE vs SPAIN, BRITAIN & PORTUGAL

British international intrigue draws Spain into war against its former French ally. The years of fighting in Spain take a heavy burden on France's Grande Armée. While the French win battle after battle, their communications and supply lines are severely tested. French units are isolated, harassed, and slowly bled to death by guerilla fighters.

The Spanish armies are repeatedly beaten, but time and again they regroup and hound the French. This drain on French resources leads Napoleon to call the conflict, "the Spanish Ulcer".

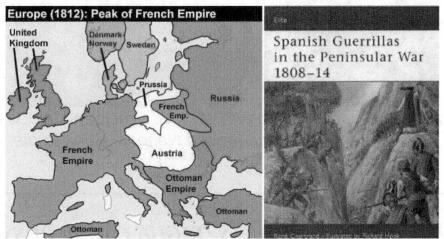

At the peak of the French Continental Empire, Spanish Guerrillas take a heavy toll on French forces.

1811
THE U.S. CENTRAL BANK IS KILLED AS BRITAIN THREATENS ANOTHER WAR AGAINST THE U.S.

Meanwhile, back in the fledgling U.S.A., the 20-year charter of Alexander Hamilton's Monster Bank is set to expire. **President James Madison** had opposed the Bank in 1791, and has no desire to renew the charter. The "Federalists" *(Hamiltonians)* in Congress favor its renewal and close relations with Britain. The

"Democratic-Republicans" *(Jeffersonians)* want to kill the Bank and view Britain with suspicion.

The vote to renew the charter is close, but the anti-Bank faction prevails. The New York-London Bank is allowed to die. At this time in history, the British are "coincidentally" escalating tensions with America. Britain is already at war with Napoleon and is blockading France. Under the blockade, US ships are being harassed and sailors taken prisoner. The young American Republic appears to be headed for a 2nd war with its ex 'Mother Country", which by now belongs to Nathan Rothschild and friends.

Author of the U.S. Constitution and 4th U.S. President James Madison allows the Philadelphia-based National Bank to die.

1811
BRITISH AND INTERNAL INTRIGUE CAUSE RUSSIA TO BREAK OFF ITS ALLIANCE WITH NAPOLEON

Napoleon and Czar Alexander I of Russia had been enjoying friendly personal relations. By 1811, however, tensions increase as Alexander comes under intense pressure from political forces within the Russian nobility to break off the alliance with France. Fearing another two-front war, Napoleon threatens serious consequences if Russia forms an alliance with Britain.

By 1812, advisers *(intriguers)* to Alexander suggest an invasion of the French Empire and recapture of Poland *(now an ally of France)*. On receipt of intelligence reports on Russia's war preparations, Napoleon prepares for a **preemptive** offensive campaign against Russia. The invasion begins on June 23, 1812.

1- Court intriguers persuaded Alexander to break off his alliance with Napoleon and join up once again with Rothschild-Britain instead.

2- Painting depicts meeting between Alexander and Napoleon during happier days.

MAY 11, 1812
BRITAIN'S PRIME MINISTER ASSASSINATED JUST BEFORE
HE IS TO MAKE PEACE WITH THE U.S.

British Prime Minister **Spencer Perceval** enters the lobby of the House of Commons. He is on his way to a meeting whose purpose is to discuss how to calm the rising tensions with the United States – an important goal for Perceval. **(22)** A man named **John Bellingham** then draws a pistol and shoots Perceval at close range. Perceval is killed. Bellingham is tried and hanged just one week later.

In 1787, Bellingham had been a midshipman on a vessel that was taken over by mutineers and sunk. In 1803, he briefly worked in Russia, where he was imprisoned for sabotaging a Russian ship, also lost at sea. These incidents suggest that Bellingham is a political radical, and not just a "crazed lone gunman". The odd manner in which Bellingham is so quickly executed, the lack of investigation into a possible broader conspiracy, his link to a mutiny, his arrest in Russia, and the looming Bank War with the U.S., all suggest that the killer is a radical patsy, used by higher authorities to eliminate a disobedient Prime Minister.

Perceval's murder will be the first in a long series of political murders, and attempted murders, which will plague Europe and America for the next 200 years. In many of these cases, it will be an emotionally unstable 'lone' radical who is used to carry out the dirty deed.

The murder of Perceval makes war with the United States inevitable.

JUNE, 1812
THE STRANGE 'WAR OF 1812' BEGINS (1812-14)

The murder of Prime Minister Perceval delays the effort to improve relations with the United States. Had Perceval lived, the British wartime policy of European trade restrictions and harassing of American vessels would have been lifted, and peace maintained.

War commences just 5 weeks after the assassination. The same Hamiltonian-Federalists, who wanted to re-charter The Central Bank also oppose Madison's decision to fight the British. After the war ends in 1814, the Federalists will be perceived as unpatriotic and their political party collapses.

Perceval's successor, **Robert Jenkinson** *(Lord Liverpool)* will later lift the trade restriction orders, which are the stated cause of the war. But by that time, the gesture is meaningless as the war is already started. Whether Liverpool was being sincere, or whether he was just trying to shift the blame for war onto the United States, is unclear.

What is known is that the House of Rothschild financed both sides of the war! **(23)**

American General Andrew Jackson will emerge as a heroic figure from The War of 1812. More on Jackson, later on.

1812
NAPOLEON'S INVASION OF RUSSIA PROVES COSTLY / TYPHUS WRECKS HIS GRAND ARMEE

The Russians avoid Napoleon's objective of a decisive engagement and instead retreat deeper into Russia. A brief attempt at resistance is made at Smolensk in August, but the Russians are defeated in a series of battles. Napoleon resumes his advance.

Owing to the Russian army's scorched earth tactics, the French find it hard to forage food for themselves and their horses. The Russians eventually offer battle outside Moscow. The Battle of Borodino results in about 44,000 Russian and 35,000 French dead, wounded or captured.

Although the French win, the Russian army has withstood the major battle Napoleon had hoped would be decisive. Napoleon's own account:

"The most terrible of all my battles was the one before Moscow. The French showed themselves to be worthy of victory, but the Russians showed themselves worthy of being invincible." **(24)**

Napoleon retreats with most of his Grand Armee intact. On the long march home, typhus wipes out most of his men.

The retreat from Russia proves disastrous for Napoleon. Contrary to popular belief, it was neither the Russian Army, nor hunger, nor the cold that wiped out most of his returning Grand Armee. It was the lice-spread disease of typhus. **(25)**

1812-1814
ROTHSCHILD'S ARMY vs NAPOLEON'S ARMEE

The Duke of Wellington's Army was funded by Nathan Rothschild

From his base in London's financial district, *("The City")* **Nathan Rothschild** single-handedly continues to finance Britain's war to defeat Napoleon. Shipments of gold to the European continent fund the Duke of Wellington's armies and also those of Britain's allies, Prussia and Austria. The Rothschild brothers co-ordinate their activities across the continent, and develop a network of agents, shippers, and couriers to transport gold across war-torn Europe. **Were it not for Rothschild's limitless fortune, the Allies would surely have had to make peace with Napoleon by now.**

*The 1934 Hollywood film **openly** portrays the Allies begging Rothschild for finance! **Boris Karloff**, best known for his 1931 role as the Frankenstein Monster, plays the part of a Prussian (German) "anti-Semitic" Count who despises the Rothschilds. Karloff is deliberately made-up to resemble the monster.*

1813
NAPOLEON SCORES MORE VICTORIES, BUT HIS FORCES ARE BEING DEPLETED

There is a lull in fighting over the winter of 1812–13 as both the Russians and the French rebuild their forces. Napoleon is then able to field 350,000 troops. Emboldened by France's failure in Russia, Prussia joins with Austria, Sweden, Russia, Great Britain, Spain, and Portugal in a new coalition. Napoleon assumes command in Germany and inflicts a series of defeats on the Coalition, culminating in the Battle of Dresden in August 1813.

Despite these stunning successes against multiple armies, the losses continue to mount against Napoleon. The French army is eventually pinned down by a force twice it's size at the Battle of Leipzig. This is by far the largest battle of the Napoleonic Wars and cost more than 90,000 casualties in total.

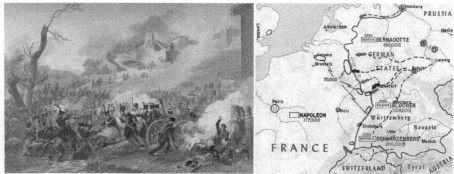

The Battle of Leipzig marks the first time Napoleon was defeated in battle.

SPRING 1814
PARIS IS CAPTURED / NAPOLEON FORCED TO ABDICATE

Napoleon withdraws back to France; his army having been reduced to 70,000 soldiers and 40,000 stragglers, against more than three times as many Allied troops. The French are surrounded as British forces press from the south, and other Coalition forces position to attack from the German states. Paris is captured by the Coalition in March 1814.

On April 2, 1814, the French Senate declares Napoleon deposed. When Napoleon learns that Paris has surrendered, he proposes that the army march on the capital. His Marshals then mutiny. They confront Napoleon and force him to announce his unconditional abdication only two days later.

"Sorry Boss. But you have to step down."

APRIL, 1814
NAPOLEON IS EXILED TO THE ISLAND OF ELBA

The combination of Rothschild's endless money, cunning British intrigue, limitless allied manpower, "the Spanish Ulcer', and the disastrous typhus-infested retreat from Russia were all just too much for the French to overcome. After Napoleon's abdication, King Louis XVIII is installed as ruler of France. Napoleon is exiled to the island of Elba off the Italian coast, where he is given authority over the island's 12,000 inhabitants.

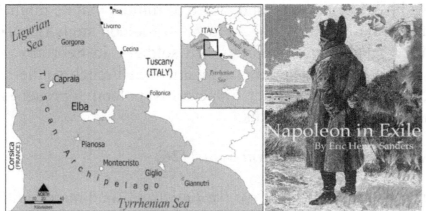

While in exile, Napoleon plans his next move.

AUGUST, 1814
THE BRITISH BURN THE WHITE HOUSE

The Redcoats burn the White House before a storm chases them away.

British forces occupy Washington DC. They set fire to the White House and other important buildings including the Treasury, The Capitol, and the Library of Congress. Less than two days after sacking Washington, the British are forced to leave when a violent hurricane tears through DC. The freak storm extinguishes fires, kills British troops, and damages many of their ships.

President Madison and the rest of the

government then quickly return to the Capitol City. Legend has it that a storm sent by "Divine Providence" drove the British away. Later that same year, Britain and the US will make peace.

FEBRUARY, 1815
THE LEGEND CONTINUES. NAPOLEON ESCAPES FROM EXILE!

Separated from his wife and sons, and aware of rumors that he might be shipped to a remote island in the middle of the Atlantic, Napoleon stuns Europe by escaping from Elba with a handful of supporters and soldiers, in February of 1815. Soon after landing on the French mainland, a regiment of French soldiers, under orders to arrest him, confronts their former Emperor. Napoleon approaches the regiment alone, dismounts his horse and shouts:

"Here I am. Kill your Emperor, if you wish." **(26)**

The soldiers respond with, *"Long Live the Emperor!"* and march with Napoleon to Paris!

King Louis XVIII flees. Napoleon quickly raises another army. He will once again confront the Rothschild-funded British and Prussians at the decisive **Battle of Waterloo** in Belgium.

He's back! Defying orders to arrest Napoleon, the troops join him instead.

52

Again financed by The House of Rothschild, The British, led by the Duke of Wellington, and the Prussians, led by Gebhard von Blucher, amass their armies near the north-eastern border of France. Napoleon is forced to preemptively attack France's enemies before they can unleash a massive, coordinated invasion of France, along with other members of this latest Allied coalition.

The **Battle of Waterloo** is fought on Sunday, June 18, 1815, near Waterloo in present-day Belgium. The French army nearly wins the great battle. It is only the late arrival of Prussian reinforcements that suddenly tilts the battle against the French.

The defeat at Waterloo marks the end of Napoleon's Hundred Days return from exile and ends his rule as Emperor once and for all. The very word "Waterloo" has since been synonymous with one's final defeat.

Napoleon's strategy to divide the British and Prussian armies, and then destroy them separately, almost worked.

JUNE, 1815
NATHAN ROTHSCHILD CAPITALIZES UPON THE BATTLE OF WATERLOO

The Rothschild Brothers utilize courier pigeons to rapidly communicate amongst themselves and their agents. The network provides Nathan Rothschild with political and financial information ahead of his peers, giving him an advantage in the financial markets. After the final defeat of Napoleon at Waterloo, Rothschild receives word of the battle's outcome long before anyone else.

Rothschild will use the "insider information" of Wellington's victory to become Britain's supreme master. He orders his brokers to sell off his holdings. Other brokers assume that Rothschild has therefore learned that Britain has lost at Waterloo. A panic sell-off drives the market down to historic lows. Rothschild then buys up the devalued market at bargain prices.

When the public learns of Britain's *victory* over Napoleon, the stocks skyrocket to new heights. Nathan Rothschild multiplies his massive fortune by 20 times!

Nathan buys up Britain after Waterloo.

The 1934 film does indeed portray Rothschild's buying-up of the London market, but makes it seem like it was the "accidental" consequence of his trying to "save" the market and not "insider trading"!

1- Rothschild's descendants (like Jacob, above) still wield enormous financial and political power.

2 – It is enough power to make star-struck groupies like Governor Arnold Schwarzenegger and Billionaire Warren Buffett (shown above with Jacob) seem like nobodies.

After the final defeat at Waterloo, Napoleon is exiled to the island of St. Helena, 1000 miles off the coast of West Africa. King Louis XVIII is installed on the throne and, predictably, allows Napoleon's "Infamous Decree" against usury to expire in 1818. The Rothschilds are back in control!

Rumors of Napoleon returning will continue to occasionally circulate throughout Europe. Napoleon is neglected by his British captors, and will finally die in 1821, at age 51, from what appears to be arsenic poisoning.

Napoleon dies. The legend lives. His coffin is still on display in Paris.

1814-1815
BALANCE OF POWER POLITICS / THE CONGRESS OF VIENNA RESHAPES EUROPE

After Napoleon's defeat, the European powers hold a series of meetings in Vienna, Austria. Political boundaries are redrawn. Old disputes are settled. These conferences are known as Vienna "Though many nations participate, the Congress is run by the "Big Four" *(Britain, Prussia, Russia, & Austria)*. The most notable decision reached at Vienna is the consolidation of 360 small German states, into a German Confederation of 38 states.

Arrangements made by the Four Great Powers ensure that future disputes will be settled in a manner that will avoid the wars of the previous twenty years. Although the Congress of Vienna preserves the "balance of power" in Europe, it does not check the spread of the Red revolutionary movements that are being born, and will spread across Europe some 30 years later.'

"Balance of Power" politics serves the interests of the Globalist planners in that it allows for a disobedient nation, or nations, to be checked, challenged, and controlled by a group of other nations of equal power. The Rothschilds and their agents will soon wield enormous financial influence in 3 of the "Big 4" nations. **Only Russia still remains free of Rothchild's reach.**

The Congress of Vienna consolidated German states and redrew the borders of Europe.

1816
THE BEAST IS BACK! THE 2nd CENTRAL BANK OF THE U.S. IS ESTABLISHED

Five years after America's Central Bank was killed, and just two years after the White House is burned, the **Second Bank of the United States** is chartered by many of the same Congressmen who voted against the re-charter in 1811. After the War of 1812, Madison and other anti-Bank Jeffersonians had a "change of heart" when they found it difficult to cover war debts. Was there a deal made to re-establish a Bank in order to call off Rothschild's British attack dogs?

The timing of the re-charter, the timing of the Perceval assassination, the timing of the war, and the sudden decision to now accept a Central Bank, suggest that the very strange War of 1812 was actually a Bank War. Like the first Bank, this one also has a 20 year charter, is also a privately held corporation, and its principal shareholders are also linked to the New York-London axis. The Bank has the power to engineer debt driven "booms" by creating money "out of thin air" and then lending it into the economy at interest.

1819
THE 2nd CENTRAL BANK OF THE U.S. CAUSES A PANIC

By 1819, the Bank has already created its first boom-bust real estate bubble. The Bank's easy debt money drove prices up, and its "tight money" adjustment drove prices down. When the bubble from **The Panic of 1819** pops; borrowers are unable to repay their loans and property values crash.

Bankruptcies and bank runs follow.

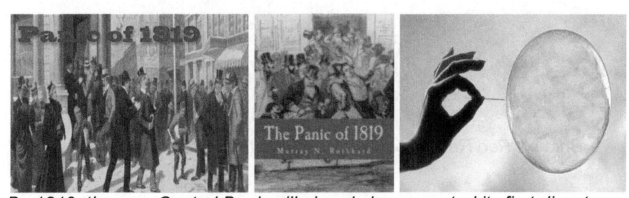

By 1819, the new Central Bank will already have created its first disastrous bubble – in real estate and also stocks.

1820
THE CATO STREET CONSPIRACY / RED RADICALS PLOT TO KILL THE UK PRIME MINISTER AND HIS CABINET

With the recent death of King George III, Revolutionary **Arthur Thistlewood** and his gang of conspirators hope to exploit his death and bring a French style revolution to Britain. At their Cato Street meeting place in London, the group plots to kill Britain's Prime Minister as well as all of his Cabinet Ministers. In the ensuing chaos, the radicals would then institute a "Committee for Public Safety" to instigate and oversee a radical Revolution similar to the murderous French Revolution of just 30 years earlier.

After the plot is uncovered, five of the main planners are executed and five others sentenced to prison. As was the case in France, Thistlewood's masters and financial backers remain in the shadows. The Red monster is still alive and growing in Europe.

Britain's Red Revolution was foiled and the traitors were hanged.

1821 – 1880

DECEMBER, 1823
THE MONROE DOCTRINE

The Monroe Doctrine is aimed at curbing European influence in 'The Americas'. **President James Monroe**'s policy states that the US will not interfere in the colonial affairs of Europe, but would regard further colonization in the America's as an act of aggression, which would trigger US intervention.

As Spanish colonies struggle for independence, Monroe seeks to prevent the establishment of puppet British or French monarchies in their place. Whether or not Spain keeps its colonies does not concern Monroe. His goal is to prevent the "balance-of-power" politics of Europe from spreading to the Americas, and thus threatening the young USA.

"Don't cross this line!"

1825
THE HOUSE OF ROTHSCHILD BAILS BRITAIN OUT OF THE "PANIC OF 1825"

The **Panic of 1825** is a stock market crash that arises, in part, out of speculative investments in Latin America. As is *always* the case, the crisis is precipitated by the expansionary monetary policy – in this case from the Bank of England. This fuels a stock market bubble. The inevitable tightening of money pops it.

The crisis leads to the closing of six London banks and sixty country banks in England; but was also manifest in the markets of Europe, Latin America, and the

60

United States. Nathan Rothschild steps up to supply enough coin to the Bank of England to enable it to stay afloat.

An infusion of gold reserves from the Rothschild-affiliated **Banque de France** also helps to save the Bank of England from complete collapse. As if the family didn't have enough wealth and power -- the House's bailout / buy up of 1825 makes them even bigger!

The Bubble Game:

With passions inflamed by the Rothschild financial press, greedy fools get all excited over easy money and rising stock prices. When the money supply is tightened, the bubble inevitably pops and stocks crash. Rothschild then steps in and buys everything up.....And the idiots NEVER figure it out.

1825
RUSSIAN CZAR ALEXANDER I DIES MYSTERIOUSLY AS ROTHSCHILD TARGETS RUSSIA FOR DESTRUCTION

After the fall of Napoleon and the Congress of Vienna, the Rothschilds have turned their hateful lust towards the Royal **Romanov Family** of Russia. The Russian Empire is an up and coming world power, possessing vast territory and resources. Like the young United States of America, Orthodox Christian Russia is also destined for greatness. And also like the USA, it is not under Rothschild's complete control.

Czar *(King)* **Alexander I** had already survived a kidnapping attempt made while he was on his way to a conference in Europe. In 1825, the Czar dies of an unexpected illness, contracted while he was again traveling far away from the safe

Capital of St. Petersburg. The death is sudden and mysterious, giving rise to "conspiracy theories." The world-shaking events that will occur over the next 100 years add much credibility to the poisoning theory. Coming events will clearly confirm that the Romanovs and their Empire have been targeted for death by the forces of the **New World Order** and its controlled gang of Red terrorists.

Nathan Rothschild wants the Romanovs dead and the enormous Russian Empire and its resources under NWO control. Czar Alexander's death was shrouded in mystery.

1832-1835
CENTRAL BANK BOSS NICHOLAS BIDDLE BATTLES WITH ANDREW JACKSON

The Charter for the **Second Bank of the United States** is due to expire in 1836. **Nicholas Biddle** is the President of the privately owned Central Bank. Biddle is an advocate of big government, public *(government)* education, and centralized banking.

In 1833, President **Andrew Jackson** begins his effort to "Kill the Bank" by withdrawing government funds from it and then letting its charter expire without renewal. Jackson hates Biddle's Bank. He accuses it of causing inflation, creating speculative bubbles, and corrupting the nation's politics. He is said to have declared to the bankers':

"You are a den of vipers and thieves. I intend to rout you out, and by the Eternal God, I will rout you out!" **(1)**

Biddle then *deliberately* causes the recession of 1834 by tightening the money supply, leaving debtors short of new currency to repay old loans. Biddle is trying to intimidate the ex-General and hero of the War of 1812, but the fiery Andrew Jackson is a fearless defender of the common people. Instead of backing down from banker pressure, Jackson turns up the heat. He threatens the bankers and wins the public to his side in **"The Bank War"**.

When he didn't get his way, Biddle deliberately damaged the economy. Jackson is determined to shut the bankers down and clean them out.

JANUARY, 1835
JACKSON PAYS OFF THE ENTIRE NATIONAL DEBT – THE FIRST & ONLY TIME IN U.S. HISTORY!

The banking dynasties watch in dismay, as Andrew Jackson becomes the first and only President in US history to pay off the entire national debt. US taxpayers are thus spared the burden of paying bond interest on debt to the Central Bankers. Jackson warns America about the danger of debt:

"I am one of those who do not believe that a national debt is a national blessing, but rather a curse to a republic; inasmuch as it is calculated to raise around the administration a moneyed aristocracy dangerous to the liberties of the country."
(2)

Deprived of the huge profits that Central Banks generate from the debts of big government, the bankers plot the destruction of Andrew Jackson.

Jackson hated debt and mistrusted the New York Bankers.

JANUARY 30, 1835
BRITISH AGENT ATTEMPTS TO KILL ANDREW JACKSON

As President Jackson leaves the Capitol following a funeral, a "deranged" man from Britain named **Richard Lawrence** emerges from behind a column and fires his pistol at Jackson. The gun misfires. Lawrence pulls out a 2nd pistol, which also misfires! Jackson attacks Lawrence with his cane. The would-be assassin is then restrained.

Lawrence plays the part of a "deranged" lone gunman, but he does suggest that Jackson's opposition to the Central Bank is what motivated his action, saying that with Jackson dead, *"Money will be more plenty."* **(3)**

The assassination attempt on Jackson is the first against an American President who defied the **New World Order** bankers. Many more attempts against conservative and nationalist Kings, Prime Ministers, and Presidents, carried out by manipulated loner fanatics, are yet to come.

The legend of the General – President Jackson grows stronger by the day.

Biddle's effort to keep the Central Bank alive fails as the charter expires. When asked in later years about what he believed was his greatest accomplishment, Jackson replied: *'I Killed the Bank."* **(4)**

The privately owned bank will go out of business completely in 1841. Biddle is arrested for fraud, but later acquitted. Jackson's heroism set the NWO bankers' efforts back many years. It will be 77 more years before the fraudulent monster of central banking resurfaces in America under the name: "The Federal Reserve System".

1- 1836 Cartoon: Jackson slaying the 'Monster Bank'

2- Jackson is still hated to this day by America's Ruling Financial Class and their prostitute "historians". In 2015, a media-hyped effort to remove Jackson's image from the $20 bill was launched.

1844
WRITER, FUTURE UK PRIME MINISTER USES FICTION TO CONFIRM THE ROTHSCHILD CONSPIRACY

Benjamin Disraeli is a Jewish writer and aspiring politician. He will become Prime Minister of Britain *(1868, and 1874)* and a dominant player of the 19th century. Long before his rise to power, Disraeli publishes **Coningsby: The New**

Generation. Though fictional, *Coningsby* is based on British politics *(Young England Movement).*

A character named Sidonia represents **Lionel de Rothschild** *(son of Nathan)*. Sidonia describes to the politician Coningsby how unseen forces - the "Sidonias" foremost among them, shape Europe's affairs. Sidonia reveals his dislike for the Romanovs *(Russian Czars)*:

"there is no friendship between the Court of St. Petersburg (Russia) and my family." **(5)**

Sidonia foretells of the Jewish role in the coming 1848 Revolutions about to engulf Europe.

"You never observe a great intellectual movement in Europe in which the Jews do not greatly participate... that mighty revolution of which so little is as yet known in England, is entirely developing under the auspices of Jews." **(6)**

Sidonia hints of subverting White nations by making the Whites disappear through "race mixing":

*"The fact is you cannot destroy a pure Caucasian race. It is a simple law of nature. **The mixed persecuting race disappears**, the pure persecuted race (Jews) remains."* **(7)**

- "persecution"' = opposition to Rothschild

Sidonia concludes his confession by speaking of the shadow rulers:

"So you see my dear Coningsby, that the world is governed by very different personages from what is imagined by those who are not behind the scenes." **(8)**

Disraeli was very close to the Rothschild Dynasty which made his career. In 'Coningsby', Disraeli uses fiction to describe the very real power and real plans of Lionel de Rothschild (right) and family.

"The mixed persecuting race disappears."

1848
'SPRING TIME OF THE PEOPLES'; PRE-PLANNED REVOLUTIONS AFFECT 50 COUNTRIES

As foretold by Disraeli, pre-planned uprisings - similar to today's "color revolutions" - begin in Sicily in January of 1848. Soon after, revolts "spontaneously" break out in 50 states throughout Europe and South America. The rebel Reds and other assorted groups demand "democracy" *(mob rule manipulated by the Banking Dynasties / Globalists).*

Although there are legitimate grievances in any nation, and many of the 1848 reformers are sincere people with noble republican visions, the higher purpose of the revolts is not to improve the lives of the people. The true goal is to subvert the authority of existing governments and install "democratic" governments that can be easily controlled by agents working for **The New World Order.**

Again, let us reiterate:

> **The New World Order refers to a movement among banking, media and academic elites - the legendary Rothschild Family foremost among them - with philosophical roots dating back to the days of the French Revolution.**
>
> **The N.W.O. envisions the future establishment of an integrated system of "Global Governance" to be erected upon the ruins of the "Old World Order" - a world based on sovereign and independent nations.**

The controlled revolutions wreak havoc, causing thousands of deaths and leading to political changes in some states. Within a year, the revolutions will have been put down, but the political structure of Europe has now been weakened by the slow poison of "liberalism". Czarist Russia, the hated enemy of the legendary Globalist **Rothschild Family**, is unaffected by the Red tumult of 1848, but not for long.

1848 was a big year for the Globalists and their controlled 'pro-democracy' mobs of Communists, republicans and assorted dupes of varying stripes.

1848
KARL MARX PUBLISHES THE 'COMMUNIST MANIFESTO'

As well-funded and well-organized revolutionary movements spread across Europe, German-Jewish "philosopher" **Karl Marx** sets forth the goals of the Communists. For all his lofty talk and empty promises of a "workers' paradise" and "social justice", the **Communist Manifesto** is just an intellectual mask for the Rothschild Family's Globalist plan to enslave humanity under a **New World Order.** Marx's grandparents were actually related to the Rothschild Family, through marriage.

The Communists call for heavy income taxes, a Central Bank with monopoly on credit, abolition of private land ownership and inheritance, state control over communication, education, manufacturing, agriculture, and medicine. Marx refers to this totalitarian scheme as 'dictatorship of the proletariat *(downtrodden masses).*

Marx's cult followers promote violence, class envy, and hostility towards free markets, family, business, tradition, and Christianity. In addition to the angry misfits, envious losers and maladjusted criminals who worship Marx; there are many well-meaning idealists who fall for Marx's empty and poisonous promises of a better world with security and prosperity for all.

These "useful idiots" are known, to this day, as "liberals" or "progressives". Their thoughtless idealism will unwittingly help the Reds and Globalists greatly.

1 & 2 - The revolutionary philosophy and false promises of Marx & Engels will destabilize Europe for many years to come. 3- George Orwell's classic, 'Animal Farm' is an allegorical expose of what idealistic Communism is really all about.

1840-1880
SEVEN ASSASSINATION ATTEMPTS ON QUEEN VICTORIA

During the 64 year reign of **Queen Victoria** *(1837-1901),* **(9)** the legendary Monarch will survive an astounding **seven** assassination attempts! Three of these failed efforts against Victoria occurred during the turbulent 1840's. These attempts, and the many other attempts and murders of European Kings in the coming years, combine to send a clear and intimidating message to the Monarchs of Europe.

Were the dark forces of the NWO behind any of the attempts on Queen Victoria? We can only speculate, but it does seem plausible. By the end of her reign, the once powerful Victoria and her heirs will have been reduced to a nostalgic sideshow. The Rothschild **New World Order** is, to this day, run out of London's financial district *(AKA "The City" of London.)* The symbolic British Monarchy survives only because its members know better than to challenge the Globalist-Zionist Bosses in London.

Victoria's power is usurped by The House of Rothschild and its agents.

FEBRUARY, 1853
ASSASSINATION ATTEMPT MADE AGAINST EMPEROR FRANZ JOSEPH OF AUSTRIA-HUNGARY

The wave of attempted murders of European Monarchs continues with an attempt on Austria-Hungary's Emperor **Franz Joseph**. The Emperor survives a stabbing by Hungarian "nationalist" Janos Libenyi, who attacks Franz from behind, stabbing him in the neck.

In addition to using Reds *(Communist & Anarchists)*, the NWO Mafia will often use mentally unstable "nationalist" tools to carry out suicidal assassination attempts and destabilize multi-national Empires.

Fortunately for the Emperor, the collar of his uniform is so sturdy that it blunts the effect of the knife. One of the Emperor's officers then strikes down the assassin with his saber, killing him on the spot. Franz Joseph will go on to live a long life. He will still be Emperor when Austria-Hungary, Serbia and Russia are manipulated into World War I following the 1914 assassination of his nephew by a Serbian "nationalist".

1853-1856
ROTHSCHILD, BRITAIN, FRANCE & TURKEY WAGE THE CRIMEAN WAR AGAINST RUSSIA

The Crimean War is fought between Russia, and an alliance of Britain, France, and the Ottoman Empire *(Turkey)*. Most of the conflict takes place on the Crimean Peninsula *(Black Sea / Ukraine)*. On the surface, the war is fought for influence over territory, **including control of Ottoman ruled Palestine**. Russian Czar Nicholas I seeks to avoid war by assuring Britain that its only interest is to protect fellow Orthodox Christians under Ottoman rule.

But Rothschild's Britain is determined to fight Russia. France will join them. The Rothschild Family finances the British-French war effort against the Czar. **(10)** After 2& 1/2 years of war, peace negotiations begin in 1856 under Nicholas I's son and successor, Alexander II. Russia and Turkey agree not to establish any naval bases on the Black Sea. The loss of Black Sea ports is disadvantageous for Russia, but she will regain the ports later on.

The results of the Crimean War foreshadow future events. It is the first direct assault on Russia by the forces of **The New World Order.**

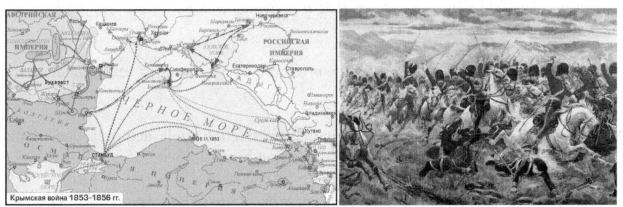

The Crimean War weakens Russia's position.

When **Charles Darwin** publishes **"The Origins of Species"** there is great skepticism over his theory that all life "evolved" from a common ancestor. The untestable, un-observable "theory of evolution" holds that a self-forming, single-cell creature, over a very long time, evolved into a fish - then an amphibian -then into a tree swinging ape - and then into a human being.

Mistaking observable adaptation for "Evolution", Darwin predicts that in time, fossil evidence will reveal the billion year progression from ocean scum to swimsuit 'super model'. After 150 years of digging, this chain of evidence has yet to materialize.

There are HUGE holes in Darwinism and his works are absolutely riddled with logical fallacies and rhetorical tricks. Yet, from its inception, Darwin has benefited from intense media and academic hype. To even *mildly* question "evolution" will get one shouted down as "ignorant" and "uneducated". This alone is evidence of its flaws!

The cult-like acceptance of Darwinism has done much to destroy faith in a Supreme Creator - and therefore the moral standards that logically derive from such faith. History shows that a people not rooted in moral principles cannot sustain self-government. They will in time degenerate and fall easy prey to tyrants.

Therefore, the fact that **Karl Marx** in his 1873 work, "Das Kapital" **writes a dedication to Charles Darwin**, is not at all surprising:

"Darwin's work suits my purpose in that it provides a basis in natural science for the historical class struggle." **(11)**

And nor is that the first and only expression of Communist excitement over Darwinism:

November 27-30, 1859: Communist icon **Friedrich Engels** acquires one of the very first copies and sends a letter to Marx telling him:

"Darwin, by the way, whom I'm just reading now, is absolutely splendid". **(12)**

December 19, 1860: Marx writes a letter to Engels telling him that Darwin's book provides the natural-history foundation for the Communist viewpoint:

"These last four weeks, I have read all sorts of things. Among others, Darwin's book ....this is the book which contains the basis on natural history for our view. **(13)** (emphasis added)

January 16, 1861: Marx writes an excited letter to his Communist friend Ferdinand Lassalle, the founder of the International Socialist movement in Germany:

"Darwin's work is most important and **suits my purpose** *in that it provides a basis in natural science for the historical class struggle."* **(14)** (emphasis added)

June 18, 1862: Marx had already *re-read Origin of Species*, and again writes to Engels: *"I am amused at Darwin, into whom I looked again"* **(15)**

1862: Marx quotes Darwin again within his 'Theories of Surplus Value':

"In his splendid work, Darwin did not realize that by discovering the 'geometrical progression' in the animal and plant kingdom, he overthrew the Malthus theory." **(16)**

German Communist leader Wilhelm Liebknecht later described just how excited the 19th Century Communist leaders all were about the new theory:

"When Darwin drew the conclusions from his research work and brought them to the knowledge of the public, **we spoke of nothing else for months but Darwin** *and the enormous significance of his scientific discoveries."* **(17)** (emphasis added)

Engels, Marx, and Liebknecht. The Big 3 legends of 19th Century Communist subversion were all obsessed with Darwinism. Why?

Indeed, "evolution" is very good for Globalism. That explains the academic and media hype behind it, as well as why **we are not allowed to question it.**

In spite of its **scientific flaws** - such as the complete lack of fossil evidence for the transitional species, the impossibility of testing the evolution hypothesis, the impossibility of species adding and losing complex chromosomes, the unobservable event of life coming from non-life, the impossibility of DNA codes writing and re-writing new and never seen before sequences, the lack of any plausible explanation for the "evolution" of *integrated complexity* present in all living organisms, and the simple fact that cross-species evolution has never been observed *(only minor adaptation of traits within a species has been observed)* - "evolution" is pushed as an indisputable fact and protected by extreme intellectual bullying as well as the force of law.

The purpose is to destroy man's faith in a Creative Intelligent Designer and the associated higher virtues that logically flow from such knowledge. In the vacuum left by "the death of God", a demoralized and degenerate people 'worship' the Government instead. As traditional families and cash strapped churches fade away, the Atheistic state takes over the charitable duties that strong families & churches used to provide.

God vs Darwin: *The Logical Supremacy of Intelligent Design Creationism over Evolution*

1- Darwin: Shhhh! You must not question 'Evolution"

2- The insanity of "Evolution" teaches that the lizard and the super-model evolved from the same common spontaneously forming one-cell ancestor.

1859
THE TERRORIST JOHN BROWN

In 1859, the abolitionist-terrorist John Brown attempts to raid a Federal armory in Harper's Ferry, Virginia. His purpose is to start a violent liberation movement among enslaved Blacks. The effort fails and Brown is tried for treason against the Commonwealth of Virginia, murder, and inciting a slave insurrection. A few years earlier, Brown and his men had also massacred five White men in Kansas.

Brown is found guilty on all counts and hanged. Southerners believe that his rebellion is just the tip of the abolitionist iceberg and represented the wishes of the Republican Party to end slavery. The **Harpers Ferry** raid in 1859 escalates already existing tensions that, a year later, will lead to secession and the Civil War. Had it not been for unreasonable psychopaths like Brown, the South would, in due time, have phased out slavery without bloodshed – as other countries already had done.

The lunatic John Brown remains a heroic figure for modern day Marxists.
(Google: John Brown Marxism).

APRIL, 1861
NORTH VS SOUTH: THE AMERICAN CIVIL WAR BEGINS

It might be a bit of an oversimplification to say that New World Order gang engineered the entire **Civil War**, aka The War Between the States, aka *(in the South)* **The War of Northern Aggression**. Regional differences of culture, interest and ideology existed since the founding of the American Republic *(recall Hamilton vs Jefferson / Jackson vs Biddle)*.

The American system of mercantilism / protectionism profits the North at the expense of the South. The perpetuation of that system is a cause of friction between the two regions. Another factor is that self-righteous New Englanders despise the more libertarian and *sometimes* less educated citizens of the South. Southerners are aware of this supercilious attitude, which in turn fuels resentment of the "Yankees".

 However, the playing off of the Northern Central Government against a southern Confederacy dovetails very nicely with how the Globalists have always operated *(and continued to operate)*. The United States is now a commercial power *mostly* outside of Rothschild control. But those political & cultural differences between the industrial North and the agricultural South have long been an issue of concern. When tensions between the South and the U.S. Federal Government come to a boil, the southern states *(Confederacy)* begin to secede from the Union. In April of 1861, after provoking a Southern attack against the Feds at Fort Sumter **(18)**, President Lincoln orders an invasion of the South.

Contrary to pop- history, the main issue of the Civil War is not about slavery.

At most, only about 3% of southerners hold slaves, and four of the Northern states are actually slave-holding states! President Lincoln does indeed oppose slavery, but he will later use the issue only as a propaganda tool to raise moral support for his true goal; saving and strengthening the Union / Federal government.

INTRIGUERS IN THE NORTH / INTRIGUERS IN THE SOUTH

Apart from those in the North whose sincere desire is to "save the union"; and apart from those in the South whose equally sincere wish is to defend their liberties, there are shady characters maneuvering behind the scenes on both sides – elements without which, the tragic war might never have happened.

THE NORTH

In American Jacobins: Revolutionary Radicalism in the Civil War Era, Jordan Lewis Reed of the University of Massachusetts explains:

*"By the late 1830s, this radical edge of the antislavery movement embarked onto two courses, both derived from and influenced by their newfound ideology. The first was towards violent direct action against slavery while the second aimed at legitimizing radical new legal theories and creating the political structure necessary to bring about their enforcement. While on the one hand **John Brown** and **Gerrit Smith** pursued militant action, on the other **Alvan Stewart** and **Salmon P. Chase** sought a political and legal redefinition of American society through the Liberty and eventually Republican parties.*

*With the coming of war in the 1860s, these two trends, violence and radical politics, converged in the Union war effort. In the midst of the Civil War and the early fight for Reconstruction, Radical Republicans and their allies in the Union Army displayed themselves as **American Jacobins**."* **(19)**

There were also many Jews energetically supporting the Northern cause. **August Belmont** a known financial agent of the House of Rothschild **(20),** is foremost among them. Belmont is a German Jew who had changed his name from Schönberg to Belmont. He is a leader of the war faction of the Democrat Party known as 'War Democrats". The Belmont Stakes horse race is named after Belmont.

THE SOUTH

There is strong Jewish influence supporting the cause of secession as well. Louisiana Senator **John Slidell** is not Jewish, but his family ties to European Jews run deep. Slidell's daughter is engaged to **Baron Frederic Erlanger**, a French Jewish financier based in Paris. Erlanger helps to fund the Confederacy, gouging the South with usurious interest rates and fees too! **(21)**

Erlanger's financing of the South, as confirmed even by today's New York Times **(22)**, is directly linked to the House of Rothschild. Slidell would later serve the Confederate States government as foreign diplomat to Great Britain and French Emperor Napoleon III.

Now the niece of the influential Senator Slidell is married to the aforementioned northern financier August Belmont *(Schönberg)*- Rothschild's Jewish boy and

Democrat boss supporting the Northern cause. After the war, "Confederate" Slidell will make his "Unionist" nephew-in-law his political protégé.

Also hooked up with Senator Slidell in this tangled North-South-Rothschild knot of financial-political intrigue is fellow Louisiana Senator **Judah Benjamin**, the Jewish big-shot who goes on to become the Confederacy's Attorney General, then Secretary of War, and then Secretary of State. There will be more on Big Benjamin in just a moment.

Through the shadowy fog of 150 years of elapsed history, we can still discern a clear pattern of divide & conquer, balance of power conspiratorial actions being played upon both sides - and with tragic consequences.

*Senator Slidell – His Jewish Son-in-Law Erlanger – His Jewish Nephew-in-Law Belmont, and Jewish fellow Senator Benjamin form an incestuous North-South connection with **direct links** (through Erlanger and Belmont) to the House of Rothschild*

General Robert E. Lee is critical of politicians on both sides:

"They do not know what they say. If it came to a conflict of arms, the war will last at least four years. Northern politicians will not appreciate the determination and pluck of the South, and Southern politicians do not appreciate the numbers, resources, and patient perseverance of the North. Both sides forget that we are all Americans. I foresee that our country will pass through a terrible ordeal, a necessary expiation, perhaps, for our national sins." **(23)**

- *Confederate General Robert E Lee*

JULY, 1861
THE BATTLE OF BULL RUN / SOUTH WINS THE FIRST BATTLE OF THE WAR, BUT FAILS TO FOLLOW-UP WITH THE 'KNOCK-OUT BLOW'

If the South is to have any chance of gaining its independence, it will have to win early, before the more industrialized and populated North can outlast them. The first battle of the war at Bull Run *(Manassas, Virginia)* is therefore critical. To make a long story short, the rebels force a Union retreat that soon turns into a full rout. The Battle of Bull Run will soon be referred to by some as "The Battle of Yankee Run" *(Yankees are the Northerners)*.

The Union Capital, Washington DC, is just miles away and now essentially undefended. It is the South's for the taking. The capture of DC and other parts north would have delivered a huge psychological blow to the North. Because many northerners aren't in favor of the war anyway; the capture of DC might very well have ended the war that same year. But instead of finishing the job, someone has decided to save the Capital - a decision that enflames the Southern press and leads to bitter finger-pointing.

The 'fall-guy' for this blunder will be War Secretary Leroy Walker. But in reality, it is the ex-war hero and ex-War Secretary and current Confederate President **Jefferson Davis** who calls the shots, not the young Walker. But it is also known that Davis relies heavily on the advice from the man whose intelligence and gift-of-gab he was awed by – Jewish Attorney General and former Louisiana Senator **Judah Benjamin**, referred to by critics as, *"Davis's pet Jew"*. **(24)**

Was it Judah Benjamin, ***the man openly admired by Solomon de Rothschild***, **(25)** who may have whispered poison in Davis's ear, telling him not to take DC and thus blowing the chance to win the game early for the South? And after Walker has been made the scapegoat and fired; who replaces him as War Secretary? None other than Judah Benjamin!

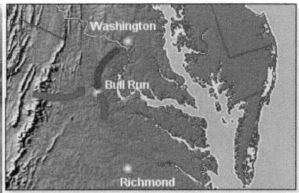

After Bull Run turned into a rout, Washington – just 30 miles away – could have been captured. Whose idea was it to halt? That of Davis --.or Benjamin?

Could the new War Secretary Benjamin's subsequent 1861 interference with the Generals, - acts so controversial that they would force a Congressional investigation - and his bizarre refusal to supply them as requested have been a ploy designed to prolong the war until the Rothschild's British and French hit-men could arrive to divvy up' America into two spheres?

Establishment historians will later claim that Benjamin's defiance of the Generals was due to a lack of supplies in the South. But given how early it was in the war, the claim that supplies were low seems like a cover story. If "lack of supplies" had been the cause of Benjamin's decisions, Generals Jackson and Beauregard would not have had reason to dislike Benjamin as they did.

Such a delaying scenario would fit perfectly with a Rothschild plan to have a long war, one in which both sides could be weakened before the British-French can arrive.

Let's take a closer look at the shady Mr. Benjamin.

Generals Jackson, Beauregard and Wise all hated Judah Benjamin.

1861-1865
JUDAH BENJAMIN – THE JEWISH INTRIGUER BEHIND THE CONFEDERATE 'THRONE'

Outwardly, the esteemed **Jefferson Davis** is the 'top dog' of the South – the President of the Confederate States of America. But behind the scenes, Judah Benjamin, with his European connections and impressive intellect, is, in the grand scheme of things, more powerful than Davis. What the banking agent Alexander Hamilton had been to George Washington, the trusted Benjamin is to Davis, *and then some.* Like Hamilton, Benjamin was also born a British subject *(West Indies)*. **There is simply no exaggerating the significance of Judah Benjamin.**

Biographer Eli Evans wrote that Benjamin:

"...achieved greater political power than any other Jew in the nineteenth century — perhaps even in all American history." **(26)**

Historian Charles Curran, in a 1967 issue of 'History Today' wrote:

Judah Philip Benjamin must be bracketed with Disraeli, who was his contemporary, as the ablest Jewish politician ever born under the British flag. But his career outdid Disraeli's in audacity. Benjamin lived three lives in one." **(27)**

Judah was a plantation owner, slave-owner and originally a Senator from Louisiana - as was the aforementioned and equally European-connected John

Slidell. Although he has no military experience, Benjamin is named the South's Secretary of War in 1861, after serving as Attorney General for several months. Many in the South loath and mistrust Benjamin. The great General Stonewall Jackson once threatened to resign over conflicts with Benjamin (28)- who was commonly referred to in the South as *"Mr. Davis's pet Jew"*. (29)

But certain people in Europe had a much higher opinion of Benjamin. In 1861, Salomon de Rothschild - grandson of dynasty founder Mayer Amschel Rothschid - described Benjamin as: *"the greatest mind in North America"* (30) That pretty much tells us all we need to know about the "southern rebel" Judah Benjamin!

In 1862, Benjamin is forced to resign as War Secretary. But Davis then appoints him as the South's Secretary of State. In this position, Benjamin will work with Swindell and Swindell's French Jewish son-in-Law Erlanger to secure not just financing from the Rothschild syndicate, but also to induce the direct involvement of Rothschild's Britain & France into the war, on the side of the South.

Judah Benjamin's face appeared on Confederate currency and bonds!

NOVEMBER, 1862
LINCOLN FIRES GENERAL McCLELLAN FOR HIS REPEATED DELAYING TACTICS

General **George B. McClellan** ably built the Union Army in the early stages of the war and achieved some early successes. But by 1862, McClellan's campaigns became notorious for timidity and sluggishness. Just like the Judah Benjamin's Confederate Army passed up a golden opportunity to capture the Union Capital *(Washington DC)* in 1861, McClellan was poised to take the Confederate Capital *(Richmond, Virginia)* in 1862 – but chose to retreat to a smaller-numbered force.

After Robert E. Lee defeats the Union at the Second Battle of Bull Run in late August, 1862, he invades Maryland. With the Confederates crashing into Union territory, Lincoln has no choice but to turn to McClellan to stop Lee.

McClellan and Lee battle to a standstill along Antietam Creek near Sharpsburg, Maryland. Lee retreats back to Virginia and McClellan ignores Lincoln's urging to pursue him. For six weeks, Lincoln and McClellan exchange angry messages, but McClellan stubbornly refuses to march after Lee.

In late October, McClellan finally begins moving across the Potomac in feeble pursuit of Lee, but he takes nine days to complete the crossing. Lincoln has seen enough. He finally removes McClellan and names General Ambrose Burnside to be the commander of the Army of the Potomac.

A picture now emerges of players on both sides of the conflict refusing to press advantages that could end the war early. We have already reviewed the intrigues of Judah Benjamin and his links to the Rothschild gang. Is there a Rothschild player that we can connect McClellan too? There is.

Two years after his removal, at a time when the Union is winning the war, McClellan will be named as the Democrat Presidential candidate to run against Lincoln in 1864. The chairman of the Democrat Party, and enthusiastic supporter of McClellan, is none other than Rothschild Jewish boy with the adopted English name – August Belmont; the nephew-in-law of Louisiana Senator and Judah Benjamin crony, John Slidell.

McClellan-Belmont-Slidell-Erlanger-Benjamin--Rothschild.

The North-South circular game is clear now. Neither side was supposed to win the War Between the States, at least not too soon. *Both* sides were meant to be bled before losing to the **New World Order**.

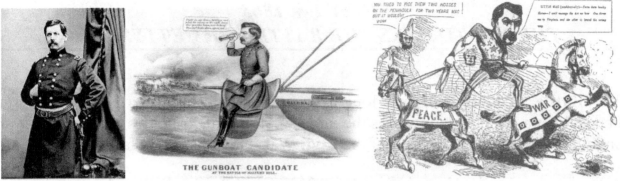

The Northern Press mocked McClellan's unwillingness to fight in numerous stories and cartoons. His past refusal to engage became an issue when he ran for President in 1964.

1861-1865
THE UNION DEFIES THE HOUSE OF ROTHSCHILD AND PRINTS ITS OWN 'GREENBACK' CURRENCY

Lincoln needs money to fund the war. He is extorted by the New York bankers, who want the Union to sell high interest bonds to them *(20%!)*, which they can resell to the banking syndicate in London.

Lincoln thwarts the bankers by issuing unbacked currency directly from the Treasury. The currency comes to be known as **Greenbacks.** The effect is inflationary, but it does prevent the Union from having to crawl to the New York-London syndicate.

Printing your own national currency is forbidden by The New World Order

The **Battle of Gettysburg** is fought in and around the town of Gettysburg, Pennsylvania. The battle involves the largest number of casualties of the entire war and will mark the turning point of the Civil War – in the North's favor.

After his success in Virginia in May 1863, Gen. Robert E. Lee leads his army through the Shenandoah Valley to begin the invasion of the North. With his army in high spirits, Lee intends to shift the focus of the war away from northern Virginia. The goal is to influence Northern politicians to stop the war by penetrating as far North as Harrisburg, Pennsylvania, or even Philadelphia.

After a grueling tussle back and forth, the Union Army beats back attacks by the Confederates and ends Lee's attempt to invade the North. For a three-day battle, the final casualty numbers are horrific.

North: 3,150 / Killed / 14,500 Wounded
South: 4,700 / Killed / 13,000 Wounded **(31)**

Brother killing brother with Rothschild agents involved in both ends.

JULY, 1863
DEADLY ANTI-DRAFT RIOTS IN NEW YORK CITY

Increasing support for the abolitionists and for emancipation of southern slaves led to anxiety among New York's Irish. From the time of Lincoln's election in 1860, the Democratic Party had warned New York's Irish and German residents to prepare for the emancipation of slaves and the resultant labor competition when southern blacks came north. To these New Yorkers, the Emancipation Proclamation was confirmation of their worst fears.

In March 1863, fuel was added to the fire in the form of a strict federal draft law. All male citizens between twenty and thirty-five and all unmarried men between thirty-five and forty-five were subject to military duty. The federal government entered all eligible men into a lottery. Those who could afford to hire a substitute or pay the government three hundred dollars might avoid enlistment. Blacks, who were not considered citizens, were exempt from the draft.

Initially intended to express anger at the draft, draft protests turned into a 4-day riot, with white Irish immigrants attacking blacks wherever they could find them. The military did not reach the city until after the first day of rioting, when mobs had already destroyed numerous government buildings, two Protestant churches, the homes of abolitionists, many black homes, and a Colored Orphan Asylum, which was burned to the ground. Lincoln had to divert 4,000 troops to control the city.

The official final death toll was listed at 119, with 2000 injured. Pro-Union newspapers later allege that some of the leaders of the riots were funded by foreign interests seeking to split the country. **(32)**

Irish New Yorkers fight the Federal Army.

1863
LINCOLN AND SECRETARY OF STATE SEWARD TURN TO RUSSIAN CZAR ALEXANDER I FOR HELP

A joint British & French entry into the war would have tipped the scales in favor of the South, and ultimately led to two American nations. Lincoln and his Secretary of State, William Seward block the scheme of Judah Benjamin by turning to Russia.

In a clear message to his old Rothschild-funded foes from the Crimean War, Czar Alexander II stations the better part of his Pacific fleet in San Francisco, and a portion of his western fleet in New York. The British & French instigators of the Crimean War get the message and are forced to back off. Judah Benjamin and the Rothschild financiers are thwarted. **Together, Alex and Abe have defied the London Bankers,** and will both pay a heavy price for it, as we shall see.

After the war, in recognition of, or payback for, Russia's help in keeping Britain & France out of the war; Seward will arrange for the purchase of Alaska from Russia after the war – an act dismissed at the time as "Seward's Folly". But now we know the reason for the "folly".

1 & 2 - The Czar and the President / UK cartoon mocks both Lincoln and Alexander

3 - The presence of the Russian Navy during the U.S. Civil War sent a strong message to Rothschild Britain & France.

OCTOBER, 1864
THE CHICAGO TRIBUNE ACCUSES AUGUST BELMONT AND THE ROTHSCHILDS OF PLOTTING AGAINST THE UNION

On 16 October 1864 on page 2, *The Chicago Tribune* reported,

"BELMONT'S CONFEDERATE BONDS (Excerpts)

"It is perhaps somewhat flattering to our national pride to know that the Rothschilds, who hold up every despotism in Europe, have concluded that it would be cheaper to buy up one of our political parties (Democrats), and in that way secure the dissolution of the Union, than to have their agents in England and France interfere and fight us.

But Irishmen and Germans have a something, which for brevity we will all a 'crop,' and this fact sticks in their crop, that the oppressors of Ireland and Germany, the money kings of Europe, not daring to carry out their first pet project of breaking down this Government by the armed intervention, of England and France,

Let Belmont state over his own signature, if he can that he and Rothschilds have not, directly or indirectly, in their own name, or in that of others, operated in Confederate stocks during this rebellion. Until he can face the music in that style it matters little what tune any of the Copperhead penny whistles may be authorized to blow, as they are very seldom authorized to state anything that is true." **(33)**

APRIL 9, 1865
GENERAL LEE SURRENDERS / SOUTHERN WAR EFFORT BEGINS COLLAPSING

With the loss of the Battle at Appomattox Courthouse, General Lee accepts surrender terms. There will be isolated fighting for a few weeks, but in essence, the game is over at this point. True Southerners had fought bravely for "Dixieland" against what they saw as a central government that was usurping the rights of the states. In the end, Northern manpower, industry, and quite frankly, the *brutality* of Generals such as Sherman and Sheridan gave the Union an advantage which could not be overcome.

The Union is preserved, at a cost of 600,000 dead. Though the differences between the North and South were very real; the bloodbath need not ever have happened. Issues such as States' Rights, slavery, tariffs etc. could all have been worked out intelligently and peacefully by wise men of good faith on both sides.

America has the John Browns, John Slidells, Judah Benjamins, August Belmonts and other assorted dupes and traitors on *both sides* to thank for the disaster. And above those puppet-players stood the 'usual suspects' - the House of Rothschild.

General Robert E. Lee surrenders to General Ulysses S. Grant at Appomattox Court House in Virginia. A sad story for both sides.

APRIL 14, 1865
LINCOLN IS KILLED / SECRETARY OF STATE SEWARD STABBED IN HIS HOME

In the closing days of the American Civil War, a massive conspiracy to decapitate the U.S. government results in the assassination of President Lincoln by an actor with ties to secret societies. **John Wilkes Booth** shoots Lincoln in the back of the head as Lincoln and his wife watch a play at Ford's Theatre. Booth escapes.

On the same night of Lincoln's murder, **Lewis Powell**, an associate of Booth, attacks Secretary of State **William Seward** in his home. Seward is stabbed in the face and neck before other men in the house subdue Powell. Seward's wife Frances dies two months later from stress caused by seeing her husband nearly killed.

Vice President Johnson and General Ulysses S Grant were also to have been killed.

The "conspiracy theorists" of the day point the finger at Judah Benjamin, who burns the official papers of the Confederate Secret Service right about this time. **(34)** Thanks to Bennie the Burner, the full story of Confederate clandestine services, and most likely the Lincoln assassination, may never be known.

Lincoln was shot from behind as he sat next to his wife. Hours later, Secretary of State Seward is nearly stabbed to death in his home.

APRIL 26, 1865
DEAD MEN TELL NO TALES! / LINCOLN'S ASSASSIN IS ALSO ASSASSINATED

John Wilkes Booth is tracked down by troops nearly two weeks later. The soldiers set fire to a barn that Booth is hiding in. Instead of taking him alive, Sergeant Boston Corbett shoots Booth in the head as he moves about in the barn. Booth's secrets die with him.

The assassin was shot after soldiers set the barn he was hiding in on fire. Why was he not taken alive so that he could be interrogated?

The *Sultana* is a Mississippi River steamboat that is tied up at Cairo, Illinois when word reaches the city that Lincoln had been shot in Ford's Theater. Immediately, Captain Mason grabs an armload of newspapers and heads south to spread the news, knowing that telegraphic communication with the South had been almost totally cut off because of the war.

While docking in Vicksburg, Mississippi, to pick up a couple of thousand recently-released Union Prisoners-of-War, *Sultana* also has some repairs done to a leaky boiler. This gives Benjamin's Confederate secret agents access to the ship.

After leaving port in Mississippi, three of the boat's four boilers suddenly explode. *Sultana* burns to the waterline, sinking near Memphis, Tennessee. An estimated 1,700 of her 2,400 passengers die **(35)** *(more than the death toll of the famous Titanic)*. The disaster will be overshadowed in the press by the just day-old killings of John Wilkes Booth and recent killing of President Lincoln.

In 1888, a St. Louis resident named William Streetor reveals that his former business partner, **Robert Louden**, made a death bed confession of having sabotaged Sultana by a weapon known as a **coal torpedo (36)** - a hollowed out prop that looked like a lump of coal but is actually packed with explosives. Enemy agents would sneak the weapons into a ship's coal supply. When shoveled into the ship's firebox – the boiler goes BOOM! Several Union ships were destroyed in this manner with substantial loss of life.

Louden, a former Confederate agent and saboteur who operated in and around St. Louis, had the opportunity and motive and may have had access to the means. **Thomas Edgeworth Courtenay**, the inventor of the coal torpedo, was a former resident of St. Louis and was involved in similar acts of sabotage against Union shipping interests. Supporting Louden's claim are eyewitness reports that a piece of artillery shell was observed in the wreckage.

Remember this fiendish little weapon – the coal torpedo – because *Sultana* will not be the last ship to mysteriously blow up.

Agent Courtenay's invention – the coal torpedo – sank the Sultana.

MAY, 1865
JUDAH BENJAMIN ABANDONS THE SOUTH AND ESCAPES TO GREAT BRITAIN

As the south collapses, Benjamin stays in the home of a Jewish merchant in South Carolina while final surrender negotiations drag on. Here, Benjamin abandons President Davis's plan to fight on, telling him that the cause is hopeless. When negotiations fail, Benjamin remains part of the group around Davis that moves on with the President.

At one point, Benjamin *(under suspicion for involvement in Lincoln's assassination)* tells Davis that he needs to separate from the Presidential party temporarily, and go to the Bahamas to be able to send instructions to foreign agents. He reassures Davis that he will rejoin him in Texas. According to historian William C. Davis, *"the pragmatic Secretary of State almost certainly never had any intention of returning to the South once gone".* **(37)**

When he bids Postmaster Reagan goodbye, the Postmaster asks where Benjamin is going. Benjamin replies: *"To the farthest place from the United States, if it takes me to the middle of China."* **(38)**

While other Confederate leaders, including the trusting fool Jefferson Davis, are being jailed and abused, Benjamin arrives in London before traveling to Paris - where his wife and daughter had been sent to live years before the war had even started. Benjamin then moves back to England and will enjoy a very profitable career and "second life" as an attorney, until his death in 1884.

Congressman John Wise, son of Confederate General and Virginia Governor Henry Wise, wrote a highly popular book about the South in the Civil War in 1899, *The End of an Era*. In it, he stated:

"(Benjamin) had more brains and less heart than any other civic leader in the South ... The Confederacy and its collapse were no more to Judah P. Benjamin than last year's bird's nest." **(39)**

Unfortunately for historians, and fortunately for the Rothschilds, Benjamin, exactly as he had done with papers pertaining to the Confederacy's secret services in 1865, burned his personal papers shortly before his death in 1884.

1 & 2 - John Wise 'End of an Era' expresses the true Southern feeling toward the scoundrel Judah Benjamin.

3 - After ditching his Confederate colleagues and the people of the South, Benjamin the Barrister went on to enjoy a hugely successful career in Rothschild's Britain.

1865
JEWISH MOGUL ESTABLISHES REUTERS NEWS AGENCY

The Reuters Telegram Company is the world's first major news organization. Established by **Paul Reuter** *(born Israel Bere Josafat),* Reuter's builds a reputation in Europe for being the first to report news 'scoops' from abroad, such as Abraham Lincoln's assassination. Almost every major news outlet in the world today subscribes to Reuters' services, which operates in over 200 cities in 94 countries in about 20 languages. The creation of the Reuters media empire marks the critical point in history when Jewish moguls begin to dominate the press of Europe and the US.

Though the Reuters family founders and heirs have since passed away, the public company today continues to vomit out pro-Globalist and pro-Zionist propaganda.

Jewish domination of the press, and thus, the public mind, began with Reuters

1865-1870
LINCOLN'S DEATH ALLOWS A RADICAL FACTION TO BRUTALIZE THE SOUTH / SOUTHERN VETS FORM THE KKK

Though his war against the South was brutal and destructive, Lincoln's post-war policy towards the defeated states was to have been one of brotherly reconciliation and rebuilding. With his sudden death, however, a radical Jacobin-like faction of the Republican Party known as the **Radical Republicans** are free to abuse and punish the southern states for their attempt at succession.

During **Reconstruction**, many supporters of the Confederacy are banned from voting while newly freed slaves are given the vote before they can be educated. Smooth talking "carpetbaggers" from the North flood the South, promising the ex-slaves "40 acres and a mule" in exchange for their votes.

Once in office, the carpetbaggers and their ex-slave allies raise heavy taxes on the conquered southerners. Criminal acts against southern citizens, as well as rapes of southern women, are common. In this atmosphere of oppressive occupation, Confederate Army veterans form a secret society known as the **Ku Klux Klan** (KKK). Klan members clad in white robes and hoods, serve as vigilante groups.

They restore order, protect white women from being raped, lynch criminals, attack Radicals, and prevent the ex-slaves from mob voting for carpetbaggers.

More than the Civil War itself, it is the vindictive oppression of the South during Reconstruction that will incite racial tensions and leave lasting scars that will take nearly a century to heal.

1- General Nathan Bedford Forrest was a founder of the KKK

2- 1915 film, "Birth of a Nation' depicts Klansmen chasing off post-war Black Union occupiers.

APRIL, 1866
THE FIRST ASSASSINATION ATTEMPT ON ALEXANDER II IS MADE BY A RED TERRORIST

One year after the murder of President Lincoln, Lincoln's ally, Russian Czar Alexander II also comes under fire. Red Revolutionary **Dimitry.Karakozov** draws his pistol and attempts to fire at Alexander. The attempt is thwarted when a quick-thinking bystander jostles his arm as he fires.

Karakozov is captured and will be executed. Ten of his accomplices are arrested and sentenced to hard labor

Alexander narrowly escaped the same fate as his ally, Abe Lincoln at the hands of a patsy named Karakozov.

1870-71
FRANCE STARTS – AND LOSES – A WAR WITH THE GERMAN STATE OF PRUSSIA

The **Franco-Prussian War** is a conflict between the French Empire of Napoleon III *(a nephew of Napoleon Bonaparte),* and the Germanic Kingdom of Prussia. Prussia is aided by a confederation of many smaller German states. The swift Prussian / German victory thwarts French ambitions in central Europe, and brings about the end of Napoleon III's rule.

After the war, the French branch of the Rothschild Family steps up with a massive bail out of the nearly bankrupt French government. The new government *(The 3rd Republic)* is again a "democracy", bought and paid for by the Rothschilds, and under their influence more so than before.

Imperial France started the Franco-Prussian War, not the Germans. Above: Prussian leader Bismarck (seated right) meets the defeated Napoleon III.

JANUARY, 1871
GERMAN STATES DECLARE UNITY / GLOBALISTS SEEK TO CONTROL NEW GERMAN EMPIRE

The Prussian / German victory over France brings about the unification of the German states under Kaiser *(King)* **Wilhelm I** of Prussia. United Germany will soon become the main economic power of continental Europe with one of the most powerful and professional armies in the world.

Meanwhile, back in England, the Globalists plot to control the new German nation. Although Jewish bankers thrive in Germany, Germany *(like Tsar Alexander's Russia),* has the capacity to shape its own destiny and thwart the ambitions of the "City of London". Not only is German politics outside of Rothschild's total control, but the fact that several German Royals are intermarried with British nobility complicates 'the City's" ability to menace Germany with British power.

It will be 48 years before the new German nation can be brought under the thumb of The New World Order. But the long-range plan goes into effect immediately. Rothschild agent and future *(as well as ex)* "British" Prime Minister Benjamin Disraeli plots against both Germany and Russia.

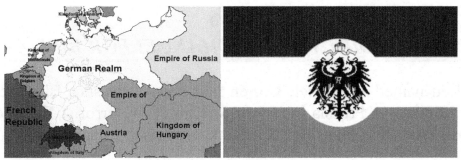

The voluntary unification of the German states gives rise to a great German Reich (Empire / Realm)

1871
THE NEW GERMAN REICH GRANTS CITIZENSHIP RIGHTS TO JEWS / THE JEWS OF GERMANY PROSPER

Otto Von Bismarck is the Chancellor of the new German Reich under Kaiser Wilhelm I. Through his skilled and energetic diplomacy, he will keep Germany out of war, and the rest of Europe at peace.

Soon after united Germany is established, Bismarck's government becomes the first European nation to grant citizenship privileges to its Jewish population. **(40)** Even Rothschild's England has yet to do this. The UK's Jewish Prime Minister *(Disraeli)* holds office because he had "converted" to Christianity. **By 1900, this remarkable people will have obtained massive influence over German commerce, education, press, politics, arts and banking.**

Bismarck, the political father of the German Reich, treated the Jews very well. They prospered in tolerant Germany.

A Jewish Red named **Frederick Cohen** had previously shot Bismarck when he was Prime Minister of Prussia in 1866. Now, in 1874, terrorist **Eduard Kullman** attempts to assassinate Chancellor Bismarck. Kullman's gunshot strikes Bismarck's hand.

Kaiser Wilhelm I and Chancellor Von Bismarck are the peacemakers of Europe, but Rothschild's **New World Order** crime gang would like these leaders dead so that mighty Germany can be subdued under their thumb.

Kullmann (on right) nearly killed Bismarck.

OCTOBER, 1873
GERMANY, AUSTRIA-HUNGARY, & RUSSIA FORM 'THE LEAGUE OF THE THREE EMPERORS

Chancellor Bismarck negotiates an agreement between the monarchs of **Austria-Hungary** *(Emperor Franz Joseph)*, **Russia** *(Czar Alexander II)*, and **Germany** *(Kaiser Wilhelm I)*. The alliance, known as **The League of the Three Emperors**, has three purposes:

1. The League serves as a mutual defense against the growing Red movements, which have menaced Europe with violence since 1848.

2. The League will avoid war amongst each other when diplomacy can resolve differences.

3. The League opposes the expansion of French and British power, as well as plots to threaten the internal order of their countries.

The military and financial power of these three Empires forms a Central-Southern-Eastern European power base that the Rothschilds and their British & French "hit men" cannot control.

There can be no New World Order until this mighty defensive coalition of Empires is somehow broken up and individually smashed.

British cartoon on left mocks The Three Emperors League. Bismarck is depicted as puppet master of the Emperors.

1877-78
RUSSIA DEFEATS THE OTTOMAN EMPIRE (TURKEY) IN THE RUSSO-TURKISH WAR

There are two main causes of the **Russo-Turkish War.** First, Russia desires to reclaim vital Black Sea territory lost in the Rothschild-financed Crimean War of 20 years earlier. The other objective, or at least, the other *stated* objective, is to liberate the Orthodox Christian Slavic populations of the Balkan states. Russia's Orthodox Christian and Slavic allies, Serbia, Montenegro, Romania, and Bulgaria, all rebel against Turkey and fight with Russia. Claims of Turkish mistreatment of Bulgarian Christians further upset the Russians.

Russia dominates the fighting, and begins advancing towards Istanbul *(Constantinople).* Dismayed that Russia may capture Constantinople and even

101

Palestine from the beaten Turkish Empire, Britain's Jewish Prime Minister **Benjamin Disraeli** pressures Russia to accept a truce offered by Turkey. Britain sends ships to the area to intimidate Russia and force a peace conference in Berlin, Germany.

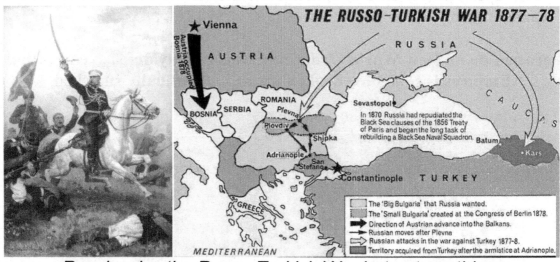

Russia wins the Russo-Turkish War but gets nothing.

MAY 11 & JUNE 2, 1878
REDS MAKE <u>TWO</u> ASSASSINATION ATTEMPTS AGAINST KAISER WILHELM I

In the days just before the important post-Russo-Turkish War international conference *(Congress of Berlin)* is due to take place in Berlin, two assassination attempts are made against **Kaiser Wilhelm I**. On May 11, '78, a Red named Emil Max Hodel fires shots at the Emperor and his daughter as they travel in their carriage. Hodel is captured and then executed in August.

Three weeks later, another Red named **Karl Nobiling** fires a gun at the Emperor. The 82 year old Kaiser is wounded, but he survives. Nobiling then shoots himself, and dies 3 months later. **The New World Order**'s secret war against The Three Emperors League, and all of Europe's Christian Monarchs, is really starting to heat up.

The War on the Three Emperors Leagues heats up with two assassination attempts against German Kaiser Wilhelm in just 3 weeks time.

JUNE, 1878
BENJAMIN DISRAELI PLAYS DIRTY TRICKS IN BERLIN

Rothschild wholly-owned British-Jewish Prime Minister, Benjamin Disraeli, dominates the conference which was called into session to settle the Russo-Turkish war. Britain, Germany, Austria-Hungary, Russia, France, Italy, and Turkey attend the **Congress of Berlin**. The Ottoman Turks still control the "The Holy Land", but Britain and the Rothschilds wish to ultimately take over Palestine. Russia is committed to the protection of Orthodox Christians throughout southern Europe and Turkey.

Before the Congress opens, Disraeli concludes a secret deal with Turkey against Russia, in which Britain will keep the strategic island of Cyprus. **(41)** This gives Disraeli an advantage, leading him to issue threats of war if Russia doesn't comply with the demands of the Turks, who had lost the war!

Another dirty pre-Congress deal is struck between Disraeli and Russia's soon-to-be *ex*-ally, Austria-Hungary. **(42)** Slavic Orthodox Christians, including the Serbs of Bosnia, are to be put under Austria-Hungary's rule. Russia and its Slavic allies had *won* the war against Turkey, but now many of the Slavs are to be transferred from Turkish rule to *Austro-Hungarian* rule. This breeds resentment among the Slavic subjects of Austria-Hungary, especially the Serbs of Bosnia who are forbidden from uniting with the independent nation of Serbia. **Court intriguers on all sides have put a permanent wedge between Russia and Austria-Hungary.**

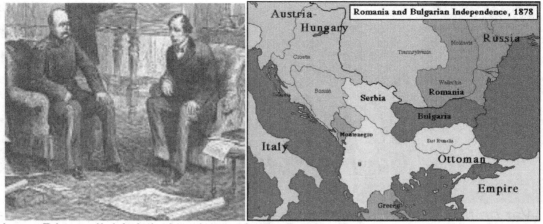

Devious Disraeli (right) dominated the Berlin Congress and undermined its host, Bismarck (left). The "victorious" Russians weren't happy about the deal, nor were their Bulgarian allies, and nor were the Serbs living in Austro-Hungarian Bosnia.

JUNE, 1878
DISRAELI'S DIRTY TRICKS CAUSE THE BREAKUP OF THE THREE EMPERORS LEAGUE

Chancellor Bismarck tries to keep the Disraeli-engineered controversies from breaking up the Three Emperors League, but the humiliation of Russia at the hands of Britain, Turkey, and Austria-Hungary is too much to bear. Russia pulls out of the League. Instead of being allied with Germany *(whom Disraeli also wants to isolate),* Russia is now cut off from her, and placed in a position where it can be played off against Germany's ally, Austria-Hungary - a classic divide & conquer scheme.

The foundation of the Great War of 1914-1918 *(World War I)* was laid at the Congress of Berlin, thanks to the dirty work of the Globalist-Zionist-Rothschild agent Benjamin Disraeli.

Upon returning to England, Disraeli boasts to Queen Victoria of how he killed the Three Emperor's League. **(43)**

By causing the Three Emperors League to split, dirty Disraeli laid the foundation for the Global bloodbaths of the coming century.

NOVEMBER 1878
DISRAELI PROVOKES RUSSIA BY INVADING PEACEFUL AFGHANISTAN

With the Three Emperors League disbanded, Rothschild & Disraeli escalate their assault on Russia. Disraeli plots to project British power along Russia's long Asian border with Afghanistan. He must sell his Afghan plot to the Parliament, the public, and to a foolish Queen that he has charmed and wrapped around his finger. Two years earlier, the deceitful flatterer had bestowed the title of "Empress of India" upon Queen Victoria.

Disraeli falsely accuses Russia of planning to conquer India *(a British colony)* via Afghanistan. The charge is ridiculous. Russia has no intention of attacking India and the Afghan and Himalaya Mountains make conquest virtually impossible. To counter the non-existent Russian threat Disraeli proposes a British occupation of Afghanistan. He writes to Victoria of his plan to: *"to clear central Asia of Muscovites (Russians) and drive them into the Caspian Sea."* **(44)**

The appeal to patriotism leads Britain into an invasion of Afghanistan, a campaign that ends very badly for the British. They withdraw in 1880 and Disraeli's influence is finally checked.

The "Great Game" in Afghanistan will be played again in 2001. Instead of a fictitious threat against India, it will be the **NWO-orchestrated attacks of**

9/11/2001, and the fictitious threat of "Al Qaeda" that will be used as the excuse to encircle Russia *(and China)* by way of Afghanistan and other Asian nations.

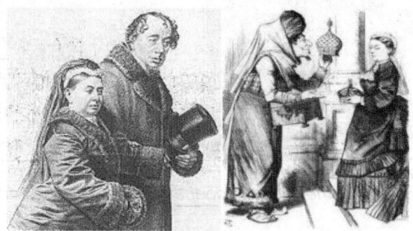

Rothschild's evil flattering agent has the foolish Queen wrapped around his finger. Cartoon depicts Disraeli crowning Victoria as Empress of India.

APRIL 1879, DECEMBER 1879, FEBRUARY 1880: THREE MORE ASSASSINATION ATEMPTS ON ALEXANDER II

The **New World Order** Red crime gang is relentless in its obsession to murder Czar Alexander II. One attempt had already failed in 1866. In April of 1879, a Red named **Alexander Soloviev** makes an attempt on the Czar in St. Petersburg.

In December of the same year, a Red group calling itself **"The People's Will"** tries to blow up the Czar by planting explosives.

Two months later, Red terrorist **Stephan Khalturin** detonates a bomb intended to kill the Czar at a dinner party. The Czar is late for dinner, but 11 others are killed and 30 wounded.

While Britain's Disraeli wages war against Russia on the diplomatic and military fronts; Rothschild's insane Red Revolutionaries attack Romanov Russia internally.

1- Soloviev fired five shots at the Czar and missed.

2- 'The People's Will" blew up a train station but didn't get the Czar either.

3- Khalturin's bomb failed to kill the Czar, but it did kill 11 others.

1881– 1910

MARCH, 1881
COMMUNIST TERRORISTS FINALLY KILL ALEXANDER II

After four previous attempts, Rothschild's Red terrorists finally succeed in assassinating Czar Alexander II of Russia. With his son Alexander III, and grandson Nicholas watching, the Marxists hurl bombs at the Czar. Alexander's legs are blown off and he bleeds to death.

Due to the presence of so many Jews in the revolutionary movement, anti-Semitic violence sweeps across Russia after the Czar's murder. These "pogroms", though exaggerated for propaganda purposes, help to trigger a wave of Jewish immigration to the United States, England, and Germany.

Many of these new immigrants bring their radical politics with them, as they continue to agitate against Christian Russia from their newly adopted nations.

The killing of Alexander II triggered massive Jewish immigration to America. Alexander is remembered as the man who liberated the serfs.

JULY 2, 1881
U.S PRESIDENT JAMES GARFIELD IS SHOT / DIES FROM WOUND INFECTION IN SEPTEMBER

The civilized world is still reeling from the brutal murder of Czar Alexander II just a few months earlier. Now America will lose its 2nd President in 16 years to an assassin's bullet. **James Garfield** is an Ohio Republican who has only been in

office 4 months. The state of Ohio will earn the reputation for producing Constitutionalist, Republican Presidents *(Garfield, McKinley, Taft, Harding)*
.

Garfield is a brilliant scholar, talented orator, and an advocate of interest-free "hard money" *(gold)* as a national currency. Like Napoleon, Andrew Jackson and Abe Lincoln before him, Garfield mistrusts the international bankers. Garfield warns:

"Whoever controls the volume of money in any country is absolute master of all industry and commerce." **(1)**

On July 2, '81, Garfield is shot at a railroad station by "crazed lone gunman" Charles Guiteau. Garfield survives and is slowly recovering, but his condition worsens after weeks of doctors needlessly probing him to find the now harmless bullet. Garfield finally dies on September 19, not from the bullet, but by infection caused by "incompetent" doctors. Garfield is the first of 4 Ohio Republican Presidents who, over the course of the coming 40 years, will either be killed, or cheated out of an election.

Garfield is shot in the back and dies 10 weeks later.

1880 - 1900
THE RED 'REFUSE' OF EUROPE INVADES AMERICA

In the wake of Czar Alexander's murder, anti-Jewish & Anti-Red uprisings sweep across the Russian Empire. Having watched his father blown apart by a Red bomb, Czar Alexander III does little to quell the public outrage *(or so it is said)*. The outbreaks, known as "pogroms", lead many Jews to flee to Germany, Britain, or the U.S. The Jews adapt well to their new lands, but the Red Jews bring their radical politics with them. In 1885, **Emma Goldman**, the notorious anarchist who will terrorize America for 30 years, arrives in New York.

In 1883, Jewish writer **Emma Lazurus** pens the '*The New Colossus*', a poem still on display at the Statue of Liberty. She forever changes the original theme of the Statue *(liberty)*, to what most people believe it now represents *(immigration)*. The poem includes the famous line welcoming the "wretched refuse":

"Give me your tired, your poor, your huddled masses yearning to breathe free, the wretched refuse of your teeming shore." **(2)**

Of course, many good European people arrive during this period, but so does much of "the wretched refuse." **An overlapping collection of Zionists, Communists, Anarchists, and money-lenders will soon spread Europe's violent Red plague throughout America's free society.**

1- 'Red Emma' Goldman began agitating as soon as she arrived in the U.S.

2- Emma Lazurus called for more "wretched refuse" to be let into America.

3- Both good people and bad Reds stared pouring into America

1882
THE ANGLO - EGYPTIAN WAR / ROTHSCHILD'S BRITAIN ADVANCES TOWARDS PALESTINE

The Zionists dream of one day capturing the Holy Land *(currently under Ottoman Turkish control)*. Recall how years earlier, with Ottoman Turkey on the brink of total defeat, Benjamin Disraeli intervened to keep the Russians away from

Palestine. Now, the Zionists are positioning their "chess pieces" towards the next step.

When the British-French **Suez Canal** opens in 1869, it is Benjamin Disraeli's Britain; *with Rothschild financing* that purchases enough shares to make Britain the main shareholder of the waterway linking the Mediterranean to the Red Sea.

By 1882, the Canal's host nation, Egypt, is being treated like a colonial subject of Britain. Always waging war under false pretenses, Rothschild's UK attack-dog picks a fight with Egypt, under the pretext of "protecting the Suez Canal." During the **Anglo-Egyptian War**, the British bomb Alexandria and invade Cairo. Rothschild's Britain becomes master of Egypt. During World War I, Egypt (*which borders Palestine*) will be a useful staging post to launch attacks on Turkey. **Palestine *(Israel)* is now within the Zionist Rothschild Family's reach.**

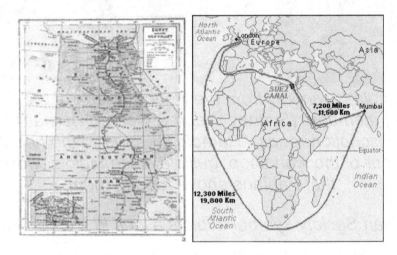

Egypt's strategic location and proximity to Palestine (future Israel) are coveted by the Zionist Rothschilds.

1884
THE SOCIALIST / COMMUNIST FABIAN SOCIETY IS FORMED

Like their openly Communist cousins, Fabian Socialists are followers of Karl Marx. **The Fabian Society** takes its name from Quintus Fabius Maximus, an ancient Roman general famous for his stealth delaying tactics. The difference between Fabians and Communists is one of tactics.

Communists work towards their goal through murder, terror, and revolution. The Fabians however, use stealth, gradualism, and 'democracy' to establish a Red world. Fabians practice *evolution instead of revolution.* Fabian homosexuals soon capture the British Labor Party. The disease spreads to the U.S. under the name of "progressivism", eventually taking over the Democrat Party and gaining a foothold in the Republican Party.

1- The stained glass window from the Headquarters of the Fabian Society depicts leading members (Sydney Webb & George Bernard Shaw) molding the world. (Inscription reads: "Remold it nearer to the heart's desire."). Beneath the floor of the workshop, gullible 'useful Idiots' worship the books that Fabians above feed to them.

2- Fabian Society symbol depicts a wolf in sheep's clothing

3- The patient Fabian Turtle's motto: "When I strike, I strike hard!"

MAY 4, 1886
MAY DAY RIOTS AT HAYMARKET SQUARE / IMMIGRANT REDS MURDER 8 CHICAGO POLICEMEN

American Reds organize massive May Day *(Illuminati Founding Day)* demonstrations in Chicago. On May 3rd, **August Spies**, a German born Anarchist Labor leader and self-styled "hero of the working man" addresses a crowd of striking union workers. The agitated mob then attacks a group of non-striking workers of the McCormick Harvesting Machine Company. To protect the non-strikers *("scabs")*, and themselves, the police fire shots on the frenzied mob; killing two of the Red union thugs.

Red agitators then spread the false rumor that the police killed the strikers in cold blood. The Reds print fliers calling for the workers to take up arms and attend a mass meeting in Chicago's Haymarket Square.

.

The following day, a line of police officers maintains order as Red speakers address the crowd. Suddenly, a pipe bomb is thrown at police lines. Reds begin firing pistols at the police and the police return fire. When the smoke clears, eight policemen lay dead and 60 others are wounded. Four of the Reds are also killed. Seven Red leaders *(most of them European immigrants)* will be tried and executed.

The monument to the dead policemen will be bombed in 1968 by terrorist Bill Ayers; the Communist friend and ghost-writer of future President Barack Obama.

JUNE, 1887
'THE REINSURANCE TREATY' / GERMANY AND RUSSIA FORM A SECRET ALLIANCE

Although the British-Rothschild agent Disraeli had destroyed The Three Emperors League *(Russia / Germany / Austria-Hungary)* back in 1878, German Chancellor Bismarck continues to work for peace. To "reinsure" the peace of Eastern Europe, and to prevent British or French intrigue from starting more wars, Bismarck's

Germany and Tsarist Romanov Russia agree to a secret treaty known as **"The Reinsurance Treaty"**.

Under the terms of the agreement, Germany and Russia agree to remain neutral should either become involved in war with a third nation. However, neutrality would not apply if Russia attacks Germany's ally, Austria-Hungary.

The two powers remain vulnerable to the Balkan controversy in Austria-Hungary *(Russia is the protector of the minority Slavic/Orthodox community under Austrian rule, and also of small Slavic states like Serbia)* Nonetheless, the Reinsurance Treaty is a very good sign that Russia and Germany will be able to work out any future differences diplomatically.

Bismarck worked to keep France & Britain from getting Germany and Russia to fight. Right: Bismarck with Russian Prince Andrey Lieven

APRIL 20, 1889
ADOLF HITLER IS BORN

At a time when the dark forces of the **New World Order** were already setting the chess pieces for the future war to enslave Germany, **Adolf Hitler**, the man who would become their greatest nemesis, is born into a very simple Austrian family.

Klara Hitler, Alois Hitler and baby Hitler

1890
NEW GERMAN KAISER DISMISSES BISMARCK / TURNS DOWN RUSSIAN OFFER TO RENEW THE REINSURANCE TREATY

Kaiser Wilhelm I passes away in March of 1888 at the age of 91. He is succeeded by his son Frederick I, who dies of throat cancer after a reign of just 3 months. Frederick's 29 year old son **Wilhelm II** then becomes Kaiser in June of 1888.

Like many young, "educated" Europeans, Wilhelm II is partially infected with the poison of "liberalism". Whereas 'Iron Chancellor"' Bismarck wants to smash the Reds of Germany, young Wilhelm is hesitant to crush the Communists. He believes that if Germany becomes more "democratic", it will pacify the Red agitators. Wilhelm II also wants better relations with the UK, the enemy of Russia. To that end, Wilhelm, *(possibly under the influence of NWO court intriguers)* turns his back on Russia, refusing repeated Russian requests to renew Bismarck's Reinsurance Treaty.

These irreconcilable differences lead Wilhelm to dismiss the legendary Bismarck in 1890. As the grandson of Britain's Queen Victoria, Wilhelm evidently believes that he can trust and befriend Britain *(which really belongs to the Rothschilds, not Victoria)*. He also believes that he can solve problems with Russia by negotiation.

Russia now feels isolated and mistrusts Germany's ally, Austria-Hungary. This leaves Russia very vulnerable to French and British intrigue. **History will prove that wise old Bismarck was right, and naive young Wilhelm was wrong.**

"Dropping the Pilot" - British cartoon mocks the dismissal of the great statesman and peacemaker. Bad move Kaiser Wilhelm!

1892
PENNSYLVANIA STEEL STRIKE TURNS VIOLENT / JEWISH RED SHOOTS AND STABS CHAIRMAN OF CARNEGIE STEEL

The **Homestead Steel Strike** turns deadly when members of the Amalgamated Association of Iron and Steel Workers threaten non-striking workers of the Carnegie Steel.Corporation. Pinkerton Security men are called in to secure the plant. Union thugs fire upon them as they arrive. The Pinkertons fire back and a 10-minute shootout leaves 2 dead from each side.

In nearby Pittsburgh, steelworkers gather in the streets, listening to accounts of the attacks at Homestead. Hundreds of them, many armed, move toward the town to assist the strikers. The Pinkertons confront the angry mob and beat them back.

The strike, and the Steel Union itself, are finally broken when the state militia arrives. Soon afterwards, **Alexander Berkman**, a Russian-born Jewish anarchist from New York, arrives and attempts to murder Henry Clay Frick, Carnegie's Chairman. Berkman had plotted with his lover, Russian-born Jewish anarchist Emma Goldman, to carry out the murder. Frick is shot and stabbed, but survives.

Berkman will serve 14 years in prison. "Red Emma" Goldman remains free and continues to openly call for violence against prominent Americans.

1- Berkman - the lover of Red Emma Goldman (yikes!) - nearly killed Frick.

1890-1894
'ANTI-SEMITISM' BREAKS OUT IN FRANCE OVER 'THE PANAMA AFFAIR' & 'THE DREYFUS AFFAIR'

The collapse of the **Panama Canal Company** in 1889, due to corruption, causes 800,000 French investors to lose their savings. Two Jews, **Cornelius Herz** and **Jacques Reinach**, play prominent roles in the political bribery aspect of the massive scandal. Their role in the massive fraud leads to a breakout of anti-Semitism.

Then, in November of 1894, a Jewish French army captain named **Alfred Dreyfus** is convicted of treason for passing military secrets to German agents. Amidst an international firestorm and charges of "anti-Semitism", the conviction is later overturned. But many French still believe that Dreyfus was guilty. **The Dreyfus Affair** deeply divides the people of France.

1 – The Panama Canal investment scandal rocked France

2 & 3- French postcard: "Museum of Horrors" depicts Dreyfus as a snake &
Dreyfus is ceremonially shunned by his fellow soldiers

1893
GLOBALIST BANKERS ENGINEER THE U.S. PANIC OF 1893

Like all bursting bubbles of economics, the **U.S. Panic of 1893** is a serious economic depression caused by excessive lending of bank notes *(monetary expansion)* followed by the inevitable tightening of loans. As always, when there is not enough new money flowing into the system to support the repayment of old loans, the end result is stock market crashes, bank runs and bank failures.

Compounding the panic is a run on the gold supply. Even though the currency is gold-backed, and although there is no Central Bank, bankers had still been able to artificially balloon the money supply with 'paper gold' issued through the scam of "fractional reserve banking".

The Democrats and President Cleveland are generally blamed for the Depression as the decline of the gold reserves stored in the Treasury fell to a dangerously low level. This forces Cleveland to borrow $65 million in gold from legendary Wall-Street banker J.P. Morgan and the Rothschilds of England. **(3)** Crawling to Morgan & Rothschild is the only way to support the gold standard. Morgan is an immensely wealthy and powerful man in his own right; but he is a "made man" - his maker being the House of Rothschild.

The simple-minded blame "Capitalism" for the distress. Many of them will turn leftward politically, even radically so. But the more astute observers place the blame elsewhere. Jewish historian Hasia Diner notes:

"Some Populists believed that Jews made up a class of international financiers whose policies had ruined small family farms. Jews, they asserted, owned the banks and promoted the gold standard, the chief sources of their impoverishment. Agrarian radicalism posited the city as antithetical to American values, asserting that Jews were the essence of urban corruption." **(4)**

Like all previous and future monetary crashes & panics, 1893 is a very good year for the Rothschilds. It marks a major American power grab for the House of Rothschild and its American agents and allies.

1- Drawing of panic at the stock exchange

2- House of Rothschild Rothschild front man J.P. Morgan

3- An "anti-Semitic" political cartoon in an issue of "Sound Money" magazine which appeared in the 1800's. Caption reads: "This is the U.S. in the Hands of the Jews", portraying Uncle Sam being crucified like Jesus.

DECEMBER, 1893
FRENCH RED BOMBS THE CHAMBER OF DEPUTIES

French Anarchist **Auguste Vaillant** throws a home-made bomb device from the public gallery of the French Chamber of deputies. The explosion injures 20 French deputies but fails to kill anyone.

Vaillant is sentenced to death and executed in February 1894. His last words were "Death to the Bourgeoisie! Long live Anarchy!"

French society was shocked by the brazenness of the Red attack.

JANUARY, 1894
RUSSIA ENTANGLED INTO A 'FRANCO-RUSSIAN ALLIANCE

Isolated from Germany and suspicious of Austria-Hungary, Russia *(which wants another crack at Turkey)*, falls into a clever trap set by France *(which wants another crack at Prussia/Germany)* and Rothschild NWO agents *(who have a much bigger picture in mind)*. **The Franco-Russian Alliance** creates an entangling military alliance between the two nations. The Russian giant can now be used to create a deadly 2nd front in any future war with Germany. **This is what German Chancellor Bismarck had worked so hard to avoid!**

The great Russian novelist **Leo Tolstoy** *(War and Peace)* passionately condemns the Franco-Russian Alliance as a French trick to entangle Russia in a future war against France's enemy *(Germany)*. Tolstoy sarcastically describes the suddenly friendly French as **"people who, without reason, suddenly professed such spontaneous and exceptional love for Russia".** **(5)**

1- Bismarck's nightmare; French magazine glorifies the Franco-Russian Alliance.

2 & 3: Tolstoy warned of the danger: "The Franco-Russian alliance cannot now present itself as anything else than what it is: a league of war." **(6)**

JUNE, 1894
REDS ASSASSINATE PRESIDENT OF FRANCE

The popular French President **Marie Francois Sadi Carnot** has a reputation for honesty and was untouched by the massive Panama Canal scandal of the 1890's. He establishes a friendship with Russian Czar Alexander III, receiving the Order of St. Andrew from the Czar himself. **(7)**

Carnot's popularity, immunity to blackmail, and close friendship with the hated Czar make him difficult for the Rothschilds to control. At this point in history, it appears that the Zionists are "removing some of their eggs" from the increasingly anti-Semitic French basket, and placing them in the increasingly Jewish-influenced German basket *(as suggested by Jewish-French Captain Dreyfus passing secrets to Germany and the attack on the French deputies)*. The one constant that remains is Rothschild's hatred for Russia.

This may explain why Carnot was stabbed to death by Italian Anarchist **Sante Geronimo Caserio.** The murder arouses horror and outrage throughout France. No King or President is safe from the Red beasts and their **New World Order** masters.

Like U.S. President Abe Lincoln before him, President Carnot befriended a Russian Czar. Carnot is then stabbed to death by the Italian Red, Caserio.

1896
GLOBALIST - ZIONIST PURCHASES THE NEW YORK TIMES

Since its founding in 1851 by Republican Henry Jarvis Raymond, *The NY Times* has been a big player in shaping public opinion. In 1896, the *Times* takes a turn to the internationalist left when it is purchased by a German-Jew named **Adolph Ochs**. In 1897, Ochs himself coins the paper's self-serving slogan: *"All the News That's Fit to Print"*

Ochs' daughter marries **Arthur Hays Sulzberger**, who becomes publisher when Adolph dies. Ochs' great grandson **Arthur Ochs Sulzberger, Jr.** is the publisher of the NY Times today. For 117 years, America's most influential rag has been in the hands of the same Zionist-Marxist family. Count on *The Times* to promote big government, Globalism, phony environmentalism, Israel, the Fed, and endless wars.

The New York Times

1896-1898
THE 'YELLOW PRESS' AGITATES FOR WAR AGAINST SPAIN

Beginning on a small scale in 1896, and building up to a comical climax in 1898, the very same New York 'Yellow Press', whose propaganda had already invented the legend of Superman Police Commissioner Roosevelt, agitates relentlessly for war with Spain, ostensibly over the "liberation" of Cuba.

Our High School History fables taught us that the Spanish-American War of 1898 was a meaningless war instigated by the Yellow Journalist William Randolph Hearst for the purpose of selling newspapers. Here's a typical history-book sample of the retarded drivel that is still being spoon-fed to captive audiences of dumbed-down students:

"It is arguable that the Spanish-American War was perhaps the most pointless war in the history of the United States. Although it was not known at the time, the war was not truly fought for territory, for markets, for principle, or even for honor. Rather, it began because William Randolph Hearst, editor of the popular New York Journal sought sensational material to print." **(8)**

Certainly, Hearst and his propaganda rival at the New York World, Joseph Pulitzer, are helping to poison the public mind against Spain while selling a lot of papers in the process. But this idiotic and incomplete analysis ignores the "big picture" of the geopolitical hand which is moving the chess pieces. The point of the imperial game is to project U.S. imperial power over the Asian Pacific. To that end, it is necessary to kick Spain out of The Philippines and Guam so that U.S. naval bases can be established there instead. It is a dirty game and, as we shall soon see, the cowboy-turned-super-cop will become a key player in the game.

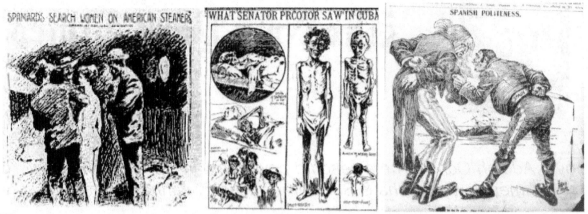

The phony, absurd, and vile atrocity stories of the warmongering Yellow Press created the momentum needed for the Spanish-America War.

APRIL, 1897
TEDDY ROOSEVELT IS NAMED ASSISTANT SECRETARY OF THE U.S NAVY / AGITATES FOR WAR WITH SPAIN

With war propaganda heating up, the charmed life and meteoric rise of **Theodore Roosevelt** (TR) continues with an appointment to the Office of Assistant Secretary of the U.S. Navy. Clearly, somebody is puffing-up this still young man, and in a big way.

Near the end of 1897, TR explains his warmongering priorities to one of the Navy's planners. Behold the chilling talk of a social-engineering psychopath who views Americans as his personal clay, and military men as cannon-fodder to be sacrificed for "the governing class." TR:

"I would regard war with Spain from two viewpoints: first, the advisability on the grounds both of humanity and self-interest of interfering on behalf of the Cubans, and of taking one more step toward the complete freeing of America from European dominion; second, the benefit done our people by giving them something to think of which is not material gain, and especially the benefit done our military forces by trying both the Navy and Army in actual practice." **(9)**

As for the pious rubbish about "liberating Cuba", we shall address that self - aggrandizing bit of bullshit shortly.

The rapid career rise of the new Assistant Naval Secretary was fueled by the same political and journalistic forces agitating for war with Spain.

AUGUST, 1897
REDS MURDER PRIME MINISTER OF SPAIN

The New World Order crime gang wants to destabilize Catholic Spain and turn it into a controllable "democracy." **Antonio Canovas** is Prime Minister of Spain. He is an advocate of a Constitutional Monarchy, and a supporter of the Catholic Church. This makes him a target of the Christian-hating Reds and their Rothschild masters. Red terrorists had previously hurled a bomb at Canovas in 1896 but the attempt failed.

While internal Red turmoil weakens Spain from within, external U.S. Globalists agitate for war with Spain over control of its Cuban and Philippines Naval Bases. Canovas will not live to see the disastrous Spanish-American War. He is shot dead by Italian Red, **Michele Angiolillo,** before the war begins.

Add Canovas to the growing list of dead Kings, Presidents, and Prime Ministers

The First Zionist Congress is held in Basel, Switzerland and is chaired by **Theodore Herzl**. Jewish delegates from across Europe agree that Palestine should be given to them. The idea of a Jewish takeover of Palestine had been floating around for decades. Whenever Russia advanced its interests in the area, Rothschild's Britain would keep Russia out.

The problem is, Palestine is 90-95% Arab, and falls under the sovereignty of the Ottoman Turks. Unless the Turks agree to give Palestine to the Jews, the Zionist dream cannot be realized.

In 1901, the Zionists will offer to arrange a reduction of Turkey's foreign debt *(owed to Zionist bankers)* in exchange for Palestine. The Sultan of Turkey bluntly refuses. Giving away the Holy Land to the Zionists would be a betrayal of Turkey's, and Palestine's, Muslim population.

Herzl refuses to give up. The British offer to give the Jews part of the African colony of Uganda. The Zionists refuse, insisting upon Palestine. Prior to his death in 1904, Herzl predicts that a world body will one day give Palestine to the Jews, and that he will go down in history as father of the Jewish State. **For Herzl's dream to come true, a European military power will have to be manipulated into taking Palestine away from the Ottomans by force.**

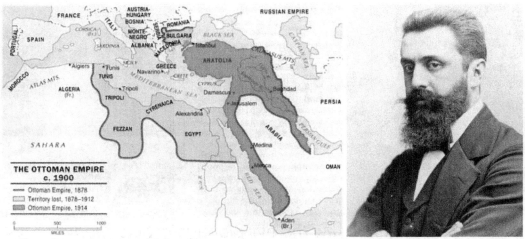

Palestine lies deep within Ottoman territory. But Herzl has a long range plan. He speaks of a "future world body" that will give the Jews a homeland in Palestine.

DECEMBER, 1897
THE DYING BISMARCK'S FINAL WARNING AND PREDICTION

Former German Chancellor Bismarck is now 83 years old and in poor health. Kaiser Wilhelm II visits Bismarck for the last time in December of 1897. Again, the wise old man warns the Kaiser to beware of the intrigues of courtiers around him, and of a European disaster that may yet still come.
.

Bismarck warns Wilhelm not to trust court advisors: ***"Your Majesty, so long as you have this present officer corps, you can do as you please. But when this is no longer the case, it will be very different for you."*** (10)

Subsequently, Bismarck makes these accurate predictions: ***"... the crash will come <u>twenty years after my departure</u> if things go on like this." ..... "One day, the great European War will come out of some <u>damned foolish thing in the Balkans</u>."*** (11)

This prophecy will be fulfilled almost to the year! Bismarck knew that a Balkan crisis could result in a 2-front war against Britain & France in the west, Russia in the east, plus an internal Red uprising on the home front.

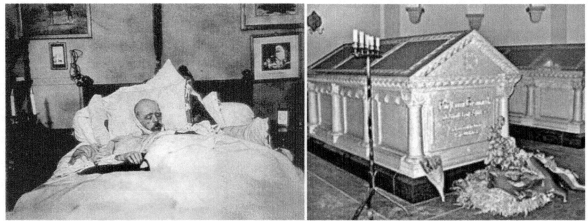

Bismarck foresaw the evil plot against Germany.

FEBRUARY 15, 1898
THE CONVENIENT SINKING OF THE USS MAINE

In January, 1898, with war propaganda now at fever pitch, Assistant Secretary Roosevelt, on his own initiative, orders the armored cruiser USS Maine to provocatively sail into Cuba's Havana Harbor *(controlled by Spain)*. In an amazing "coincidence", the ship just blows up, resulting in the deaths of 266 men. The warmongers of the New York Yellow Press, stirred up by Roosevelt's false accusation of Spain, finally have the 'casus belli' *(cause for war)* that has eluded them. What good "fortune", eh?

Without a trace of evidence, and in spite of strong Spanish denials, the treacherous TR proclaims Spain as the guilty party. Pressure grows on a reluctant President McKinley to ask Congress for a Declaration of War. Knowing that Spain is innocent, McKinley resists.

The official position of the U.S. government today is that "coal dust accumulation" caused the horrific, and unprecedented, explosion. But astute students of history understand how such events are often engineered by the clandestine services of the "victim" nation itself.

Speaking of "coal dust" and clandestine services, recall how during Civil War days the secret service of the Confederacy developed a "**coal torpedo**" – a hollowed-out device that resembled a lump of coal, but was actually packed with explosives. Enemy agents sneak the weapons into a ship's coal supply. When shoveled into the

130

ship's firebox – the boiler goes BOOM! This nasty little weapon caused great loss of life during the Civil War; and was probably the means used by Secretary Roosevelt used to blow up the Maine.

1- The mysterious and deadly blast was immediately followed by the false accusations of the Yellow Press and their darling Teddy Roosevelt.

2- Was it a coal torpedo? You know it was!

FEBRUARY 25, 1898
TR ORDERS THE U.S. NAVY TO PREPARE FOR WAR

Just 10 days after the battleship *Maine* explodes, the Secretary of the Navy leaves his office and Roosevelt becomes Acting Secretary for four hours. TR wastes no time in cabling the Navy worldwide to prepare for war, ordering ammunition and supplies, bringing in "experts" and going to Congress to ask for authority to recruit as many sailors as needed. All the while, Spain continues to protest its innocence.

TR orders the squadrons to prepare for the war that he wants so badly.

Even after the strange explosion on the Maine, President McKinley, Speaker of the House Thomas Brackett Reed, and America's business community had all urged a negotiated solution to the manufactured crisis in Cuba. **McKinley even communicates with the Pope in hopes for a peaceful mediation. (12)**

But the warmonger coalition in Congress and the New York Press is now too strong. Feeding off of Roosevelt's vile slanders, the Yellow Press runs headlines such as "Spanish Murderers" and "Remember the Maine". It is interesting to note that when McKinley finally surrenders to the inevitable, he never mentions the sinking of the USS Maine. That's because he knows that Spain is innocent and, unlike Roosevelt, isn't willing to lie to the American public.

*Neither the Pope, nor the innocent Spaniards, nor the U.S. President was able to beat back the insane war mania and press propaganda which followed the destruction in the Maine. **The Congressional and media pressure on McKinley forced him to finally ask for a war declaration.***

APRIL 12, 1898
TR ORDERS NAVY TO ATTACK SPAIN'S PACIFIC FLEET

Within hours of the war declaration, "Assistant" Secretary Roosevelt again takes matters into his own hands by issuing an order for America's **Asiatic Squadron**, stationed in British Hong Kong, to "protect commerce" - by destroying the Spanish fleet based in the Philippines. Try not to laugh, dear reader; but some warmongers justify this outrageous act of aggression as a necessary defensive strike aimed at preventing a Spanish attack on California!

The Battle of Manila Bay takes place on May 1 and it is an absolute rout. Commodore Dewey not only destroys the Spanish fleet, but also captures the harbor of Manila - effectively a U.S. body of water ever since. On June 20, a U.S. fleet commanded by Captain Henry Glass, also captures the island of Guam - a U.S. territory ever since.

And finally, in July, the House and Senate work their way around the 2/3 Senate requirement for annexing Hawaii by voting on a joint resolution instead. **The "emergency" of the war is what finally enables the establishment of a huge base in Hawaii** *(Pearl Harbor)*. This is against the wishes of most native Hawaiians.

Philippines, Guam, Hawaii; yes, the war with Spain turned out to be very good for the warmongering Globalist imperialists of that era. Hey Teddy! Wasn't this holy war of yours supposed to be about "liberating" ***Cuba***?

The war for "Cuba's freedom" was really all about controlling Asia.

MAY 6, 1898
TR RESIGNS AS ASSISTANT NAVAL SECRETARY TO BECOME A FAKE "WAR HERO'

The totally lopsided war will end in August, after just 3 and 1/2 months. But not before the war's most important instigator, Teddy Roosevelt, steps down from his position and volunteers to "fight". The grand-standing clown serves just long enough to build his resume as a "war hero". His mythical achievements as the fearless, horse-mounted leader of the "The Rough Riders" and "hero of San Juan Hill" will be hyped by the very same Yellow Press which propagandized for the wicked little war in the first place.

In reality, the Battle of San Juan Hill, which actually took place at Kettle Hill, was only a minor supporting skirmish, *fought on foot*, in which Americans outnumbered Spaniards 15-1! It was actually the Buffalo Soldiers of the 10th Cavalry and 24th Infantry Regiments that had already done the heavy fighting, not TR's "Rough Riders". **(13)**

Prior to charging up the essentially undefended hill, the dramatic little Caesar, who had the only horse, rode back and forth between rifle pits at the forefront of the advance up Kettle Hill, **an advance that he urged despite the absence of any orders from superiors.** He was forced to walk up the last part of the hill when his poor horse became entangled in barbed wire.

The mythical "war hero" later wrote about his imaginary role in the non-battle:

"On the day of the big fight I had to ask my men to do a deed that European military writers consider utterly impossible of performance, that is, to attack over open ground an unshaken infantry armed with the best modern repeating rifles behind a formidable system of entrenchments. The only way to get them to do it in the way it had to be done was to lead them myself." **(14)**

The great glory-hound recalled the Battle of Kettle Hill *(part of the San Juan Heights)* as "the great day of my life" and "my crowded hour". But it will not be until 2001 that "the war hero" is posthumously awarded the Medal of Honor for his actions. The reason why *TR's* request for the Medal of Honor was denied at the time was because Army officials, who knew the truth about his headline-grabbing, make-believe "heroism", blocked his nomination. **(15)**

Idiotic false propaganda turned TR into an instant "war hero". But TR's commanding officers knew the San Juan Hill story was fake.

"I am entitled to the Medal of Honor and I want it."

- *Teddy Roosevelt, in a letter to a friend, written upon his return to New York* **(16)**

SEPTEMBER, 1898
REDS MURDER EMPRESS ELISABETH OF AUSTRIA-HUNGARY

Elisabeth of Austria is the wife of Emperor Franz Joseph I, and thus Empress of Austria and Queen of Hungary. Despite warnings of possible assassination attempts, the sixty-year-old Elisabeth is traveling incognito to Switzerland.

On September 10, 1898, Elisabeth and her lady in waiting leave their hotel on the shore of Lake Geneva, on foot, to catch the steamship. The two walk along the promenade when a 25-year-old Italian Anarchist named **Luigi Lucheni** approaches them. Lucheni suddenly stabs Elisabeth with a 4-inch file inserted into a wooden handle.

Lucheni had originally planned to kill the Duke of Orléans, but the French noble had left Geneva earlier. Failing to find him, the assassin selects Elisabeth when a Geneva newspaper reveals that the elegant woman traveling under the pseudonym of "Countess of Hohenembs" was the Empress Elisabeth of Austria.

After Lucheni strikes her, the Empress collapses and dies soon afterwards. Lucheni is soon apprehended as anger and grief sweep Autria-Hungary.

Murderous Reds of unstable mind are being incited by propaganda and unseen handlers to blindly serve the bloodlust of The New World Order.

NOVEMBER, 1898
THE "WAR HERO" IS ELECTED GOVERNOR OF NEW YORK

Almost immediately after leaving the Army in August, 1898, the legend-in-his-own-mind is tapped by the kingmakers of New York to run as the Republican Party candidate for governor. As one would have come to already expect of the raging narcissist, TR campaigns vigorously on his war record as the "hero" of San Juan Hill. The mendacious mythology is multiplied by the Yellow Press. 'Colonel" Roosevelt wins the election by the historically narrow margin of just 1%. So many good things happening for Theodore Roosevelt!

His brief 2-year Governorship is marked by a flurry of busy-body activity in which TR casts himself as the champion of "little guy" against the big bad corporations. Like his mythical charge into the imaginary gunfire of San Juan Hill, this simplistic narrative is based on smoke and bullshit. In reality, TR was a wholly-owned creation of the very Wall Street Finance Kings that he claims to be crusading against.

The other notable, and typical, development of TR's Governorship was the very strange innovation of holding press conferences not on a weekly basis; not on a daily basis, but *twice* each day! Ostensibly, this was done to "stay connected with the middle-class". In reality, the two-a-day pressers serve as further evidence that

TR is a self-obsessed, attention-seeking megalomaniac who should never have been allowed anywhere near the levers of state power.

Then, as now, the gullible public loves a "war hero". TR shamelessly rode his fictitious battlefield heroism into the Governorship of New York.

1899-1900
U.S. VICE PRESIDENT GARRET HOBART DIES / TR IS IMPOSED UPON McKINLEY AS NEW VICE PRESIDENT

Just 55 years of age, Vice President Garret Hobart dies of strange heart ailment in November, 1899. Hobart is a constitutional conservative. His untimely death conveniently creates an opening for the Progressive-Globalist faction that has infiltrated the Republican Party.

The very same faction of warmongers that had imposed the phony Spanish-American War upon McKinley will soon impose TR onto the Presidential ticket for the 1900 election. This effort is also supported by some in New York who wish to be rid of the meddlesome do-gooder Governor and his excessive interference in commerce.

The Globalists are now "just one heartbeat away" from having their first puppet installed in the White House. ***Was Hobart poisoned to pave the way for the Globalist TR's stunning rise?*** Subsequent events suggest that Hobart's oddly convenient death was likely part of a plan.

Step 1: TR's military record is exaggerated by the Yellow Press *(San Juan Hill)*.
Step 2: The "War Hero" is then rocketed into the Governorship of New York
Step 3: When Hobart dies, the "the war hero" is forced upon a reluctant McKinley.

The popular McKinley is re-elected. In September, Roosevelt coins the phrase for which he is best known: *"Speak softly and carry a big stick, and you will go far."* **(17)** Spoken like a true sociopath. So many good things are happening for Theodore Roosevelt!

An unexpected death (poison?) turns McKinley-Hobart into McKinley-Roosevelt. The Yellow Press cartoon image at center depicts a "reluctant" TR, in "war hero" uniform, having to be seduced by the 4 maidens (North, South, East, West) into joining the McKinley 1900 ticket as Vice President.

1899-1902
THE BOER WARS / ROTHSCHILD INVADES SOUTH AFRICA

The **2nd Anglo-Boer War** is the first major war of the 20th century. *(The 1st war was a brief conflict won by the Boers in 1881)* Boers are descendants of German, French & Dutch settlers who arrived in South Africa in the 1600's. Hard working Boers develop the virgin land and build prosperous, free republics. Like flies to feces, the discovery of diamonds in the 1800's attracts British/Zionist immigration and intrigue.

Rothschild agent **Cecil Rhodes** *(for whom the Globalist "Rhodes Scholarship" is named)* and Jewish mogul **Barney Barbato** establish the **DeBeers** company, which will control the world's diamond production. In December of 1895, a band of 500 British adventurers had attempted to seize control of South Africa in an "unofficial" armed takeover. The failed raid is led by Rhodes's personal friend, Leander Starr Jameson.

Undaunted by the raid's failure, the aggressors continue to foment war against the Boers, with Zionist newspapers in the UK being the most vocal. The Boers ask

Britain to withdraw its troops. The Brits refuse. The 2nd Boer War begins in October of 1899.

The British wage a cruel war, even starving women and children in filthy concentration camps. They instigate and arm Black tribes to "kill the Boers." The Boers finally submit and accept British rule, *(up until 1961)*. The Jewish Oppenheimer Family - whose business ties with the Rothschilds go back more than 100 years **(18)** -, will dominate **DeBeers**, and South Africa's media. To this day, the **Globalists** are using Blacks to wage war against Boers.

Many women & children died in Rothschild Britain's concentration camps.

JULY 29, 1900
REDS ASSASSINATE THE KING OF ITALY

In May of 1900, Red terrorist **Gaetano Bresci** leaves his home in Paterson, NJ and returns to Italy. He proceeds to stalk **King Umberto**, arriving in the town of Monza on July 26. The King, who had survived a Red assassination attempt in 1878, arrives on the evening of the 29th in an open air carriage and begins distributing medals to the Italian athletes gathered.

After a short word of congratulations, Umberto descends the platform and gets back into his carriage. As he sits, Bresci bursts from the crowd brandishing a revolver and fires four times. The King dies seconds later, having been hit three times in the chest. Bresci is tackled by police agents and arrested.

Mamma Mia! The King of Italy is dead!

The charmed political life of the cowboy-super cop-war hero Roosevelt continues when **Leon Czolgosz**, a Red terrorist, shoots President McKinley at close range. It was the speeches of the notorious Red subversive, Emma Goldman, which moved Czolgosz to "do something heroic" and thus become famous.

McKinley appears to be making a strong recovery, before suddenly weakening and dying on September 14, 1901. Just shy of his 43rd birthday, the ultra-ambitious Theodore Roosevelt becomes the youngest President in U.S. history. A Red bullet has put a "progressive" in the White House.

And again, so many good things are happening for Theodore Roosevelt!

McKinley dies. TR is sworn-in as President. The rapid rise of TR is complete.

1- Leon **Czolgosz**: The immigrant Red's bullet put a big government "Progressive" into the White House.

2- Cartoon later depicts TR and Wall Street bosses welcoming Karl Marx.

1901-1907
TR FIGHTS THE PHILIPPINES WAR AND MORO REBELLION

The shameful Philippines War and subsequent Moro Rebellion grow out of the equally shameful Spanish-American War – the "splendid little war" as TR refers to it.

During TR's war of Asian aggression, **5,000 Americans and 20,000 Filipinos are killed, with as many as 100,000 more natives dying of disease. (19)** This is the Philippine independence movement's reward for rising up against Spain, based on America's empty promises. The formerly Spanish-speaking natives are then converted to the English language, which they speak to this day.

1- TR's long-since forgotten Philippines War got 5,000 Americans killed
2- American troops waterboard-torture a Philippine rebel.

1903
TR ORCHESTRATES A REVOLUTION IN COLUMBIA

Contrary to TR's post-Presidency boasts, and also contrary to official U.S. history fables, the phony Pharaoh of America did not "build the Panama Canal". The concept was long in the works before TR even arrived on the scene. At most, TR can be credited with expediting the stalled project; but the manner in which he did this amounts to yet another shameful and uncalled for episode of Rooseveltian "big stick" bullying.

Irritated by Colombia's reasonable request for better terms for what is to become the Panama Canal, TR foments a fake revolution in the Panama region of Colombia. As a show of intimidation, TR also orders battleships into the area. The result is the newly formed puppet state of Panama. Colombia ends up being screwed out of any lease payments for the Canal! **(20)**

Teddy tosses a spadeful of Panama dirt on the capital city of Colombia.

THE MAN BEHIND THE EGG—From the *Times* (New York)

1- Cartoon depicts TR's militaristic bullying of Columbia.

2- The Yellow Press and modern court historians would have you believe that TR single-handedly conceived and built the canal with his own two hands!

3- Cartoon mocks TR's intrigues which broke up Columbia and created the Panama puppet state.

APRIL, 1904
THE 'ENTENTE CORDIAL' / UK & FRANCE FORM AN ALLIANCE / GERMANY IS SUSPICIOUS

The Entente Cordiale is a series of agreements signed between France and Great Britain. The agreements settle issues regarding colonial expansion and also mark the end of a centuries-old era of on and off conflict between France and Britain.

Germany views the new alliance with great suspicion, especially because France had already allied itself with Russia in 1892. *The "chess pieces" of Europe are clearly being set in preparation of the Big Game to come.*

The Rothschild-Anglo-French alliance will one day entangle the U.S. These nations will serve as the military "hit men" of the **New World Order**.

German cartoon: John Bull (UK) walks by with his French whore as Germany, saber at the ready, looks on with suspicion.

1905
ZIONIST BANKERS & REDS ATTEMPT REVOLUTION IN RUSSIA

The attempted **Russian Revolution of 1905** is a wave of political uprisings, massive labor strikes, and terrorist acts against the government of Russia. The Reds *(under orders from their Rothschild / Schiff masters)* use the discontent surrounding the lost war with Japan *(financed by Schiff)* to foment the revolution. From 1905 to 1909, Red terrorists will kill 7,300 people and wound about 8,000.

Though the Jewish-inspired Red Revolution is suppressed, Tsar Nicholas II is forced to make "democratic" concessions which weaken his power and set him up for a future attempt. Nicholas makes a critical mistake by showing mercy to Red leaders such as Lenin and Trotsky. Instead of executing the Marxist leaders, the Russians merely arrest or deport them.

Lenin finds his way to Switzerland, and Trotsky ends up in New York after escaping from prison. The exiled Communists will one day return, with more money from the Zionist bankers, to terrorize Christian Russia once again.

1- Trotsky (center) and his Jewish-Marxist gang hung out in New York.

2- Jewish Wall Street banker Jacob Schiff weakened Russia by financing Japan's victorious war effort

FORBIDDEN HISTORY: QUOTE TO REMEMBER

"The Jews have undoubtedly to a large extent furnished the brains and energy in the revolution throughout Russia." (21)

George von Longerke / US Ambassador to Russia

FEBRUARY 17, 1905
REDS MURDER GRAND DUKE OF RUSSIA (The Czar's Uncle)

Russia's **Grand Duke Sergei Alexandrovich** is the brother of the late Czar Alexander III. Their father, Alexander II *(Lincoln's ally)*, is murdered by the Reds in 1881. The Grand Duke is a very influential figure during the reign of his nephew and current Czar, Nicholas II.

The Grand Duke meets the same sad fate as his father when a Red terrorist named **Ivan Kalyayev** hurls a bomb at the Duke's carriage. The bomb lands on his lap, obliterating the Duke and his carriage beyond recognition. Duchess Elizabeth, the Grand Duke's wife, withdraws from public life, founding a convent and dedicating herself to helping the poor. The Reds will eventually murder her and her nun-maid in 1918.

Another Romanov is murdered. The Communist killer got so close that the Duke's blood splattered on his own face.

1905
THE MYSTERIOUS PROTOCOLS OF THE LEARNED ELDERS OF ZION IS PUBLISHED IN RUSSIA

Russian Professor **Sergei Nilus** publishes a full version of **The Protocols of the Learned Elders of Zion**, a controversial document discovered a few years earlier. The *Protocols* are alleged to be the minutes of a secret meeting of Jewish elites in which a master plan for world domination, to be completed over the next 100 years, is laid out in chilling detail.

The *Protocols* tell of Jewish control of world banking, world media, Communism, liberalism, and political parties of every type. The master plot includes plans to:

- Destroy the Catholic Church and all Christianity
- Promote Atheism
- Wage class warfare / labor against management
- Overthrow Tsarist Russia

- Corrupt the morals of the people
- Promote senseless "modern art" and dirty literature
- **Use anti-Semitism to keep "lesser Jews" cohesive**
- Manipulate women with ideas of "liberation"
- Create economic depressions and inflations
- Create "controlled opposition" to themselves
- Use state debt as a weapon to enslave countries
- Subvert and control all existing governments
- Install tainted politicians that can be blackmailed
- Manipulate college students with phony idealism
- Assassinate world leaders
- Spread deadly diseases
- Use balance of power politics to control nations
- Commit acts of terrorism
- Promote sports and games in order to divert people from politics
- Start a World War which will include the USA
- Set up world government after an economic crash

Some allege that the *Protocols* were forged by Russian security agents in order to convince the Tsar Nicholas II of the **New World Order's** existence. Although the authenticity of the document remains in question, world events of the coming decades will match the *Protocols* so closely that the document becomes a worldwide sensation during the 1920's and '30's. Forgery or not, whoever wrote it had an unusual knowledge and spooky prescience.

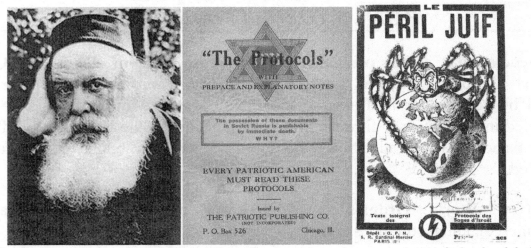

Professor Nilus translated the Protocols; since re-translated widely.

MARCH 25, 1906
ZIONIST-OWNED NEW YORK TIMES PUBLISHES FALSE CLAIM THAT 6 MILLION JEWS FACE EXTERMINATION IN RUSSIA

The New York Times
Published: March 25, 1906
Copyright © The New York Times

Dr. Paul Nathan's View of Russian Massacre

STARTLING reports of the condition and future of Russia's 6,000,000 Jews were made on March 12 in Berlin to the annual meeting of the Central Jewish Relief League of Germany by Dr. Paul Nathan, a well-known Berlin publicist, who has returned from an extensive trip through Russia as the special emissary of Jewish philanthropists in England, America, and Germany, to arrange for distribution of the relief fund of $1,500,000 raised after the massacres last Autumn.

Dr. Nathan paints a horrifying picture of the plight and prospects of his coreligionists, and forecasts at any hour renewed massacres exceeding in extent and terror all that have gone before. He left St. Petersburg with the firm conviction that the Russian Government's studied policy for the "solution" of the Jewish question is systematic and murderous extermination.

Dr. Nathan read to the meeting a circular addressed to the garrison of Odessa, calling upon the soldiers to "rise and crush the traitors who are plotting to upset the holy Government of the Czar and substitute for it a Jewish empire."

He concluded with an appeal to the Jewish money powers of the world to arrest Russia's career as a borrower. The financiers of the world should call a halt not only for humanitarian reasons, but for practical reasons. Russia's bankruptcy is an established fact, he added.

WENATCHEE DAILY

VOLUME I.—NO. 300.   WENATCHEE, WASHINGTON, WEDNESDAY, JUNE 20, 1906

MAY EXTERMINATE JEWS IN RUSSIA

Bloody Anti-Jewish Campaign is so Well Organized That Few Jews and Very Little Jewish Property Will Survive

London, June 20.—Leopold J. Greenburg, honorary secretary of the English Zionist Federation, received a telegram this morning from a member of the Russian douma, stating that the bloody anti-Jewish campaign in Russia is so well organized and so vigorously supported by the bureau of an attempt on the life of General Trepoff, commandant of the palace, by a well dressed woman masquerading as Princess Narishbin.

According to the rumor, the woman gained admittance to the palace and when Trepoff appeared she drew a revolver, but before it was fired she was seized.

The story is denied by the police.

BEVERIDGE BILL PASSES THE HOUSE

Washington, D. C., June 20.—The beef inspection bill passed the House today.

Senator Beveridge and the President

PASSAGE OF RATE BILL STILL IN DOUBT

Three Amendments are Giving Trouble and Arguments Have not Yet Been Reached on Several More

Washington, June 20.—From present indications the conferees on the railroad rate bill will not reach an agreement until some time next week, which in all probability will be the last week of the session. The purpose of withholding their report, it is said, is to avoid a repetition of the long de-

Smaller newspapers later picked up the "6,000,000" claim too.

MAY 31, 1906
REDS NEARLY ASSASSINATE KING & QUEEN CONSORT OF SPAIN ON THEIR WEDDING DAY

The wedding day of the popular **King Alphonso XIII of Spain and Queen Consort Victoria Eugenia** *(granddaughter of England's Queen Victoria)* is marred by yet another Red assassination plot. **Mateu Morral Roca**'s bomb is concealed in a bouquet of flowers, which he launches at the Royal couple from a nearby balcony. The deadly flower-bomb misses its mark, but several bystanders are killed.

The New World Order's murderous war against Spain, and all of western civilization, continues.

The King & Queen-to-Be were almost killed, in church, on their wedding day, by yet another crazed Anarchist dupe of the New World Order.

1907
TRIPLE ENTENTE BRINGS EUROPE CLOSER TO WAR!

The Triple Entente *(from French* entente, *"agreement")* is a military alliance between the UK, France, and Russia, concluded after the signing of the British-Russian Entente in 1907. Of course, Rothschild Britain is not allying with Russia out of any friendship. The Globalist goal is to draw Russia into fighting Germany & Austria-Hungary from the east. After Russia, Germany, and Austria-Hungary exhaust themselves, all three former allies can then be subverted from within by Communists and/or liberals, controlled by the Globalists.

The Triple Entente is the counterweight to the 1882 **Triple Alliance** *(or Central Powers)* of Germany, Austria-Hungary, and Italy. Rothschild & Warburg agents are also at work within The Triple Alliance. Italy later switches sides and is replaced by the Ottoman Empire *(Russia's nemesis)*. The two alliances have been cleverly set up as mechanisms for the purpose of triggering the coming world war to rearrange Europe, and the world. One little incident in the Balkan region of southern Austria-Hungary is all that it will take to ignite the two alliance powder kegs, and drag the powers of Europe *(and America)* into a massive war.

The New World Order and its agents will skillfully manipulate the patriotic passion of the various nations so as to bring about a disaster that will benefit Zionism, Communism, and Globalism.

Germany & Austria-Hungary boxed-in by The Triple Entente. The 3 ladies in the Russian propaganda poster represent France, Russia and Britain.

1907-1909
TR SHOWS OFF THE 'GREAT WHITE FLEET'

The **Great White Fleet** was the popular nickname for the U.S. Navy battle fleet that TR ordered to sail around the world from December 1907 to February 1909. TR's ostentatious and unnecessary "big stick" intimidation consists of 16 battleships divided into two squadrons, along with various escorts. The vulgar display of military power marks the completion of America's Rooseveltian transition from a peaceful republic to a violent global bully that is prepared to intervene around the world.

"USA! USA! USA!"....The jingoistic and militaristic ugliness that is modern "American exceptionalism" originated with the mad Globalist TR.

Jewish psychologist Sigmund Freud is a press-hyped charlatan whose "insights" will play a major role in breaking down and obliterating the sexual mores needed to stabilize a family-based society – a critical objective that The New World Order has *always* promoted.

Freud is a neurotic himself who projects his own weird obsessions onto his patients and into his writings. He smokes 20 cigars a day, and does not quit even when he is diagnosed with cancer of the jaw. **(22)** Freud will be operated upon many times before the disease finally kills him.

Freud's "Seduction Theory" claims that many mental disorders are due to repressed, or even imagined memories of seeing or hearing adults engaging in various forms of sexual activity. Schizophrenia, he argued, was caused by unresolved feelings of homosexuality.

Everything with Freud is about penis envy, sexual desire for one's mother, and the alleged evils of "repression" *(sexual self-control)*. His imagination is his only check in reality. In short, Freud's destructive message to the West is that "repressed sexuality" is the root of insanity. Indulge. Indulge. Indulge. That's bad for society – but good for those who wish to destroy it.

Hyped by the Globalist press, Freud's sex-obsessed fraud has done great damage to European and American thought and culture.

EARLY 1900's
THE RISE OF THE HOUSE OF ROCKEFELLER

In the early 1900's, wealthy non-Jewish, "Anglo" elites *(JP Morgan, Rockefeller, etc.)* have formed alliances with Jewish Dynasties such as the Rothschild, Warburg, and Schiff Families. Drunk on their power and wealth, these families believe it is their birthright to control humanity under their **New World Order.**

The most prominent of the U.S. Globalists is **John D Rockefeller Sr.,** who founded Standard Oil in 1870. Rockefeller's fortune, adjusted for inflation, makes him the richest American in history *(net worth of 700 billion in 2013 dollars!)* His son, John Jr. inherits the Rockefeller Empire and expands it into banking. He will raise 5 sons who take the family's crime operation into the 21st century.

'Puttin' on the Ritz.'John D. and his son, John Jr. Their offspring would influence world affairs for the next 100 years.

OCTOBER, 1907
WALL STEET BANKERS ENGINEER THE PANIC 1907

The New York bankers have artificially inflated the stock market with easy loans. When lending is then tightened, the bubble pops. Stocks crash nearly 50% and bank runs follow. The New York Times and the Wall Street bankers use the **Panic of 1907** to make a case for establishing a European-style Central Bank *(as Karl Marx envisioned).*

A few years later, Senator Robert Owen (OK) accuses the Bankers,

"The Panic was brought about by a deliberate conspiracy for the enrichment of those who engineered it." **(23)**

JP Morgan, John D Rockefeller, Jacob Schiff, and **Paul Warburg**, all declare that the lesson of the Great Panic is that the U.S. needs a Central Bank. In fact, nine months *before* the crisis, **Schiff** warned, in a speech to the Chamber of Commerce:

"unless we have a central bank with control of credit resources, this country is going to undergo the most severe and far reaching money panic in its history." **(24)**

How "prophetic" indeed!

Rothschild-connected Jacob Schiff and friends engineered the bank runs of 1907 in order to set the stage for the re-establishment of the Central Bank that Andrew Jackson had killed 70 years earlier. Senator Owen (right) figured this out.

FEBRUARY 1908
RADICALS ASSASSINATE BOTH THE KING _AND_ CROWN PRINCE OF PORTUGAL

The Royal bloodbath in Europe continues as assassins murder **King Carlos of Portugal** along with his son and heir to the throne, **Prince Luis Filipe**. The assassins, **Alfredo Costa and Manuel Buiça**, are linked to the secret **Carbonari**

153

Society. They had also wanted to murder the Queen. Their hope was to provoke a revolution.

Similar to the case with Abe Lincoln's murder, the assassins are executed on the spot before they can talk, suggesting that the conspiracy may have included elements within the government. Although panic ensues, a revolution does not materialize. Prince Manuel *(younger son of the King)* succeeds his father.

The heads of Europe are revolted, partly due to King Carlos's popularity, and also the brutal manner in which the assassination was planned and orchestrated.

Father and son, killed by radicals; both of whom were immediately killed.

1908
TR APPOINTS WALL STREET FRONT MAN TO MONOPOLIZE AMERICA'S CURRENCY & CREDIT

One year after the seemingly engineered Panic of 1907, TR and Congress establish the "**National Monetary Commission**" to study the crash and make suggestions. In stark contradiction of Roosevelt's careful crafted image as "the scourge of the Wall Street Robber Barons"; Senator Nelson Aldrich, the son-in-law of John D. Rockefeller, is named as Chairman. The NMC later suggests the establishment of a privately owned Central Bank for America - which will eventually come into being in 1913 as "The Federal Reserve".

The on-again and off-again harm that the Fed has caused to America ever since is beyond the scope of this work and too far removed from the direct subject matter. The essential takeaway point here is that TR's well-publicized battles against the New York "Robber Barons" are a publicity sham. Indeed, TR's NMC, assembled during TR's final months in office, aims to hand over the whole damn money supply to the Rockefellers ,Warburgs, Schiffs, Morgans and Rothschilds!

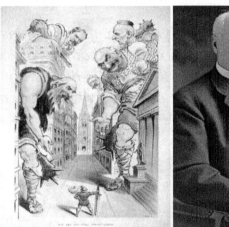

1- The Yellow Press myth of TR as the slayer of the giant "capitalists" is as phony as the "cowboy" and "war hero" legends. It was Wall Street fat cats who were behind TR all along. TR's National Monetary Commission began the process of handing over the money supply to the Global Banking Mafia.

2- Nelson Aldrich, an in-law and trusted agent of the Rockefellers   3- Papa Rockefeller and son John D. Jr. strolling in their top hats.

1905-1908
MARK TWAIN NAILS TR TO THE LITERARY CROSS

One thing that great writers all have in common is the uncanny ability to read human nature and to see through the facades of our behavior. The legendary **Mark Twain** had TR all figured out. His brutal and illuminating words, accumulated over a period of 6 years, speak for themselves.

"He is magnificent when his ears are pricked up and his tail is in the air, and he attacks a lightning express, only to be lost in the dust the express creates. **(25)**

Mr. Roosevelt is the Tom Sawyer of the political world of the twentieth century; always showing off; always hunting for a chance to show off; in his frenzied imagination the Great Republic is a vast Barnum circus with him for a clown and the whole world for audience; he would go to Halifax for half a chance to show off and he would go to hell for a whole one. **(26)**

We are insane, each in our own way, and with insanity goes irresponsibility. Theodore the man is sane; in fairness we ought to keep in mind that Theodore, as statesman and politician, is insane and irresponsible. **(27)**

Our people have adored this showy charlatan as perhaps no impostor of his brood has been adored since the Golden Calf, so it is to be expected that the Nation will want him back again after he is done hunting other wild animals heroically in Africa, with the safeguard and advertising equipment of a park of artillery and a brass band. **(28)**

Great writers instinctively sense the flaws and facades of the human character. That is why Mark Twain despised the show-off "circus clown" Roosevelt.

1908
ROTHSCHILD'S 'YOUNG TURKS' REVOLUTION WEAKENS THE OTTOMAN EMPIRE

The Young Turks, *(like Young England years earlier)* are a group of Globalist backed "progressives" who work to undermine the Sultan of the Ottoman Empire and bring about "democracy". In 1908, the Young Turks, supported by elements within the military, stage an uprising against the Sultan. Because the Young Turks have penetrated the army, the Sultan is forced to submit to concessions which weaken his power.

The **"Committee of Union and Progress"**(CUP), emerges from its previous conspiratorial darkness and becomes a powerful force in Turkish parliamentary politics. As is the case in Europe, Jewish reformers play a leading role in the Young Turks/CUP *(Carasso, Bey, Russo, Jabotinsky etc.)*

This latest "chess move" advances Globo-Zionist plans. The Sultan had strongly opposed the establishment of a Jewish state in Ottoman Palestine. Now, with so many prominent Jewish Young Turks on the rise, the Zionists have some friendly partners in Turkey to work with.

1- Jewish 'Turk' Carasso worked for Rothschild.

*2- Young Turk leader **Mustafa Kemal Atatürk** preaches Globalism:*
" Mankind is a single body and each nation is a part of that body."

1909
RETIRED PRESIDENT TR GOES ON A SAFARI RAMPAGE

After 7 years in office, TR decides to not seek re-election. He entrusts his 'Progressive' agenda to his friend, William Howard Taft. Ever-hungry for the limelight, the fake tough-guy with the childhood inferiority complex goes on an African safari and again proves his manhood by killing every majestic creature that he can point a rifle at. The numbers of animals that TR and his group, including his son, kill for "science" is staggering.

More than 1000 large animals, including 512 big game animals and six rare White Rhinos, are gunned down in TR's great expedition. **(29)** Tons of salted animals and their skins are shipped to Washington's Smithsonian Museum, which has to pass some off to other museums. When criticized for the shocking number of animals so senselessly slaughtered, Roosevelt, in typical narcissist fashion, replies: *"I can be condemned only if the existence of the National Museum, the American Museum of Natural History and all similar zoological institutions are to be condemned"*. **(30)**

Although the safari was ostensibly conducted in the name of science, it was really a self-aggrandizing political and social event as it was a hunting excursion. In 1910, TR, as expected, publishes a book about his great adventure, *African Game Trails*. Theodore Roosevelt is truly a sick man.

After a 10 year run of killing U.S. sailors and Philippine natives, ex-President Roosevelt took to killing elephants, rhinos, giraffes and lions as a hobby.

"He is hunting wild animals heroically in Africa, with the safeguard and advertising equipment of a park of artillery and a brass band."

- Mark Twain **(31)**

Edward Gibbon's description of the shocking excesses of the megalomaniac and degenerate Roman Emperor Commodus (depicted by Joachim Phoenix in the 2000 movie 'Gladiator'), is very similar to TR's well-publicized safari slaughter:

From the Wikipedia entry on Commodus:

"Commodus was also known for fighting exotic animals in the arena, often to the horror of the Roman people. According to Gibbon, Commodus once killed 100 lions in a single day. Later, he decapitated a running ostrich with a specially designed dart and afterwards carried the bleeding head of the dead bird and his sword over to the section where the Senators sat and gesticulated as though they were next. Dio notes that the targeted senators actually found this more ridiculous than frightening, and chewed on laurel leaves to conceal their laughter. On another occasion, Commodus killed three elephants on the floor of the arena by himself. Finally, Commodus killed a giraffe, which was considered to be a strange and helpless beast." **(32)**

Commodus also had an inferiority complex for he could never measure up to his learned philosopher-king father, Marcus Aurelius. Likewise, the Columbia Law School dropout TR knows that he can never measure up to American Presidents of the past.

More proud photos from the great American Emperor-Gladiator:

Hippo – Cheetahs – Antelope

Giraffe – Zebra – Decapitated Bull Elephant "Trophy"

1900-1920
NEW AMERICAN ZIONIST KINGPINS EMERGE

The Rothschild orbit includes other Zionist bankers who emerge as giants in their own right. These "American" moguls will dominate the coming 8-year Presidency of their pathetic puppet, Woody Wilson.

- **JACOB SCHIFF:** The Schiff Family shared a home with the Rothschilds in the 1700's. Schiff helped Japan defeat Russia in 1905. He will also help to found / fund the comig NAACP and the ADL.
- **BERNARD BARUCH:** Baruch first introduced Woodrow Wilson to the wealthy Jewish community of New York City. According to one account, *"Baruch led Wilson as one would a poodle on a string".* **(33)** During World War I, Baruch will head up Wilson's War Industries Board, making him the most powerful figure in U.S. industry.

- **THE WARBURG BROTHERS:** German banker **Paul Warburg** will soon become the "Father of the U.S. Federal Reserve" – a private banking and stock manipulation syndicate which collects interest for the privilege of printing the nation's currency. His son James will set up the **United World Federalists** in 1947 to *openly* promote world government. **(34)** His brother, **Max** is a very powerful banker in Germany, and his other brother, **Felix**, a 'philanthropist', uses his fortune to promote Globo-Zionist causes.

Jacob Schiff   Paul Warburg   Felix Warburg   Bernard Baruch

Other Zionist power players of that era

Louis Brandeis   Samuel Untermyer   Chaim Weizmann   Rabbi Wise

"Against Our Better Judgment" by journalist and historian Alison Weir reveals how early Zionists manipulated Wilson, and others.

The **NAACP** *(National Association for the Advancement of Colored People)* is the most well-known Black American organization. What is not widely known is that its founders are all Jewish! **(35)** Early Jewish founders include Julius Rosenwald, Lillian Wald, Rabbi Emil Hirsch, and Rabbi Steven Wise. A black Communist named **W.E. Dubois** is cleverly put up as the NAACP's front man.

In 1914, Jewish Professor Joel Spingarn becomes Chairman and recruits for its board Jewish leaders such as Jacob Billikopf, Rabbi Stephen Wise, and the all mighty Jacob Schiff. Zionist money has long controlled this "civil rights" group.

By design, the Zionist run NAACP draws blacks away from the positive influence of the Black-American conservative **Booker T. Washington**., a popular Black leader who believes in America's founding principles and seeks to build bridges between whites and blacks.

The liberal Democrat NAACP represents the opposite of what the Republican Booker T. stands for. The NAACP is a Globalist Marxist tool that serves to divide and incite Americans while herding black voters *(who they do not care about!)* into the left-wing political camp. As a result, even today, 90-95% of black voters blindly vote for Democrat Party candidates.

Conspirators such as the "Red Rabbi" Stephen Wise created and controlled the NAACP for their war against Whites. Communist WE Dubois (center)) was the front-man used to neutralize the influence of Booker T Washington.

After amassing huge fortunes during the 19th century, the name Rothschild is now synonymous with power and wealth. The family is known for its art collecting and palaces. By the end of the 19th century, the Rothschild Family owns about 40 palaces, of a scale and luxury unparalleled even by the Royal families..The soon-to-be British Prime Minister **Lloyd George** states, in 1909, that **Lord Nathan Rothschild** *(son of Lionel)* ***"is the most powerful man in Britain"***. **(36)**

The French and Austrian branches of the Rothschild syndicate also hold similar power *(though to a lesser degree)* over those nations. Their agents also influence American and German politics and finance. Together with other Jewish banking dynasties *(Schiff, Warburg, Baruch, Lazard et al)* and also Anglo-American allies and agents *(Rockefeller, JP Morgan et al.)* the Globo-Zionist House of Rothschild is the beating heart of the self-perpetuating **New World Order** crime syndicate that carries on to this day.

'Lord' Nathan Rothschild (left) - the son of Lionel (center) became the new patriarch of 'The Family'. His great great grandson Nathan is a rising superstar of International Finance today

Cyrus Scofield is a small time politician and career criminal. In 1873, he is forced to resign his position as a District Attorney because of crooked financial transactions which include accepting bribes, stealing political contributions, and securing bank notes by forging signatures. He serves jail time for forgery charges.

A heavy drinker, Scofield later abandons his wife and two daughters. His wife finally divorces the drunken crook in 1883. As so many con-men do, Scofield then claims to have "found Jesus". He is ordained as a Minister and then claims to have a Doctor of Divinity degree, but this degree is never verified.

After several mysterious trips to Europe and New York; Scofield publishes the notated reference Bible that bears his name. The **added side notes** in **Scofield's Bible** inject a very weird "End Times" prophecy into Christianity. Because of Scofield's altered Bible, many Christians today believe that Jesus will return to save his followers from the "end times" (The Rapture), only after Israel is established, and that **"God will bless those who bless Israel."**

This biblical alteration, *at the hands of a known criminal*, marks the beginning of a powerful force in American politics known as **"Christian Zionism."** Many millions of "Evangelical" Christians have been mentally infected with Scofield's poison. Christian Zionists are even more fanatical in their support of Israel than the Jewish Zionists are. **The Scofield Bible is very good for Zionism!** The question is; who did the con-man Scofield meet with while in New York and Europe?

Con Man Scofield warped Christianity to serve his paymasters. Christian-Zionist pastors like John Hagee will later wield influence on Israel's behalf.

1909
THE 'MELTING POT' OPENS ON BROADWAY! WARM & FUZZY GLOBALIST PROPAGANDA CONTAINS A 'POISON PILL'

Jewish Globalist writer **Israel Zangwill** coins the demeaning term **"Melting Pot"** to describe an America in which all races and cultures are blended into a new people. When 'The Melting Pot' opens on Broadway, it is critically acclaimed *(hyped)* by the Zionist Press, and publicly praised by Teddy Roosevelt. **(37)**

Like all Globalist schemes, this concept sounds like a noble ideal, but, in reality, the "multi-cultural" dissolution of the European people *(Whites)* is a critical long range goal of the "anti-racist" Globalist & Zionist elite - who keep their bloodlines intact as they seek to dominate a de-Europeanized, non-White new world.

The long-term vision of Israel Zangwill and his type is to 'melt' (and even kill) Whites out of existence.

1910-1912
MONEY KINGS OF NEW YORK USE TR TO RUN A 3RD PARTY CAMPAIGN TO REMOVE TAFT

To thwart the Republican Taft's re-election bid, TR, with backing from some big Wall Street financiers, quits the GOP and runs again for President as a 3rd party candidate *(Progressive / Bull Moose Party)*. Many years later, a well-connected businessman named **Benjamin Freedman** tells the real story of how the historic election plot of 1912 originated in his father's home.

From a Freedman speech given in 1974:

Benjamin Freedman's speeches and writings reveal the "inside story" of that period in history

"Jacob Schiff came back to New York - he was at that time head of The American Jewish Committee, - and in my father's home - I was a young man then- in the presence of many prominent men , names that are familiar to many people that are here. That is a fact. Now, what happened?

They ganged up in New York, to get rid of Taft. I was a protégé of Mr. Bernard Baruch - a name that I think you are all familiar with. His father was a doctor, Dr. Simon Baruch, who had brought me into the world, and Bernard Baruch was a visitor at our home all the time. He courted my sister; one of my sisters. So the stage was set to get rid of the Republican Party and the Republican President and put in their own party and their own President. But it was very difficult, because, after the Cleveland Depression -President Cleveland was a Democrat- we had the worst depression ever seen anywhere. And that swept the Republican Party into power, because they advocated protective tariffs to protect the working man against the cheap labor of Europe and to protect the infant industries of the United States against foreign competition.

Mr. Schiff came back to New York and the stage was set. And I, as a young man, got into the act. What I am telling you now, I saw with my own eyes, heard with my own ears, but I make it brief. The stage was set: "How can we get rid of the Republican Party; how can we get rid of Taft" - and Mr. Baruch was picked out as the leg man. He was a smart man!

They set up the National Democratic Headquarters at 200 Fifth Avenue, which was the site of the old Fifth Avenue Hotel, now an office building, and Mr. Henry Morgenthau, Sr., the old man, the father of the one you all know, was made chairman of the Finance Committee. I was made his confidential assistant in liaison with the Treasurer, who was Mr. Rollo Wells of St. Louis, - the Andrew Mellon of his time. And I was right in the middle! I saw everything that went on, because I handled all the books that had the cash contributions in them. Mr. Jacob

Schiff and the Jews put up the money to launch this Party and they looked around for a man to put up as President. To make a long story short, they got Woodrow Wilson, a rascal who wasn't worth the powder to blow him to hell!

They got Woodrow Wilson, the man who had more ego than any man I have ever read about, they got him to head the Democratic Party. And they got into difficulties, because the Democrats only got the Electoral votes in the South; where the people in agriculture wanted cheap goods from Europe. But the North wanted the Republicans. They found out they could not elect a President in the United States. So, I handled the money; I was the leg man, the errand boy.

They trotted Theodore Roosevelt out of the political "moth-balls". They told him, "You are the indispensable man. You are the only man who can save the United States." And with his ego they formed the "Bull Moose Party" and Mr. Jacob Schiff and the Jews throughout the world - they got plenty of money from England - they formed the Bull Moose Party. And in that way they split the Republican vote between Roosevelt and Taft, and Mr. Wilson walked in with a minority of the popular vote - the lowest man -and I knew the inside of his private life, which I don't want to go into here-. But never was a lower rascal in the White House, and I've known plenty of them since that time! **(38)**

1- Seated behind TR is New York financier and Rothschild agent, Jacob Schiff (gray beard) - America's richest and most well-connected Money King at the time.

2- Financier Bernard Baruch set up TR's 'Bull Moose' scam.

3- The famous photo of TR riding a Bull Moose has since been confirmed as a doctored-up FAKE. **(39)**

NOVEMBER, 1910
SECRET MEETING ON JEKYLL ISLAND PLOTS THE CREATION OF A NEW U.S. CENTRAL BANK

The same forces that deliberately created the Panic of 1907, and the Monetary Commission of 1908, continue to advance their plot to impose a "solution" to the very crises that they engineered. **Senator Nelson Aldrich** *(maternal grandfather of Nelson & David Rockefeller)* invites top bankers to attend a secret conference at the Jekyll Island hunting club in Georgia. Meeting under the ruse of a duck-shooting excursion, the conspirators plot to recreate a privately owned Central Bank for America.

The "duck hunt" on Jekyll Island includes Senator Aldrich, Henry P. Davison *(the front man for financier **J.P. Morgan**)*, National City Bank President **Frank A. Vanderlip**, and the "Father of the Fed", the recent German Jewish immigrant and Rothschild agent, **Paul Warburg.** From the start, the group proceeds covertly. They avoid the use of last names as they meet quietly at Aldrich's private railway car in New Jersey.

Details of the secret Jekyll Island meeting will not emerge until years later. ***It is later <u>openly acknowledged</u> that the Warburg-Rothschild Central Bank, (which will be established in 1913 as the Federal Reserve System), was conceived at the Jekyll Island meeting.***

Writing in his autobiography 25 years later, Jekyll Attendee Frank Vanderlip reveals:

*"There was an occasion, near the close of 1910, when I was as secretive—indeed, as furtive—as any conspirator. ..I do not feel it is any exaggeration to speak of **our secret expedition** to Jekyll Island as the occasion of the actual conception of what eventually became the Federal Reserve System. We were told to leave our last names behind us. We were told further that we should avoid dining together on the night of our departure. We were instructed to come one at a time and as unobtrusively as possible to the railroad terminal on the New Jersey littoral of the Hudson where Senator Aldrich's private car would be in readiness attached to the rear-end of a train to the south.*

Once aboard the private car we began to observe the taboo that had been fixed on last names. We addressed one another as Ben, Paul, Nelson and Abe. Davison and

168

I adopted even deeper disguises abandoning our first names. On the theory that we were always right, he became Wilbur and I became Orville after those two aviation pioneers the Wright brothers. The servants and train crew may have known the identities of one or two of us, but they did not know all and it was the names of all printed together that would've made our mysterious journey significant in Washington, in Wall Street, even in London. Discovery we knew simply must not happen." **(40)**

1-

'The "Creature from Jekyll Island": by Edward Griffin is a must read!

2- *FLASH FORWARD 100 YEARS**...The 'Banksters' **OPENLY** celebrate the 100th anniversary of the conspiratorial meeting at Jekyll Island. Zionist Fed Chairman Ben Bernanke and Zionist ex-Chairman Alan Greenspan are both in attendance at the conference entitled **"A Return to Jekyll Island: The Origins, History, and Future of the Federal Reserve"** - held exactly 100 years after the original 1910 meeting, and in the exact same building! Ben Bernanke (l) / Alan Greenspan (r)

1911 – 1920

TR had groomed Taft to be his "progressive" successor. But he is disappointed when Taft turns out to be his own man on issues such as tariffs and "trust busting". Ironically, Taft actually breaks up more monopolistic trusts than Roosevelt ever did -- a fact which should have made him beloved by the "progressives". But Taft ran afoul of TR when he tried to break up J.P. Morgan's U.S. Steel, which happened to be a trust that TR supported. Roosevelt accuses Taft of not knowing a "good" trust from a "bad" one. Once again, the exaggerated myth of TR being the arch-enemy of the Rockefeller-Morgan crowd reveals itself as public propaganda.

Taft had also angered Jacob Schiff by refusing to apply economic sanctions to Czarist Russia. With the Rothschild-Schiff gang behind him Roosevelt turns against his old friend and viciously criticizes his successor. Taft is hurt and stunned by TR's venom, but he remains firm in his Constitutionalism. Taft hits back at the Progressives, stating, *"They (Progressives) are seeking to pull down the temple of freedom and representative government."* **(1)**

Due to TR's petty vindictiveness, the ideological differences undermine the friendship and personally hurt Taft to his core. The friendship between the two men is destroyed when TR launches continuous insults at the honorable Taft and then, at the urging of Baruch, Schiff and company, runs for President as third party spoiler.

Never before, and never since, has an ex-President so publicly interfered and undermined the Presidency of his successor. The Taft-Roosevelt split is the beginning of a deep divide in the Republican Party that still exists *(though Constitutionalist Republicans are very few now.)*

Taft was a good man and a good President. The cartoons above mock the hypocrisy of TR's "good trust / bad trust" comment; and his attacks on Taft.

1912
A STAGED ASSASSINATION ATTEMPT ON TR RUINS TAFT'S CHANCES

In the fall of 1912, Taft still has a chance to win reelection; but that chance is about to disappear. Just 3 weeks before the election, an "October Surprise" comes in the form of an "assassination attempt" against TR.

On October 14, 1912, just moments before he is set to deliver a typically Rooseveltian 50-page speech, TR, we are told, is shot with a Colt .38 by an Anarchist fanatic named **John Flammang Schrank.** The bullet is first said to be a "flesh wound" that "lodged in his chest". Afterwards, the story changes to that of a bullet "safely lodged" against TR's rib, after having been slowed down by both his steel eyeglass case and the thick speech he was carrying in his jacket.

.22 caliber

9mm

.357 caliber

.45 caliber

As far as bullet sizes go, the .38 caliber *(a measure of diameter)* is one of the larger size bullets. But "Superman" TR felt no pain?

TR takes a clean handkerchief to cover the "wound" as he heads for the stage, where one of his bodyguards is attempting to explain what has just happened to the audience. Someone in the crowd shouts out: *"Fake! Fake!"* **(2)**

True to his self-promoting form, TR the drama queen wastes no time in proclaiming to the crowd:

"Friends, I shall ask you to be as quiet as possible. I don't know whether you fully understand that I have just been shot." **(3)**

The horrified audience in the Milwaukee Auditorium gasps as the theatrical TR unbuttons his vest to reveal his bloodstained shirt. Then comes the proud boast:
"It takes more than that to kill a bull moose." **(4)**

Now the crowd is really buzzing as the legend of TR reaches new heights of super-humanism. The babbler continues before launching into yet another 90-minute speech about nothing:

"But fortunately I had my manuscript, so you see I was going to make a long speech, and there is a bullet - there is where the bullet went through - and it probably saved me from it going into my heart. The bullet is in me now, so that I cannot make a very long speech, but I will try my best." **(5)**

Right on cue, Schrank claimed that the spirit of President McKinley had told him to avenge his murder by killing TR. In an open letter to the American people, Schrank writes:

"To the people of the United States: In a dream I saw President McKinley sit up in his coffin pointing at a man in a monk's attire in whom I recognized Theodore Roosevelt. The dead president said—'This is my murderer'—avenge my death." **(6)**

There were indeed some Taft supporters who believed that the murder of McKinley in 1901, also carried out by a deranged "Red", was part of a plot to install TR as President. This event makes Taft supporters look bad. Schrank's "dream", coupled with TR's whining about the "vicious attacks" against him, damages the Taft campaign while creating sympathy for the "wounded" and "tough" TR.

The very strange event is directly responsible for drawing many votes away from Taft. A reasonable person has to wonder if the assassination stunt and the McKinley murder were both staged by the same invisible hand that has guided fanatical 'Red' assassins since the days of the French Revolution; and has also guided the rocket-like career of TR all along.

Should the disbelieving reader be inclined to dismiss the staged shooting scenario as an irresponsible "conspiracy theory", your suspicious author here invites you to jam a .38 thick screwdriver through your chest and to your rib. Then, attempt to speak loudly for a full 90 minutes. Go ahead. Try it; and do let us all know how you make out.

TR will not win the election, but he will, with the help of this oh-so-convenient "October Surprise", and exactly as Schiff & Baruch had intended all along, steal enough votes to propel fellow "progressive" Woodrow Wilson into the Presidency with just 41% of the vote. Schrank is committed to a mental hospital for the remaining years of his life. The alleged bullet in TR is "never removed". That figures!

1- After the "shooting", the sympathetic press hyped the "wounded" TR's "heroic" speech.

2- The would-be "assassin" Schrank and the police officers share a good laugh. What's the joke, gentlemen?

More bloodshed in Europe! The Russian Prime Minister **Pyotr Stolypin** is a dedicated reformer who wants to improve the quality of life for Russia's peasants. Stolyypin is a hard-liner when it comes to dealing with violent Red revolutionaries. But he also understands that a thriving and growing middle class is the real key to depriving the Reds from gaining support among the poor and uneducated.

While attending a performance at the Kiev Opera House, the popular Prime Minister is shot at close range by a Jewish double agent named **Dmitri Bogrov** *(born Mordekhai Gershovich)*. Bogrov is a member of the Ohkrana, a Russian police force that has been infiltrated by Red spies. The murder of Russia's Prime Minister is carried out in front of the Czar and his two eldest daughters.

Prime Minister Stolypin (left) – killed at the Opera by another Red.

1912
THE 'ALDRICH PLAN' FOR A CENTRAL BANK IS QUICKLY KILLED IN THE U.S. CONGRESS

Senator Nelson Aldrich introduces his bill to establish a Central Bank *(The Aldrich Plan)*. The scheme *(hatched at Jekyll Island)* is transparent, and Aldrich's name is too closely linked to the Money Masters of New York. Congressman Charles A Lindbergh Sr. *(father of the famous aviator)* declares:

"The Aldrich Plan is the Wall Street Plan. It means another panic, if necessary, to intimidate the people. Aldrich, paid by the government to represent the people, proposes a plan for the trusts instead." **(7)**

Opposition to Aldrich's scheme is so strong, that the bill to create a Central Bank is never even brought to the floor for a vote.

1- Charles Lindbergh Sr. and Jr.   2- 1912 anti-Bank cartoon

3- A known Wall Street stooge; Senator Aldrich's name was too toxic.

NOVEMBER, 1912
NEW WORLD ORDER GANG RE-CAPTURES THE U.S. PRESIDENCY WITH THE ELECTION OF WOODROW WILSON

Understanding that popular U.S. President William Howard Taft would never involve America in Rothschild' schemes; the Globalists had recruited **Woodrow Wilson**, a Princeton professor who had been rocketed to Governor of New Jersey, then to Democrat nominee for President.

To steal Republican votes from Taft, ex-President Roosevelt runs as the Progressive Party candidate *(aka Bull-Moose)*. The divide & conquer trick works. **Due to TR's meddling; Wilson wins with just 41% of the vote.**

After decades of strategic political preparation, the **New World Order** now has 7 major goals its wants to achieve in the coming decade, and the right puppet in the White House to do it:

1. Establish a Central Bank in the U.S.
2. Impose an Income Tax on America so that State debt to the Central Bank can be collateralized with human labor
3. Trigger the long planned Triple Entente-Triple Alliance war to reshape Europe
4. Entangle the U.S. in the coming war and World Organization
5. Finish off Russia and convert the Eurasian giant into a Red tyranny
6. Establish a World Political Body under the pretext of "world peace"
7. Carry out Herzl's plan to steal Palestine from the Turks and Arabs.

TR's interference undermined Taft (center) and enabled Puppet Wilson (right) to become President and make a HUGE mess of the world.

NOVEMBER, 1912
REDS MURDER ANOTHER PRIME MINISTER OF SPAIN

The liberal reformer **Jose Canalejas** became Prime Minister in 1910. While in office, he works to turn Spain into a more democratic state. But that's not good enough for the Reds. On November 12, 1912, while shopping in a Madrid bookstore, Canalejas is fatally shot by anarchist **Manuel Pardiñas**.

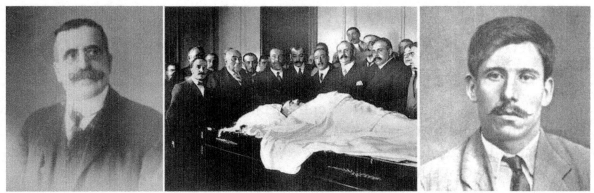

Even liberals like Canalejas (left) aren't safe from the never-ending Anarchist bloodbath. Pardinas on right.

DECEMBER, 1912
WORLD PRESS HYPES THE 'PILTDOWN MAN' HOAX

Much of the world press excitedly hypes the discovery of the fossilized remains of an "apelike human ancestor". The skull and jawbone of this "missing link" are found at a gravel pit in Piltdown, England. It will be another 40 years before **"Piltdown Man"** is exposed as a hoax, a combination of an orangutan jawbone and a human skull.

Up until the Global Warming Hoax of the present day, Piltdown Man is the most famous scientific hoax ever. During its 40 year run, the Piltdown Hoax will do much to undermine public faith in God - an important goal for the Globalists who always work to break down the civilizing and stabilizing influences of religion and morality.

'Reconstruction' of the Piltdown skull by J.H. McGregor (1914)

Respected scientists fell hook, line and sinker for the 40-year hyped hoax!

A new bill for establishing a new Central Bank for the United States is already pending. If the government is to now borrow counterfeited money from a privately owned Central Bank, *(by selling Bonds to the Bank)* the Central Bankers must have assurance that the Government can pay them back, *plus interest.*

A Marxist style 'Progressive Income Tax" will now turn American workers into **human collateral** for the Zionist bankers. **The Revenue Act of 1913** adjusts American tariffs, and it also institutes an Income Tax of 1-7%, but only for the wealthiest Americans. Naturally, empty promises are made that the initial rates, as well as the income ranges subject to tax, will not be changed.

It's hard to believe, but about 100 years ago, self-reliant Americans paid ZERO income tax – and still had roads, courts, schools, police, & military!

OCTOBER 1913
ZIONIST CROOKS ESTABLISH THE A.D.L. (ANTI-DEFAMATION LEAGUE)

The **ADL** *(Anti-Defamation League)* is founded by Sigmund Livingston in response to the 1913 trial of **Leo Frank**. Frank is a Jewish factory manager in Georgia who raped and murdered a young employee named **Mary Phagan**, and then tried to frame a black man for the crime. After oddly being spared the death penalty, angry Georgians would later storm the prison and hang Frank themselves.

The charter of the ADL states:

"The immediate object of the League is to stop, by appeals to reason and conscience and, if necessary, by appeals to law, the defamation of the Jewish people. Its ultimate purpose is to secure justice and fair treatment to all citizens alike and to put an end forever to unjust and unfair discrimination against and ridicule of any sect or body of citizens." **(8)**

The ADL's true purpose is to protect Rothschild's Mafia from exposure. **Anyone who dares to call attention to the workings of the New World Order or the Federal Reserve will be denounced by the ADL as "anti-Semitic."** The ADL continues, to this day, to destroy political and journalistic careers.

Rapist killer Leo Frank is lynched. The ADL still claims he was innocent!

DECEMBER 23, 1913
WOODROW WILSON SIGNS THE FEDERAL RESERVE BANK INTO LAW

A few cosmetic changes are made to the old Aldrich Bill and the bill is then renamed **'The Federal Reserve Act'**. Minnesota Congressman Lindbergh Sr. is not fooled:

*"This is the Aldrich Bill in disguise ...This Act establishes the most gigantic trust on earth. When the President signs this bill, the invisible government by the Monetary Power will be legalized. The people may not know it immediately, but the day of reckoning is only a few years removed. **The worst legislative crime of the ages is perpetrated by this banking bill.**"* **(9)**

The bill passes anyway, on December 23, after many Senators and Congressmen had left town for Christmas! Puppet President Wilson quickly signs the bill creating the privately owned **Federal Reserve System**. Weeks earlier, Wilson had already enacted the nation's first Income Tax *(needed to pay interest to the bankers after they set up their Central Bank!)*

The Fed Board: Warburg (standing-left) Frederic Delano, uncle of FDR (seated-right)

After the Fed is up and running, Lindbergh adds:

"The financial system has been turned over to the Federal Reserve Board....The system is private, conducted for the sole purpose of obtaining the greatest possible profits from the use of other people's money." **(10)**

The "Federal Reserve System" is neither "Federal", nor does it contain "reserves", and nor is it part of a decentralized "system" The new Central Bank now has the power to create money out of thin air, and then lend it to the nation's banks and U.S. Treasury *at interest.* To this day, the 'Fed plagues America with constant inflation, housing & stock bubbles, artificial booms, recessions, and depressions. Its money-creating tricks enable Big Government to borrow endlessly from the Fed. Behind its academic façade, **the Fed is just a counterfeiting, loan sharking, and insider trading operation all in one.**

The member banks which own the Fed are controlled by the Rothschild-Warburg-Schiff Axis. To conceal the Jewish influence, Paul Warburg, *(the Fed's true founder)* is not named Chairman. Instead, he is appointed Chairman of the New York Branch of the Fed *(the most important seat).* Today however, there is no need to conceal the Fed's Zionist face. **Every Fed Chairman since 1970** *(with exception of William Miller's 1 year term in 1978-79)* **has been Jewish.** *(Burns, Volcker*, Greenspan, Bernanke, Yellen).*

* Volcker is Jewish by lineage, not by practice. **(11)**

Left to Right: Yellen, Volcker, Greenspan, Bernanke. Why can't non-Jews serve as Fed Chairmen anymore?

JUNE 28, 1914
A DOUBLE MURDER LIGHTS THE BALKAN FUSE

To kick off their long-awaited, pre-planned World War, the **New World Order** uses "Serbian Nationalists." A secret society known as **Young Bosnia**, possibly working with **The Young Turks**, plots the murder of an Austrian Royal.

Serbia is an Orthodox Christian nation under the protection of Russia. **Due to Disraeli's past schemes, many Serbs also live under Austro-Hungarian rule *(in Bosnia)* instead of under Serbian sovereignty.** This situation has always caused friction, both within Austria-Hungary, and also between Russia and Austria-Hungary.

Archduke Franz Ferdinand is heir to the Habsburg Family throne of Austria-Hungary. While traveling through the Bosnian city of Sarajevo with his wife, Sophie, a bomb is thrown at the Archduke's open car. He deflects the bomb with his arm and it explodes behind him. The royal couple insists on seeing all those

183

injured at the hospital. After traveling there, they decide to go to the palace, but their driver takes a wrong turn onto a side street, where another assassin named **Gavrilo Princip** spots them. He shoots Sophie in the stomach and Franz in the neck. Franz is still alive when witnesses arrive to give aid. His dying words to Sophie are, *"Don't die darling. Live for our children."* **(12)**

The world is shocked. The fateful prophecies of Tolstoy and Bismarck are about to come to pass.

SUMMER 1914	POST ASSASSINATION CHAIN-REACTION SETS EUROPE ON FIRE
JUNE 29	Anti-Serbian riots erupt in the Austro-Hungarian city of Sarajevo.
JULY 7	Austria-Hungary convenes a Council of Ministers to discuss the situation.
JULY	**The Zionist Austro-Hungarian press of Vienna fans the flames of anti-Serbian sentiment. False reports of a Serbian conspiracy are circulated.**
JULY	Kaiser Wilhelm II of Germany, at the request of Russian Tsar Nicholas *(his cousin)*, attempts to restrain his Austro-Hungarian ally by encouraging Austria-Hungary to talk with Serbia. **(13)**
JULY 28	Austria-Hungary gives in to war hysteria and declares war on Serbia.
JULY 29	To defend its Serbian ally, Russia mobilizes it armies against its former 'Three Emperors League' ally Austria-Hungary.
AUGUST 1	**Beyond both the Tsar and the Kaiser's control**, the Triple Alliance / Triple Entente time bomb is triggered. Germany declares war on Russia for its mobilization against its ally Austria-Hungary.
AUGUST 1	Ignoring German pleas to not enter the conflict, France begins advancing towards Austria-Hungary in support of its Entente ally, Russia.
AUGUST 3	Facing the dangerous 2-front war that France & England had engineered, *(and that Bismarck had feared)* Germany quickly advances towards France, through Belgium, while at the same time confronting Russia in the east.
AUGUST 4	Great Britain enters the war on the side of France & Russia.
SEPTEMBER 5	**London Agreement: Triple Entente allies France, Russia, & UK agree that no member shall make separate peace with Germany or Austria-Hungary.**
OCTOBER 28	Russia's southern rival, the Ottoman Turkish Empire, enters the war on the side of Austria-Hungary and Germany.
In just a few weeks' time, Europe is now aflame in war as the Globalist-Zionist press in France, England, Austria, and Germany whip up a mutually destructive nationalist fervor among the European nations.	

1 & 2: Surrounded by the Great Powers of the Triple Entente, peaceful Germany was forced to quickly advance in two directions.

3: The 'Willy-Nicky" cables clearly reveal how the Russian and German Emperors both tried to avoid war, **(14)** *but were powerless to stop the dark forces controlling events.*

1914-18
EARLY GERMAN VICTORIES / FOLLOWED BY STALEMATE

After Germany's westward march towards Paris stalls, the Western Front bogs down into a bloody stalemate with trench lines that change little until 1918. In the East, the Russian army successfully fights against the Austro-Hungarian forces but is then forced back by the German army. Additional fronts open after the Ottoman Empire *(Turkey)* joins the war *(on Germany's side)* in 1914. Italy switches sides and joins the Entente powers in 1915.

At sea, the British Navy blockades Germany. German U-boats will counter the blockade, and sink many British merchant ships carrying arms and supplies.

Not one inch of German territory was ever lost during the Great War.

To counter the lies of the Allied propagandists, 93 of Germany's leading scientists, scholars and artists sign their name to **"The Manifesto of the 93".** The document denounces the lies aimed at Germany, and declares unequivocal support of German military actions. Perhaps the most notable of the accomplished signatories is **Wilhelm Roentgen,** the Nobel Prize winning physicist who discovered "X-rays".

The Manifesto reads:

"As representatives of German Science and Art, we hereby protest to the civilized world against the lies and calumnies with which our enemies are endeavoring to stain the honor of Germany in her hard struggle for existence—in a struggle that has been forced on her.

The iron mouth of events has proved the untruth of the fictitious German defeats; consequently misrepresentation and calumny are all the more eagerly at work. As heralds of truth we raise our voices against these.

It is not true that Germany is guilty of having caused this war. Neither the people, nor the Government, nor the Kaiser wanted war.

It is not true that we trespassed in neutral Belgium. It has been proven that France and England had resolved on such a trespass, and it has likewise been proved that Belgium had agreed to their doing so. It would have been suicide on our part not to have preempted this.

It is not true that the life and property of even a single Belgian citizen was injured by our soldiers without the bitterest defense having made it necessary.

It is not true that our troops treated Louvain brutally. Furious inhabitants having treacherously fallen upon them in their quarters, our troops with aching hearts were obliged to fire a part of the town, as punishment. The greatest part of Louvain has been preserved..

It is not true that our warfare pays no respects to international laws. It knows no undisciplined cruelty. But in the east, the earth is saturated with the blood of women and children unmercifully butchered by the wild Russian troops, and in the west, dumdum bullets mutilate the breasts of our soldiers.

It is not true that the combat against our so-called militarism is not a combat against our civilization, as our enemies hypocritically pretend it is. Were it not for German militarism, German civilization would long since have been extirpated..

We cannot wrest the poisonous weapon—the lie—out of the hands of our enemies. All we can do is to proclaim to the entire world, that our enemies are giving false witness against us.

Have faith in us! Believe that we shall carry on this war to the end as a civilized nation, to whom the legacy of a Goethe, a Beethoven, and a Kant, is just as sacred as its own hearths and homes." **(15)**

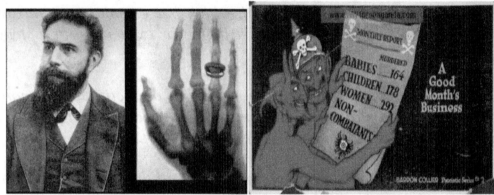

As the discoverer of 'X-rays', Wilhelm Roentgen was able to 'see through' the Allies' anti-German atrocity propaganda.

Again with the 6 million???

APPEAL FOR AID FOR JEWS
New York Times; Dec 2, 1914

APPEAL FOR AID FOR JEWS.

American Committee Tells of Suffering Due to the War.

The American Jewish Relief Committee, called into being at a conference of more than 100 national Jewish organizations which was held at Temple Emanu-El on Oct. 25 to consider the plight of more than 6,000,000 Jews who live within the war zone, has elected Louis Marshall Chairman, Cyrus L. Sulzberger Secretary, and Felix M. Warburg Treasurer, and has issued the following appeal:

MAY 7, 1915
UK LORD OF THE ADMIRALTY WINSTON CHURCHILL SETS UP THE LUSITANIA TO BE SUNK / 1200 CIVILAINS KILLED

The UK wants to draw America into the war. Lord of the Admiralty **Winston Churchill** and Wilson's Marxist advisor, **Edward Mandell House**, believe that if Germany can be baited into sinking a British ship with Americans on board, the U.S. will be forced into the war. **(16)** Unbeknownst to its passengers, the luxury liner **Lusitania** is carrying arms and explosives destined for Britain. **(17)**

Sailing from New York, Lusitania is loaded with 600 tons of explosives, 6 million rounds of ammunition, 1200 cases of shrapnel shells, and some American passengers. The German embassy in Washington is aware of this and tries to warn American travelers by placing ads in U.S. newspapers, which are refused in most cases. **(18)**

As Lusitania approaches the Irish coast, it is ordered to reduce speed, and its military escort ship, *Juno*, is withdrawn. **(19)** Churchill knows that German

U-Boats are in the area. **He purposely slows down the Lusitania and calls off** *Juno*, **leaving the Lusitania as a sitting duck.** A German torpedo hit ignites the munitions, causing a secondary explosion which sinks the massive liner in just 18 minutes! *Nearly 1200 of its 1959 passengers are killed, including 128 Americans.* The American press vilifies Germany, but makes no mention of the smuggled munitions *(or perhaps a pre-planted bomb?)* which really sank the Lusitania.

During the 1950's, the British Navy attempts to destroy the historical evidence of the *Lusitania* explosion by **dropping depth charges onto the sunken liner.**

1- Mad Dog Churchill

2 & 3 - Globalist NY Times, claimed TWO torpedoes hit.

1915-16
IN SPITE OF THE LUSITANIA SINKING, WILSON DELAYS U.S ENTRY INTO THE WAR

The Lusitania incident plays a role in turning American sentiment against Germany, but it is not yet time for America to make its entry. **The Zionists are waiting to achieve maximum leverage before ordering Wilson to finally pull the trigger.** For the time being, Wilson will just verbally condemn the Lusitania attack, while keeping America out of the war and cruising towards re-election in November, 1916.

The British are disappointed. UK politicians, journalists, and the certifiably insane Teddy Roosevelt all mock Wilson as being timid. In an effort to keep America inflamed, the British fabricate a story about German school children being given a holiday to celebrate the sinking of the *Lusitania*. Other false tales tell of German soldiers nailing babies to church doors in Belgium!

The British know that they will eventually need American help if they are to gain the advantage over The Triple Alliance / Central Powers. **The Zionists know this too, but they are biding their time, setting up the UK and the US for the right moment,** *and the right deal.*

Wilson intends to drag America into the war, but his 1916 re-election campaign promises say otherwise.

1915
ROTHSCHILD'S 'YOUNG TURKS' COMMIT GENOCIDE OF 1.5 MILLION ORTHODOX CHRISTIAN ARMENIANS

During and after the Great War, Jewish-led, **"Young Turks"** take advantage of the fact that both Christian Russia and the Ottoman Sultan are now unable to protect the Christian minorities of the Ottoman Empire.

A policy of mass killings, burnings, and deadly forced marches kills off most of the Armenian population of Turkey. Orthodox Assyrians and Greeks are also murdered by the Young Turks.

To this day, the systematic genocide of 1915-16 is ignored or denied by the current government of Turkey.

Rothschild's 'Young Turks" got away with genocide! To this day, Armenians still seek recognition of the event, but in vain.

DECEMBER, 1916
GERMAN KAISER TRIES TO STOP THE WAR

The Battle of Verdun rages for 10 months, resulting in 306,000 battlefield deaths *(163,000 French and 143,000 German)* and 500,000 wounded. That's an average of 30,000 deaths for *each* of the 10 months of the battle!

Taking place in north eastern France, Verdun is the longest and most devastating battle of **The Great War.** By the end of Verdun, the war has broken down into a stalemate, but Germany still holds an advantage. In December of 1916, Kaiser Wilhelm offers to negotiate peace with The Entente Powers. **But Britain and France deliberately make impossible demands upon Germany as a condition for even negotiating.**

In spite of Germany's sincere efforts to stop the madness, somebody wants this senseless bloodbath to continue. But who? ..... *And why?*

Battle of Verdun / Kaiser Wilhelm wanted peace all along.

By December 1916, the Central Powers have a clear advantage. France has suffered horrible losses. Russia is facing internal Red revolutionary chaos. Britain is under U-Boat blockade, *and not one square inch of Germany has been occupied.* Germany offers generous peace terms. Basically, Kaiser Wilhelm is willing to just call off the war and return to how things were.

That's when the Zionists make their move to fulfill Herzl's plan! **Chaim Weizman** and **Nathan Sokolow** approach the British with a dirty deal. The Zionists offer to use their international influence to bring the U.S. into the war on Britain's side, while undermining Germany from within. **The price that Britain must pay for U.S. entry is to steal Palestine from Ottoman Turkey** *(Germany's ally)* **and allow the Jews to settle there. (20)**

Though the official declaration of British support for a Jewish homeland is not to be made public until 1917 *(Balfour Declaration)*, **the agreement was, in fact, reached in December of 1916.** Soon after that, Zionist agitated anti-German propaganda was unleashed in the U.S. while the Zionists and Marxists of Germany begin to undermine Germany's war effort from within.

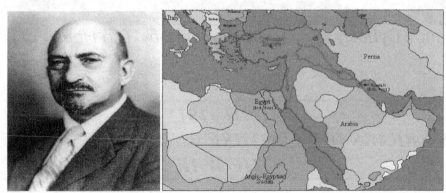

Chaim Weizman made the British an offer they couldn't refuse. In return, the Zionists want to see the Turkish Empire busted up and Palestine given to the Jews.

FEBRUARY, 1917
THE 'FEBRUARY REVOLUTION' TOPPLES RUSSIA'S ROYAL ROMANOV FAMILY

As the Russian economy deteriorates and the war becomes unpopular, the **'February Revolution'** begins. Communists, Progressive Socialists, and disaffected soldiers combine to destabilize the already weakened reign of Czar Nicholas. The Tsar is forced to abdicate his throne and put under house arrest pending exile. Jews worldwide celebrate the abdication of the Russian Czar.

A "center-left" coalition government consisting mainly of Socialists and Communists is established. A power struggle between the Democratic Socialists and the hard-core Communist *(Soviet-Bolshevik)* faction follows.

The Romanov Dynasty is over – conquered by The House of Rothschild.

APRIL, 1917
WILSON BREAKS HIS PROMISE AND BRINGS THE U.S. INTO THE WAR

During the weeks following the Zionist-UK dirty deal to steal Palestine, the Zionists deliver on their end of the bargain. **An intense propaganda campaign is suddenly unleashed in America.** The 1915 Lusitania incident is resurrected, along with hype over German U-boat warfare. A German contingency plan to ally with Mexico if the U.S. enters the war *(Zimmerman Note)* is falsely portrayed as a plot to attack America.

Citing various phony pretexts, on April 2nd, 1917, Wilson, who, according to Benjamin Freedman, was under blackmail over an affair he had when he was a Princeton professor, asks Congress for a Declaration of War. Congress complies. Regular forces of the small US military begin arriving in Europe, but it will be months before the full force of drafted men can be deployed.

Zionist Fred Rothman's iconic poster portrays Germans as monster "Huns"

APRIL, 1917
EXILED REDS BEGIN RETURNING TO RUSSIA

The terrorist Red leaders that Czar Nicholas had only exiled in 1905 now begin returning to Russia. **Vladimir Lenin** arrives from Switzerland, via Germany, with a stash of Zionist banker gold. **Leon Trotsky** arrives from New York with more money and a gang of Marxist-Jewish thugs. **(21)**

The Zionist-funded Communists immediately undermine the new provisional government. A violent coup is attempted in July, but the Bolshevik Reds are held back. Democratic Socialist **Alexander Kerensky** becomes Prime Minister as Bolshevik leaders go underground.

Back from Brooklyn, the killer Leon Trotsky (left) will join Lenin (center) in seeking to oust Kerensky (right)

APRIL, 1917
EDWARD BERNAYS FORMS PROPAGANDA COMMITTEE

Wilson establishes the **Committee on Public Information** (CPI) for the purpose of manipulating public opinion in support of the war. **Edward Bernays**, *"the father of American propaganda"* is a CPI member. A nephew of the psychoanalyst Sigmund Freud, Zionist Bernays boasts of his ability to control the public mind. He calls his scientific methods for controlling public opinion, *"the engineering of consent."* In his 1928 book, **Propaganda**, Bernays explains:

"The conscious and intelligent manipulation of the habits and opinions of the masses is an important element in democratic society. Those who manipulate this unseen mechanism of society constitute an invisible government which is the true ruling power of our country. - We are governed, our minds are molded, our tastes formed, our ideas suggested, largely by men we have never heard of. It is they who pull the wires that control the public mind." **(22)**

Bernays and his CPI co-conspirators portray the American war effort as a holy crusade *"to make the world safe for democracy"*, while at the same time spreading hate-filled propaganda directed towards Germany and its Emperor, Wilhelm II.

"Babies & Bayonets."

In Europe and America, Germany was now the target of hateful and ridiculous war propaganda.

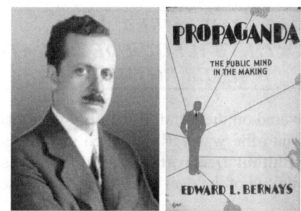

Bernays wrote the book on propaganda and manipulation; literally.

JUNE, 1917
WILSON SIGNS MILITARY DRAFT INTO LAW / VICIOUS HATE PROPAGANDA USED TO ATTRACT VOLUNTEERS

America's military is very small, but its capacity to field and equip an army is great. The unpopular draft is instituted in 1917. By the war's end, under the idiotic pretext of ***"making the world safe for democracy"*** *(Bernays' slogan)*, more than 2 million unsuspecting American men will have been sent to fight for Globalism and Zionism.

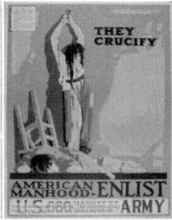

U.S. propaganda posters encouraged men to enlist by accusing the German "mad brutes" of crucifying women and children.

NOVEMBER, 1917
BRITAIN ISSUES 'THE BALFOUR DECLARATION' TO BARON WALTER ROTHSCHILD

The Zionists have delivered on their end of the dirty deal made with the British in 1916. American entry into the war was delivered as promised. By formally, and *publicly*, issuing **"The Balfour Declaration"**, Lord Balfour is assuring the Zionists that Britain will fulfill its end of the deal after the war– the theft of Palestine!

The Declaration is delivered to the 'Baron' **Walter Rothschild**. It reads, in part:

"His Majesty's government views with favor the establishment in Palestine of a national home for the Jewish people, and will use their best endeavors to facilitate the achievement of this object." **(23)**

The extraction of this promise from the British is one of the main reasons why the senseless war was kept going, and why America was finally dragged in. In Israel today, Balfour Day *(November 2nd)* is widely celebrated. The Palestinian Arabs observe it as a day of mourning.

"Dear Lord Rothschild" - Baron Walter Rothschild (left) received the Balfour Declaration from Lord Balfour.

OCTOBER 25, 1917*
'RED OCTOBER' / COMMUNISTS SEIZE CONTROL OF ST. PETERSBURG!   *NEW STYLE GREGORIAN CALENDER: NOV 7, 1917

Socialist Prime Minister Kerensky struggles to keep a bad economy afloat, an unstable coalition government together, and a tired Russian nation in the war. The time is ripe for the Reds to stage another violent attempt at power. This time, Trotsky, Lenin and their evil gang will succeed. With backing from some Red troops - *many of whom had been brainwashed in 1905 Japanese POW camps by communist reading materials paid for by Jacob Schiff* **(24)** - the Capital City of Petrograd *(St. Petersburg)* is seized during the **October Revolution**, *(aka "Red October")*.

Kerensky flees for his life and the new Soviet regime immediately moves to pull Russia out of the war *(before Germany can beat them)*. Outside of Petrograd, the pre-dominantly Jewish Red government is not recognized as legitimate. A bloody civil war between the Jewish-led Reds and the Christian "Whites" is now in the making.

Red rabble-rouser Vladimir Lenin incites the hungry mobs.

FORBIDDEN HISTORY: QUOTE TO REMEMBER:

"The Bolshevik leaders here (Russia), most of whom are Jews and 90 percent of whom are returned exiles, care little for Russia or any other country but are internationalists and they are trying to start a <u>world-wide social revolution.</u>" **(25)**

David R. Francis, U.S. Ambassador to Russia, January 1918

1918-1921
'REDS' vs 'WHITES' / CIVIL WAR IN RUSSIA

After the fall of St. Petersburg to the Reds, a counter-revolutionary civil war will tear Russia apart for three more years. The various opponents of the 'Reds' are collectively referred to as 'The Whites', led mainly by **Admiral Kolchak**.

When it becomes apparent that a Red revolutionary army composed solely of workers and some ex-Tsarist troops is far too small to put down the counter-Revolution, Trotsky institutes mandatory conscription of the peasantry into the Red Army. Opposition to Red Army conscription is overcome by terror tactics. Hostages and their families are tortured and killed when necessary to force compliance.

Admiral Kolchak's Whites vs Trotsky's Reds

JANUARY, 1918
WILSON LAYS OUT A 14 POINT PEACE PROGRAM / GERMANY AND AUSTRIA-HUNGARY RESPOND POSITIVELY

Had it not been for America's 1917 entry into the war, the stalemated parties would have ceased fighting on their own and millions of lives would have been saved. But it would not be until 1918 that sufficient numbers of trained American recruits would be ready to deploy in combat operations.

Before fresh new rivers of American blood would be shed *(117,000 Americans would die of combat or disease-related causes between April and November of 1918)*, both Germany and Austria-Hungary again communicate their desire for a peaceful resolution; just as they had previously been proposing to make a mutually acceptable peace with Britain and France all along.

In an address before the U.S. Congress, the puppet warmonger Wilson is forced to admit that, in response to his recent "14 Points" Statement, **Germany and Austria-Hungary have indeed expressed general agreement with Wilson's high-sounding proposals. (26)** But in the very next breath, Wilson casually dismisses these promising peace overtures *(referring to them as 'peace utterances')* as unacceptable.

Wilson's New York handlers *(Baruch, Schiff, Warburg, Morgenthau, Brandeis etc)* want their long-awaited war for Globalism *(the pre-planned 'League of Nations')* and Zionism *(the British theft of Palestine)*; and they certainly are not about to allow Germanic peace proposals to derail the NWO Express.

The most astonishing of Wilson's lies is his rosy description of what the eventual post-war peace is to be like. The fact that so many naive and war-weary Germans will later buy into Wilson's empty promises, will contribute to Germany's bizarre unconditional surrender and disarmament in November of that same year, 1918.

1- Wilson "Tells Germany She May Be Equal"
2- Wilson's phony peace talk carried the poison pill of the Globalists'
"League of Nations". (World Government)

1918
GLOBALIST BIO-WEAPON? / MYSTERIOUS 'SPANISH FLU' KILLS 50 – 60 MILLION PEOPLE WORLDWIDE

The **1918 Flu Pandemic** *(Spanish Flu)* is an unusually severe influenza pandemic. The virus originates at a military base in Kansas. It spreads to Europe, then Asia and Africa. Victims suffer horribly. Within hours of feeling the first symptoms of fatigue, fever, and headache, they turn blue. *Sometimes the blue color is so dark that it is difficult to determine a patient's original skin color!* Victims cough with such force that they tear their abdominal muscles, as foamy blood exits from their mouths, noses, and ears.

The final death toll of the disaster is higher than that of the War! In India, 17,000,000. In the U.S. 600,000, UK: 250,000, France: 400,000, Japan: 390,000, Germany: 400,000.

Several oddities suggest that the epidemic may be a bioweapon, aimed at the Central Powers, which somehow backfired and infected everyone! Consider the following:

1. Place of its origin *(a military base in Kansas)*
2. Coincidental timing of the flu's beginning *(same time that the full US force arrives in Europe)*
3. Strange effects of the illness *(blue skin / blood from nose & mouth)*
4. Odd way in which it targets 20-35 year olds *(military age)* instead of weak infants and elderly
5. The odd way in which it struck in 3 separate waves
6. German soldiers affected in greater numbers worse than Entente troops.
7. Inexplicable, coincidental manner in which epidemic abruptly ends as soon as the war ends

Scientists have never explained why the virus mutated into such a deadly form, why it suddenly stopped without a cure, why it targeted the young, and why it has never reappeared.

 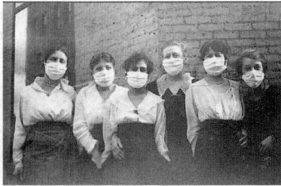

Globalist bio-weapon gone out-of-control?

SPRING, 1918
AFTER SUCCESFUL SPRING OFFENSIVE, GERMAN TROOPS 'STABBED IN THE BACK' BY HOMEFRONT JEWS

The Reds of Russia can't fight a civil war at home and an external war at the same time. Lenin and Trotsky have no choice but to take Russia out of the war. Before the American troops can be deployed in large numbers, Germany diverts its troops from the pacified eastern front and stages a major western offensive.

The operation begins in March with an attack on British forces in France. The Germans advance 40 miles and Paris is just 75 miles away! **The Spring Offensive** is so successful that Wilhelm declares March 24 a National Holiday.

At this exact critical point, Marxists & Zionists in Germany stab their countrymen in the back. Marxist Trade Union leaders order factory strikes which deprive German troops of critical supplies. **(27)** The Jewish owned press, **which had fanned war passions in 1914,** suddenly turns sour on the war and begins ripping on the German military. German morale begins to fall quickly, as does industrial output. Recent recruits arrive at the frontline with a defeatist attitude as anti-war protests and general discontent spread throughout Germany.

The Great Offensive comes to a halt just as the Americans begin to arrive. German Zionists are betraying Germany so that Palestine can be taken from Germany's Turkish ally and given to the Jews *(Balfour Declaration)*. German Jewish Marxists and "Democratic Socialists" also see a German defeat as a means to destabilize the nation and stage a revolution.

After the war, the treasonous betrayal of 1918 becomes known as **"The Stab-in-the-Back."** Modern liberal "historians" dismiss this allegation as a "legend", but there is nothing mythical about it. **On the brink of final victory, Germany was betrayed from within - plain & simple.**

Post-war cartoons depict Zionist-Marxists stabbing German soldiers in the back.

It had taken about a year for America to get its military drafted, trained, and deployed under American command. By summer of 1918, 10,000 fresh troops arrive *daily* at the front. About 120,000 of them will die in the Great War, 90,000 in combat, 30,000 from disease. In addition to the badly needed fresh blood, the French and British war machines are now being re-supplied by the industrial output of mighty America.

With the breakdown of the Spring Offensive, the tide turns against Germany and its allies. The Allied counter attack, *(100 Days Offensive)* begins in August. At the **Battle of Amiens**, the Allies advance 7 miles into German-held territory in just 7 hours. Back in Germany, the Jewish Press ignores the devastating effects of the Jewish-led factory strikes and Jewish-inspired defeatism. Instead, the newspapers blame General Erich Ludendorff for the recent German setbacks!

Fresh American boys arrived to kill German boys as the Jewish press of Germany shamelessly shifted the blame onto General Ludendorff.

1- Come on man! Join me in dying for Wilson's lies!

2- Dead American trapped in barbed-wire. If his mother, father, wife, kids could have watched him die -what would they say to Professor Wilson?

Little did TR know that Wilson and the British had already been plotting to drag America into Europe's war. Wilson just needed to wait until after his 1916 reelection was secured. Among the young Americans to die is 20-year old Quentin Roosevelt, the youngest son of Theodore Roosevelt, who was killed in aerial combat over France in 1918. Roosevelt is said to have been deeply affected by his son's death. TR dies himself just 6 months later.

The wartime death of TR's youngest son finally gave TR a taste of the pain that his warmongering had dished out to so many others.

JULY 16, 1918
CZAR NICHOLAS AND HIS ENTIRE FAMILY ARE BRUTALLY MURDERED

Czar Nicholas II had hoped to be exiled to the UK while Kerensky was in power, but his British "ally" had refused to take him in. The **Bolsheviks** *(Communists)* now hold Nicholas, his wife Alexandra, his four daughters and young son under house arrest. Their Red captors force them to live on rations.

As a boy, Nicholas had witnessed the bombing murder of his grandfather, Alexander II, in 1881. Nicholas's tragic error was in failing to execute the Red scum, such as Lenin and Trotsky, after their failed 1905 revolution. Now, his misguided mercy returns to haunt him, and his family.

On the evening of July 16/17, 1918, the royal Romanov Family is awakened at 2AM, told to dress, and then herded into the cellar of the house in which they are being held. Moments later, Jewish Reds storm in and gun down the entire family, their doctor, and three servants in cold blood. Some of the Romanov daughters are stabbed and clubbed to death when initial gunfire fails to kill them. News of the brutal murder of the Romanovs will send shock waves throughout Russia, and all of Christian Europe.

A beautiful family - shot and stabbed to death like animals! As the shooting began, the Czar tried to shield his young son.

1918
BRITISH DIVERT MANPOWER SO AS TO FINISH OFF THE OTTOMAN EMPIRE AND STEAL PALESTINE

Britain's previous campaign against the Turks had ended in failure *(Gallipoli)*. Now, with fresh and strong Americans arriving to fight the Germans in Western Europe, British troops are freed-up to concentrate on the Ottoman Empire. Britain covets the oil fields of the Middle East, but the UK also has a debt to repay to the Zionist bosses who dragged the U.S. into the war.

Assisting the Brits in the effort to steal Palestine are 10,000 American Jews who enlist to fight not alongside their fellow Americans in Europe, but with the British, who intend to seize their future home, Palestine. **(28) See: The Jewish Legion**

During this time, British airplanes drop leaflets over Germany. **Printed in Yiddish, the Balfour leaflets seek to win Jewish support in Germany** by promising the Jews a 'homeland' in Palestine after they have won the war. **(29)**

1- Vladimir Jabotinsky (left) led Jewish units in the fight against Turkey.
2- Leaving the Americans to do the heavy lifting against Germany, the British head south to dismantle the Ottoman Empire.

1918
LENIN & TROTSKY ESTABLISH THE 'COMMUNIST INTERNATIONAL' / VIOLENT RED PLAGUE GOES GLOBAL

"All Power to the Workers" really means all power to the New World Order!

With the Russian Civil War raging, the *Communist International*, known as **"The Comintern"**, is established in Moscow, Russia. The Comintern states *openly* that its intention is to fight *"by all available means, including armed force, for the overthrow of the international "bourgeoisie" (the entrepreneurial class) and for the creation of an international Soviet republic (world government)."* **(30)**

From 1918-1922, Comintern-affiliated Parties form in France, Italy, China, Germany, Spain, Belgium, the U.S. and other nations. All Communists operate under the direction of the Soviets, who are themselves financed by the same international bankers that created the Federal Reserve and brought about the Great War.

SEPTEMBER, 1918
THE 'RED TERROR' IS ANNOUNCED IN RUSSIA

The Russian Communists plan to strategically use terror to intimidate their White adversaries into submission. On orders from Lenin and Trotsky, the **"Red Terror"** is announced by the Jewish Red **Yakov Sverdlov**. The Red Terror is marked by mass arrests in the middle of the night, executions, and hideously creative tactics of torture. As many as 100,000 Russians are murdered in the Red Terror, carried out by Jewish-run **Cheka** (secret police).

Among the atrocities committed, often in view of victim's family members, are:

- 40,000 White prisoners publicly hanged in the Ukraine
- Burning coals inserted into women's vaginas
- Crucifixions
- Rapes of women of all ages
- Victims submerged in boiling oil or tar
- Victims doused with petrol and burned alive
- Victims placed in coffins filled with hungry rats
- Victims soaked with water and turned into human ice-cubes in winter
- Priests, monks, and nuns have molten lead poured down their throats

(31)

The demoralizing terror takes a heavy psychological toll on the frightened Russian people. By 1922, many are broken into submission to the Cheka monsters.

1 & 2 - The horror of the Jewish Red Terror frightened Europe. Not since the days of Genghis Khan have so many Europeans been so brutally murdered.

3- Yakov Sverdlov was a mass murdering beast.

NOVEMBER 11, 1918
THE GREAT WAR ENDS / 'THE NOVEMBER CRIMINALS' BETRAY GERMANY TO THE GLOBALISTS

By the fall of 1918, it is clear that Germany can no longer win the War. Its policy now is *"to not lose it either."* As he had in 1916, the Kaiser offers to negotiate peace on terms favorable to all. Though Germany cannot win, the Allies are not able to win either. Germany's Eastern front with Russia is closed. There are no Allied troops on German soil, the Capital, Berlin is 900 miles safely away from the front, and the German military is very capable of defending the homeland from any invasion.

But the home front is collapsing. Treasonous politicians, Marxist labor union leaders, and Zionist media moguls, combine to demoralize the people and destabilize Germany. The Kaiser is forced to step down, exiling to Holland. On November 11, '18, Marxists and liberals of the newly formed **"Weimer Republic"** *(formed in the city of Weimar)* lie down and roll over for the Allies!

Incredibly, at a time when the Allies <u>do not have a single soldier on German soil</u>, the Weimar traitors order the military to lay down their arms and withdraw from the front.

Based on Wilson's empty promises of *"peace without victory"*, the 'November Criminals' place Germany at the total mercy of the **New World Order.**

1- The armistice trap was signed in a railway car in Compiegne, France.
2- Patriotic German cartoon depicts politicians stabbing German troops in the back. 3- Jewish Reds seize Berlin that very day

"Berlin Seized by Revolutionists" (Reds)

In 1915, Jewish Reds **Rosa Luxemburg** and **Karl Liebknecht** founded the "**Spartacus League**" *(named after NWO / Illuminati founder Adam Weishaupt's code name of "Spartacus")*. In 1919, the group becomes the **Communist Party of Germany**.

That same month, the Spartacists, aided by Jewish-Hungarian Red **Bela Kun**, take advantage of the post-war chaos, and stage a coup in Berlin. Kaiser Wilhelm, fearing the same fate as Tsar Nicholas, flees to Holland. He now regrets his past liberalism and denounces the "Jewish influence" that ruined Germany.

The Communist takeover of Berlin is short-lived as veterans known as the '**Freikorps**' reclaim control from the Reds and their followers. Luxemburg and Liebknecht are captured and executed. The "Freikorps" has saved Germany from the same deadly fate that has befallen Russia, but the new "democratic socialist" Germany will soon face other serious problems. Just like the hard core Reds of Russia pushed aside the socialist Kerensky, the Reds of Germany will keep trying to grab absolute power from the "democratic socialists" of Weimar.

The German Freikorps saved Germany from the Soviet-style Communist bloodbath that Jewish Reds Luxemburg and Liebknecht were planning.

NOVEMBER, 1918
INJURED GERMAN ARMY CORPORAL REACTS BITTERLY TO NEWS OF THE SURRENDER

As a 25-year-old 'starving artist', **Adolph Hitler** had volunteered to fight for Austria in 1914. By that time, both of his parents had passed away. Afflicted with tuberculosis during youth, Hitler was rejected for military service. Hitler then pleaded with Bavarian authorities to allow him to fight for Germany. He served with great distinction, and was promoted to Lance Corporal after being awarded the German **Iron Cross 2nd Class** for bravery. In October '16, he was badly wounded and spends two months in a military hospital. He could have stayed home but chose to return to the frontlines.

In August of '18, Hitler is awarded the prestigious **Iron Cross 1st Class**. In October 1918, he is blinded by a British poison gas attack. While recovering his eyesight, Hitler hears of Germany's shameful capitulation. He is confused and outraged. The sacrifice and suffering of the German soldiers had been for nothing. The brave unknown painter from Vienna wants answers, and he won't rest until the 'November Criminals' *(his term)* are exposed and Germany's honor restored.

Hitler, seated left, was a heroic and highly decorated soldier.

JANUARY, 1919
THE PARIS PEACE CONFERENCE

The **Paris Peace Conference** is the meeting of the Allied victors to financially crush Germany and determine the new borders of the defeated nations. The

Globalists devise a series of treaties *(Paris Peace Treaties)* that reshape Europe and the world. At its center are the leaders of the three 'Great Powers': **Woodrow Wilson** *(U.S.)*, Prime Ministers **David Lloyd George** *(U.K.)* and **Georges Clemenceau** (France). *Germany is not invited and will have no say in the final decisions.*

The Globalists will dismantle existing nations and create new ones. Austria-Hungary and Turkey are carved up; their disparate peoples re-assigned to new states. The Conference also creates the framework for a future World Government, **The League of Nations**.

A Zionist delegation is also present. They had brought America into the war, and now it is time to collect payment for services rendered *(Balfour Declaration)*. Former Arab territories of the Ottoman Empire are separated from Turkish rule and broken up into small states. Palestine is to become a British protectorate. **See: British Mandate**

The Zionist statement establishes the Jew's claim to a piece of Palestine, guaranteed by The League of Nations and exactly as Herzl had predicted in 1897! Jews from all over the world may now immigrate to British Palestine, but in controlled numbers. **The Arabs of Palestine *(a 95% majority)* were not consulted about this deal, and they are angry.**

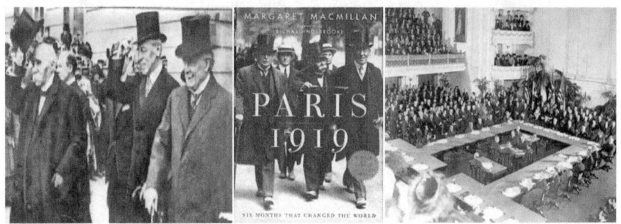

Clemenceau, Wilson, & George front for the Globalist gangsters in Paris.

During the Russian Civil War, Jewish-Hungarian, **Bela Kun** fights for the Reds. As a commander, Kun orders the killings of thousands of anti-Communists.

With the collapse of the Austro-Hungarian Empire, Kun sees an opportunity to impose Communism in Hungary. In November '18, his Red gang returns to Hungary with money given to him by the Russian Reds. He founds the Hungarian Communist Party on November 4, '18.

The **Hungarian Soviet Republic** is soon established. Kun reports directly to Lenin and is the dominant personality in the government during its brief existence. Kun's first act is to nationalize *(confiscate)* all private property. After an anti-communist coup attempt in Hungary in June '19, Kun organizes a response in the form of a Red Terror, carried out by secret police and mostly Jewish irregular units. Red Tribunals condemn 600 prominent Hungarians to death. Kun's Reds are removed from power after an invasion by Romania. Kun flees to The USSR.

Bela Kun: Yet another Rothschild rabble-rouser on a soap box.

JUNE, 1919
GERMANY IS GANG-RAPED BY THE 'TREATY OF VERSAILLES'

Out of the **Paris Peace Conference** comes the barbaric and infamous "**Treaty of Versailles**". The cruelty of the Treaty is today recognized even by liberal historians. With Germany disarmed by its new government, the Globalists & Zionists proceed to rape the German nation; **a nation that did not want war, had tried to avert the war, and had offered to make peace on numerous occasions after the war had begun.**

The Treaty contains 440 clauses, 414 of which are dedicated towards punishing Germany for a <u>war that was imposed upon her.</u>

Among the key provisions that a disarmed Germany and Austria *(Treaty of St. Germaine)* are forced to accept *<u>at gunpoint and while under a hunger blockade</u>* are:

1. Germany must accept 100% responsibility for the war.
2. German armed forces restricted to 100,000 men.
3. The industrial German Rhineland will be occupied by French troops for 15 years.
4. Kaiser Wilhelm II *(safe in Holland)* should be tried for *"offenses against international morality"*.
5. The German region of West Prussia is given to the new nation of Poland.

Two million West Prussians are forcefully expelled from their homes, and East Prussia is left isolated from the rest of Germany!

6. The German Sudetenland region is put under the rule of the new nation of 'Czechoslovakia'.
7. The new state of Austria is forbidden from uniting with their brothers in Germany.
8. Germany is stripped of African colonies. Britain, France, & Belgium take them.
9. The coal-rich Saar region of Germany is placed under League of Nations control for 15 years. During this time, its coal is to be shipped to France.
10. The Baltic Sea port city of Danzig is separated from Germany and declared a "free city."
11. Germany is forced to pay massive war reparations in the form of money and

natural resources. The crushing debt payments *(equal to 1 Trillion dollars in modern currency)* will devastate the German economy and soon cause a hyperinflationary monetary collapse. **(32)**

Defenseless Germany is kept under the hunger blockade until she agrees to the harsh terms. About 100,000 Germans die as a result of the <u>post-armistice</u> food blockade. (33) The unjust and inhumane Treaty of Versailles will breed resentment and anger for year to come.

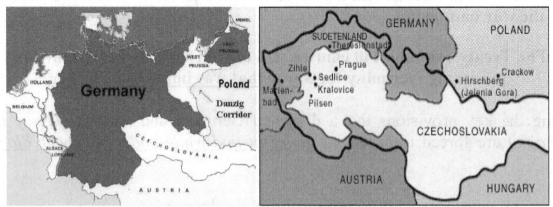

1- West Prussia is given to the new state of Poland. East Prussia is cut off from the rest of Germany!

2- German Sudetenland is assigned to the new state of Czechoslovakia

---

OCTOBER, 1919
PRESIDENT WILSON IS PARALYZED BY A STROKE / THE PUBLIC IS KEPT UNAWARE FOR 1 ½ YEARS!

The Zionist-Globalist pressure on Woodrow Wilson is too much for the feeble Princeton Professor to handle. The **New World Order** Bosses have ridden their blackmailed puppet very hard since 1912. Now, Wilson is being ordered to undertake an intense, year-long cross-country campaign to win public support for US entry into the world government blueprint known as 'The League of Nations' *(established at the Paris Peace Conference).*

During his grueling propaganda train tour, Wilson suffers a massive stroke that leaves him paralyzed. For the next 17 months, the enfeebled President lies in bed on the brink of death, barely able to write his own name. *The outside world knows nothing of this.*

All communication with the "dummy" President goes through his wife, Edith. Wilson never fully recovers and will die in 1924. His horrible legacy of treason *(The Fed, Income Tax, Zionism, World War I & Globalism etc.)* haunts America to this very day.

Even when healthy, the dummy was only good for ceremonies. Wilson's grueling 'League of Nations' train tour campaign wore him down.

NOVEMBER, 1919
MAJOR SETBACK FOR GLOBALISM! U.S. SENATE REFUSES TO JOIN THE LEAGUE OF NATIONS

After an intense, yearlong campaign to win support for entry into the League of Nations, the now incapacitated President Wilson and his Rothschild-Globalist masters are dealt a devastating blow when the Senate fails to approve U.S. membership. **Globalist pressure forces the Senate to vote three times,** but the necessary 2/3 majority *still* cannot be reached.

Leading the opposition to membership in the infant World Government are Senators **Henry Cabot Lodge** (R-MA), **Warren Harding** (R-OH), and **William Borah** (R-ID).

The American people now realize that the very strange war that they had just fought served no American interest at all. Americans want no more of Europe's affairs and just want to "return to normalcy." But the Globalists will keep on scheming against the people until they finally get their **New World Order.**

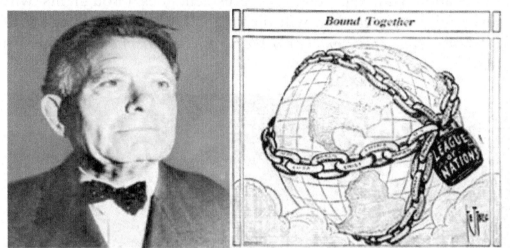

1- Senator Borah led the opposition to the New World Order trap.

2- 'Bound Together": even then, certain cartoonists smelled the global trap.

1919
UNKNOWN ADOLF HITLER SPARKS A MOVEMENT

When Adolf Hitler joins the **German Workers Party** (DAP) in 1919, he becomes only the 7th member of the nationalist group. The now 30-year old, self-educated artist from Austria has little money and no political connections. But his oratorical, organizational, and marketing talents propel him to leadership of the tiny band of brothers. Hitler's mesmerizing beer-hall speeches stop onlookers in their tracks. He denounces the Versailles Treaty, the occupation, the 'November Criminals', the Marxists, the Press, and the international bankers.

DAP membership then grows rapidly, recruiting unemployed young men and disgruntled ex-soldiers betrayed during the war. Hitler appeals to veterans because he himself was a frontline soldier, twice decorated for serious injuries sustained, and twice more for conspicuous bravery on the battlefield.

To draw recruits away from *both* the rival "right" Nationalist and "left" Socialist Parties, Hitler simply adds 'National' and 'Socialist' to the Party's name, making it NSDAP. *(They never called themselves "Nazis"!)*. To draw people away from the Reds, Hitler also uses red flags, with a symbol of the ancient Aryans of Asia.

Hitler designed the NSDAP flag. The "swastika" was a symbol of the ancient Asian Aryan peoples who settled in Europe.

Adolf Hitler: A talented painter with a dream to save Germany.

1919
RED TERROR EXPLODES ACROSS AMERICA!

What modern day liberal historians mockingly refer to as "**The First Red Scare**", is nothing to laugh about. Coming just 18 years after the Reds murdered President McKinley, the 1919 "Red Scare" is marked by a campaign of Communist/Anarchist terror and radical political agitation, set against the backdrop of Lenin's ongoing bloodbath and Wilson's crashing economy.

In April, 30 booby-trap mail bombs are sent to prominent Americans. After the 1st bomb fizzles, and the 2nd injures the wife of a US Senator, the remaining 28 are intercepted by postal authorities. On May 1 *(May Day)*, Reds stage large rallies that lead to violence in Boston, New York, and Cleveland. Two die and 40 are injured as patriots clash with immigrant Reds.

Later that year, 8 more bombs are mailed, killing 2 innocent people. The home of anti-Red **Attorney General A. Mitchell Palmer** is also bombed, and heavily damaged. Fortunately for Palmer and his family, the bomb detonates prematurely, killing **Aldo Valdinoci**, the Italian anarchist planting it. In September, Marxist Union leaders organize steel strikes, soon followed by coal strikes. The 'Red Scare' is no joke! The Reds mean business, and Americans are rightfully concerned.

1- Cartoon: Anarchist Bomber sneaks up on Lady Liberty

2- Attorney General Palmer's home was bombed by Reds.

1919 -1920
THE 'PALMER RAIDS' CRIPPLE THE U.S. REDS

The efforts of Attorney **General A. Mitchell Palmer** weaken the Reds greatly. Opposed by the pro-Red ACLU, undermined by some in the Wilson Cabinet, and undeterred by the bombing of his own home, Palmer presses on with his roundups and investigations. Palmer's Federal Agents often rough up the foreign Reds, including many Russian-Jewish radicals, as well as Italian and East European Anarchists.

In November 1919, Palmer deports 249 foreign Reds, including top leaders such as "Red Emma" Goldman, who inspired and praised the 1901 McKinley murder. Palmer then focuses on the Marxist labor strikes, leaving his young assistant *(and future FBI Director)* **J. Edgar Hoover**, to fight the foreign Reds. Hoover rounds up 3000 more radicals. In all, 5000 radicals are arrested, 556 of which are booted out of America. **(34)** Good riddance!

Palmer's efforts to contain the murderous Red cancer were heroic.

Lord of the Admiralty and Lusitania war criminal **Winston Churchill** is a supporter of Zionism *(Jewish state in Palestine)*, but opposed to Jewish Communism. Although both movements trace back to the same Rothschild Crime Family, they sometimes appear - **to this day**- to operate at cross-purposes, and in conflict with each other.

In an editorial appearing in the Illustrated Sunday Herald entitled, '*Zionism vs Bolshevism*', Churchill argues that Jews should support Zionism as an alternative to Communism; missing the fact that both movements emanate from the same source. The future Prime Minister rails against *"the schemes of the International Jews"*:

"This movement among the Jews is not new. From the days of Weishaupt to those of Karl Marx, and down to Trotsky (Russia), Bela Kun (Hungary), Rosa Luxembourg (Germany), and Emma Goldman (United States), **this worldwide conspiracy for the overthrow of civilization and for the reconstitution of society on the basis of arrested development, envious malevolence, and impossible equality, has been steadily growing.** *It played, as a modern writer, Mrs. Webster, has so ably shown, a definitely recognizable part in the tragedy of the French Revolution……It has been the mainspring of every subversive movement during the Nineteenth Century; and now at last this band of extraordinary personalities from the underworld of the great cities of Europe and America have gripped the Russian people by the hair of their heads and have become the undisputed masters of that enormous empire."* **(35)**

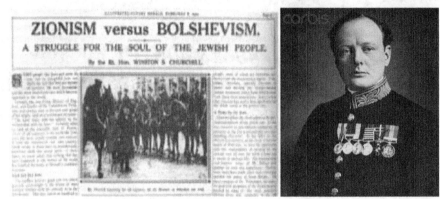

Zionism vs Bolshevism is a precursor of today's Neo-cons vs. Globalists rivalry.

SEPTEMBER, 1920
AMERICAN REDS BOMB WALL STREET / 38 DEAD

In New York, a horse drawn carriage stops on the Wall Street Financial District's busiest corner. The driver leaves the scene. Inside of the carriage, 100 pounds of dynamite with 500 pounds of iron shrapnel are set to explode in a timer-set detonation. The horse and wagon are blasted into small fragments. The 38 victims, most of who die within moments of the blast, are mostly young people who work as messengers, clerks, and brokers. Many of the wounded suffer severe, disfiguring injuries.

Prior to the blast, flyers were found in a nearby Post Office. Written in red ink, the flyers promised violence if political prisoners were not released. At the bottom was written: "American Anarchist Fighters." The actual perpetrators will never be caught, but the terrorist Red movement in America is clearly behind the mass murder.

The Red bomb overturned automobiles. The nation was shocked.

1920 - 21
GLOBALIST 'THINK TANKS' FORM IN BRITAIN AND AMERICA / ELITES RECRUITED TO JOIN THE NEW WORLD ORDER

At the Paris Peace Conference, Globalists from the U.S. & Britain had agreed to establish sister "think tanks" that will dominate the affairs of both nations. In 1920, the Fabian dominated **Royal Institute of International Affairs** *(now Chatham House)* is founded in London. In 1921, the **Council on Foreign Relations (CFR)** is established in New York with "Father of the Fed" Paul Warburg serving as its first Director.

"Chatham House Rules" of secrecy govern the members of both clubs. Membership is by invitation only. Members may discuss generalities of group meetings, but are expected to remain discreet concerning who attends the meetings and what is said.

Up until the present day, the membership rolls of **CFR & Chatham** have included top names from politics, media, banking, business, and academia. The membership rolls include a variety of Globalists, Communists, Zionists, ambitious careerists, and well-meaning dupes. The chosen few recruited by the world government builders often find themselves on a fast track to greater fame and fortune.

1- The Manhattan based CFR is the seat of America's Oligarchy. Rothschild ally Paul "Father of the Fed" Warburg is its first Director.

2- Obama speaks before his Council co-conspirators.

1921 – 1930

Lenin's oppression of the Russian people breaks their strength and will to resist. **The Famine of 1921** is partly due to the folly of central economic planning, as well as to a deliberate effort to kill off any Russians still not willing to support the Red takeover. The Communists ran the money-printing presses to finance their civil war and welfare schemes. When inflation follows, they impose price controls, causing farmers to lose money by farming. Compounding the shortage is the Red seizure of seeds.

 The horrific famine is then used to selectively feed those regions submissive to the Reds, and starve out those loyal to the Whites.

Starving Russians and Ukrainians resort to eating grass, or even cannibalizing the dead. The horror escalates when Lenin deliberately blocks foreign relief efforts. When the death toll reaches 10 million, Lenin finally allows relief. Were it not for the mostly American aid, the death toll for Lenin's cruelty would have doubled.

Starving children and corpses of the 1921 Soviet Famine

MARCH, 1921
FOR THE THIRD TIME IN 23 YEARS, REDS MURDER A PRIME MINISTER OF SPAIN

Eduardo Dato became Prime Minister of Spain for the first time in 1913. In 1915, he left that position, but would return to it for a short while in 1917, and then, for a third time in 1920.

On March 8, 1921 in Madrid, while being driven from the parliament building and in front, Dato was assassinated by three anarchists, **Lluís Nicolau, Pere Mateu, and Ramon Casanelles**, who were riding a motorcycle.

1 & 2- Dato was killed in a motorcycle drive-by shooting.

3- The bullet riddled car.

JULY, 1921
NEW YORK TIMES PUBLISHES SOVIET CLAIM THAT 6 MILLION JEWS FACE EXTERMINATION BY 'WHITE' COUNTER-REVOLUTIONARIES

BEGS AMERICA SAVE 6,000,000 IN RUSSIA

Massacre Threatens All Jews as Soviet Power Wanes, Declares Kreinin, Coming Here for Aid.

Copyright, 1921, by The Chicago Tribune Co.
BERLIN, July 19.—Russia's 6,000,000 Jews are facing extermination by massacre. As the famine is spreading, the counter-revolutionary movement is gaining and the Soviet's control is waning. This statement is borne out by offical documents presented to the Berlin Government, which show that numerous pogroms are raging in all parts of Russia

Yet again!

1921 - 23
THE BRIEF AND VERY SUCCESSFUL PRESIDENCY OF WARREN G HARDING

Pledging a "return to normalcy", Warren Harding (R-OH) is elected President in 1920. An opponent of entry into the League of Nations, his victory over James Cox (D-OH) and his VP running mate Franklin D Roosevelt (TR's cousin), is the largest Presidential landslide in U.S. history (60%-34%)

In his inaugural address, Harding lays the smack-down upon the Wilsonian Zio-Globalists:

*"The recorded progress of our Republic, materially and spiritually, proves the wisdom of the inherited policy of noninvolvement in Old World affairs. Confident of our ability to work out our own destiny, and jealously guarding our right to do so, **we seek no part in directing the destinies of the Old World. We do not mean to be entangled.** We will accept no responsibility except as our own conscience and judgment in each instance may determine.*

*We sense the call of the human heart for fellowship, fraternity, and cooperation. We crave friendship and harbor no hate. But America, our America, the **America built on the foundation laid by the inspired fathers, can be a party to no permanent military alliance.** It can enter into no political commitments, nor assume any economic obligations which will subject our decisions to any other than our own authority."* **(1)**

Harding inherits a severe Wilsonian Economic Depression. He quickly moves to slash income taxes, and will cut government spending by 50%. With the private economy now freed from the parasitic dead weight of big government, an historic economic boom soon follows. Harding is undoing Wilson's damage, and returning the country to the days of William Howard Taft *(who he names as Chief Justice of the Supreme Court).*

Harding's support for free markets, limited government, low taxes, neutral foreign policy, and his refusal to grant diplomatic recognition to the murderous Soviet Union, are all positions that anger the Globalists. An intense newspaper smear campaign regarding "scandals" in Harding's administration is unleashed against the highly popular President. In spite of the hate campaign, Harding remains extremely popular.

1- Harding (left) crushed Cox & FDR in the 1920 election and put America back on the road to recovery and happiness.

2- American glory days: Harding with baseball legend Babe Ruth

*

1- Harding's inaugural address rejected Globalism.

2- Globalist owned "Yellow Press" discovered "scandals" on Harding.

1920 – 1922
HENRY FORD PUBLISHES 'THE INTERNATIONAL JEW: THE WORLD'S PROBLEM'

American auto manufacturer and icon Henry Ford publishes a 4-volume set of booklets exposing the operations of the Globalist Jewish elite. Ford's investigations reveal a hidden influence over American politics, the Fed, the press, organized crime, theatre, art, and music. German NSDAP members read and distribute translated copies of Ford's work. Hitler himself has a copy in his office, along with a photo of Ford.

Because of Ford's national stature and vast wealth, many take the warnings of **The International Jew** very seriously. After withstanding years of intense pressure and a libel suit aimed at him, Ford eventually backs off of his crusade, even closing his newspaper, *The Dearborn Independent,* in 1927.

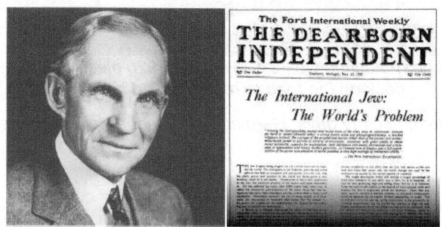

Ford knew all about the New World Order.

JULY, 1922
REDS ATTEMPT TO ASSASSINATE THE PRESIDENT OF FRANCE

Alexandre Millerand is the President of France. On July 14, 1922, an anarchist named **Gustave Bouvet** makes an attempt to assassinate him.

As Millerand and other dignitaries travel in a procession of three carriages along the Champs-Élysées; Bouvet draws a revolver from his pocket and fires two shots at the second car, which he mistakenly believes the President is riding in. Both shots go wide due to a bystander grabbing Bouvet's arm before he can aim.

Bouvet drops the gun and is quickly subdued. He is found to be carrying another revolver and 25 cartridges in his pockets. Upon interrogation, he declares that he intended to shoot the President "in order to make an example."

Millerand & Bouvet The Reds have an endless supply of disaffected and brainwashed young assassins who show no fear of being captured or executed.

1922
THE REDS WIN THE RUSSIAN CIVIL WAR / THE 'SOVIET UNION' (U.S.S.R.) IS FORMALLY ESTABLISHED

At the conclusion of the Red Terror, Red Famine, and Red-White Civil War in 1922, Lenin and Trotsky formally establish the Soviet Union with its capital city in Moscow. The former Russian Empire is now also known as the USSR *(Union of Soviet Socialist Republics)*.

The Communist giant spans Eurasia. Of its multi-ethnic "republics" the Russian republic is by far the largest and most populated. The well-known criminal brutality of the Soviets shocks the world, as do the Communist declarations to overthrow all other nations. For these reasons, three consecutive Republican Presidents *(Harding, Coolidge, Hoover)*, will refuse to diplomatically recognize the Soviet Union.

Phony symbolism: the Hammer & Sickle on Soviet flag symbolize Communist love for "the workers." The enormous Russian Empire is now the evil Soviet Empire.

OCTOBER, 1922
'THE MARCH ON ROME' / BENITO MUSSOLINI'S FASCISTS SAVE ITALY FROM THE COMMUNISTS & LIBERALS

The global economic Depression that follows World War I gives the Reds and socialists an opportunity to agitate in post war Italy. **Benito Mussolini** and his Fascist Party decide to act before the "democratic" Reds can get any stronger.

In October of '22, Mussolini declares before 60,000 people at the Fascist Congress in Naples: **"Our program is simple: we want to rule Italy."** Fascist "Black-shirts" capture the strategic points of Italy. Mussolini then leads a March of 30,000 men on the Capital City of Rome. On October 28, a sympathetic King Victor Emmanuel III, whose father had been murdered by a Red in 1900, grants political power to Mussolini. Mussolini is supported by veterans and the business class.

The corrupt left-wing political parties are eventually shut down. Under "Il Duce's" rule, the pro-business Fascist Party takes control and restores order to Italy. Fascism combines an honest and sound monetary system with a mix of free enterprise and state regulated corporatism.

Mussolini's 'March on Rome': "Communism is a fraud, a comedy, a phantom, a blackmail." (2)

JANUARY 11, 1923
FRANCE INVADES GERMANY'S RUHR REGION AFTER GERMANY IS LATE ON EXTORTION PAYMENTS

More than four years have passed since Germany's complete and total surrender at the end of The Great War. The poor & hunger-stricken German nation is now having difficulty in making the massive reparations extortion payments imposed by The Treaty of Versailles. Having already destroyed the value of Germany's currency, the Allies now demand to be paid in timber and coal. Extortionist allied troops move in for a "shakedown."

In a further humiliation of an already occupied Germany *(Rhineland)*, 60,000 troops from Belgium, France, and the French African colonies expand the occupation into the defenseless Ruhr *(an industrial region of Germany)*. While German children go hungry, the Allies collect their stolen loot of physical German commodities. Machine gun posts are set up in the streets as Allied troops take food and supplies from German shopkeepers. Other than stage passive demonstrations, there is nothing the disarmed, humiliated, and hungry German people can do about the French abuse.

Shaking down Germany! France and Belgium expanded the occupation of industrial parts of Germany. The invaders killed 132 disobedient Germans.

AUGUST 21, 1923
THE SUDDEN AND STRANGE DEATH OF PRESIDENT HARDING

While recovering from a strange sickness that had stricken him in San Francisco, President Harding shudders and dies suddenly during a conversation with his wife. Doctor's cannot agree on the cause of his strange death. Within an hour of his demise, Harding's body is embalmed and placed in a casket. The following morning, the body is on a train, headed back to Washington Incredibly, *no autopsy is performed.* **(3)** The suspicion of a deliberate poisoning plot rages throughout America.

The sudden death of the 57-year-old statesman, who successfully reversed Wilson's damage in just 29 months, remains a mystery. Of course, liberal 'historians' today rate Harding as "the worst President ever."

Crowds of mourners watched the train carry the body of President Harding back to DC.

1923
GERMAN SUPER-INFLATION WIPES OUT MIDDLE CLASS

With Allied troops occupying the Ruhr, and the German Mark losing its value to inflation, Germany in '22-23 goes through a horrific *hyperinflation*. The socialist Weimer Government and the Warburg/Rothschild Central Bank resort to massively expanding the money supply, mostly to cover the crushing debt imposed by the Versailles Treaty, but also to keep the Weimar Republic's welfare state afloat.

The life savings of the German people is wiped out as *prices double every 2 days for 20 straight months!* Workers are paid daily, so that they may go food shopping before prices double again. Many Germans refer to their devalued money as **"Judefetzen"**, *(Jewish confetti).* **(4)**

This leads to more chaos and another attempt by the Communists to stage a revolution. As they had during the war, the Marxist Trade Unions call for strikes at a time when Germany is most vulnerable. To pacify the striking workers, the Weimar / Reichsbank complex pumps even more paper debt money into the economy.

1- Germans needed wheelbarrows full of paper money to go shopping.
2- 20 BILLION Marks for a postage stamp!   3- Mark wallpaper.

NOVEMBER, 1923
'THE BEER HALL PUTSCH' / HITLER ATTEMPTS A COUP IN BAVARIAN CITY OF MUNICH

Righteous anger is boiling over the hyper-inflation and the new French-Belgian occupation. Hitler decides that the time is right to seize power from the local government in Munich. Hoping that war veterans will join the revolt and move against the national government in Berlin, Hitler uses a rally in a Munich 'Beer Hall' to launch a coup.

The local uprising, or "putsch", is ignited by Hitler's moving speech, but fails to sustain itself as troops open fire on the nationalist rebels, killing 16 of them. Hitler and others are arrested and tried for treason. At his trial, Hitler uses the occasion to spread his ideas, which are then published in the newspapers. The judge is impressed, and issues a lenient sentence for the rebels. Though the Munich coup has failed, the legend of the great orator grows, attracting new followers by the day. Membership in Hitler's NSDAP tops 20,000 by year's end.

A crowd turned out to support Hitler. Hitler and Ludendorff were arrested.

After Harding's sudden death/assassination, America doesn't know what to make of **Calvin Coolidge** *("Silent Cal")*, the new President. It is believed that Coolidge will serve the remaining 19 months of Harding's term, and then be replaced at the Republican Convention in 1924. But after continuing Harding's policies, Coolidge is now very popular. He is nominated to run against Democrat John Davis. Remarkably; Davis is also a conservative!

The Globalists put up Robert La Follette (R-WI) as the Progressive nominee. On Election Day 1924, Coolidge carries 35 states, Davis wins 12, and La Follette wins only his home state!

A period of peace & prosperity known as **"The Roaring Twenties"** has the Constitutional Republicans riding high. What's a Globalist to do? They can't just keep killing Presidents! The "Fed" will begin laying a financial time bomb beneath the nation's prosperity. When the bomb finally explodes in 1929, the era of Constitutional Republicanism will be swept away for good.

"I want the people of America to be able **to work less for the government and more for themselves.** I want them to have the rewards of their own industry. **This is the chief meaning of freedom.**"

- Calvin Coolidge

The unknown "Silent Cal" turned out to be just as good as Harding!

JANUARY 21, 1924
LENIN DIES / PSYCHOPATH KILLER JOSEPH STALIN TAKES OVER THE USSR

When Lenin dies in 1924, **Joseph Stalin**, Secretary of the Communist Party Central Committee, skillfully outmaneuvers Red Army leader **Lev Trotsky** to take leadership of the USSR. Stalin will eventually expel Trotsky from the Party, then from the USSR itself. Finally, he will have his Marxist rival axed through his brain by a Soviet agent in Mexico.

Stalin's brutality instills fear not only in the enslaved people of the Soviet Union, but also in the hearts of fellow Communists that the paranoid Stalin believes may challenge his leadership. The egomaniac renames a city after himself *(Stalingrad)*, and erects statues of his likeness in town squares. From time to time, Stalin will "purge" many of his own Red comrades, as well as wives. He dumps his first wife, and drives his second, *(as well as one of his sons)* to suicide.

In years to come, Stalin's chilling crimes against humanity will make Lenin's Red Terror and Red Famine seem like minor infractions by comparison.

Lenin (l) was a pussycat compared to the genocidal Stalin and his Jewish 'right hand man' Lazar Kaganovich. It was Kaganovich who ordered the demolition of Russia's grand and historic Christ the Savior Cathedral (right).

FORBIDDEN HISTORY: QUOTE TO REMEMBER:

"You must understand, the leading Bolsheviks who took over Russia were not Russians. They (Bolshevik Jews) hated Russians. They hated Christians. Driven by ethnic hatred they tortured and slaughtered millions of Russians without a shred of human remorse. It cannot be overstated. Bolshevism committed the greatest human slaughter of all time. The fact that most of the world is ignorant and uncaring about this enormous crime is proof that the global media is in the hands of the perpetrators."

Aleksandr Solzhenitsyn, Russian historian and literary figure (5)

AUGUST, 1924
THE DAWES PLAN / ZIONIST BANKERS REFINANCE GERMANY'S DEBT

In 1924, a refinancing of Germany's reparations debt, as well as Allied debt to the US Treasury *(which in turn is indebted to the Fed)* is worked out. The terms are still harsh, but the German economy and currency are temporarily stabilized. In 5 years the Dawes plan will also fail, and be replaced by the Young Plan. The reality of the **Dawes Plan**, named after US Vice President Charles Dawes, is that Dawes himself has little to do with it. It was the Zionist-Globalist bankers imposing the new plan. Former UK Prime Minister **David Lloyd George** reveals:

"The international bankers dictated the Dawes reparations settlement. The protocol, which was signed between the allies and Germany, is the triumph of the international financier. Agreement would never have been reached without the brutal intervention of the international bankers. They swept statesman, politicians, and journalists aside, and issued their orders with the imperiousness of absolute Monarchs, who knew there was no appeal from their ruthless decrees. The Dawes report was fashioned by the Money Kings." **(6)**

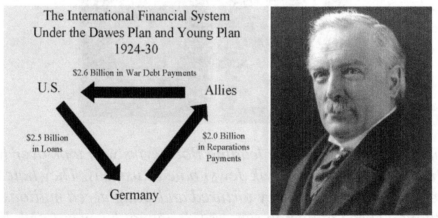

The circular Dawes Scam reworked Germany's debt. David Lloyd George confirmed that it was the International Bankers, not the politicians, who dictated the terms.

During his imprisonment of 1924, Hitler had dictated **'Mein Kampf'** *(My Struggle)*. His close associate **Rudolf Hess**, imprisoned with Hitler, typed out the dictation for the book, which was published in 1925. In it, Hitler places the blame for Germany's sorry condition upon a Global conspiracy of Marxists and Finance Capitalists.

According to Hitler, this global conspiracy for world government, directed by Jewish bankers, engineered Germany's loss of The Great War, the Russian Revolution, the Versailles Treaty, and the resulting hyperinflation that devastated Germany. He accuses the elite Marxist Jews of Germany of controlling newspapers and banking, fomenting wars, and corrupting the art, culture and morality of Europe.

Mein Kampf combines elements of a political manifesto and an autobiography along with discussions of history, philosophy, and economics. Originally written for the followers of National Socialism, *Mein Kampf* quickly grows in popularity, making Hitler a wealthy man.

Mein Kampf was first written in prison. Hitler spoke while Hess (4th from left) typed. The book is still banned in U.S. occupied Germany today.

David Sarnoff was born in a small Jewish village in Tsarist Russia and immigrated to New York in 1900. At the age of 15, he joined the Marconi Wireless Telegraph Company of America, starting a 60-year career in electronic communications.

By 1919, Sarnoff is General Manager of RCA radio. In 1926, Sarnoff's RCA forms NBC, the first major broadcast network in the U.S. Sarnoff is instrumental in building the AM broadcasting radio business which became the preeminent public radio standard for the majority of the 20th century. During World War II, he will serve under General Eisenhower as a "Communications Consultant" *(psychological warfare)*. **(7)** Sarnoff, who had no military experience, would be awarded the rank of Brigadier General.

When television in America is born under the name of the National Broadcast Corporation, the first TV show aired at the New York World's Fair and was introduced by Sarnoff himself. Leadership of RCA-NBC eventually passes down to Sarnoff's eldest son, **Robert Sarnoff**, one of the husbands of Felicia Schiff-Warburg of the two famous banking families. Franklin Roosevelt Jr. *(son of FDR)* was also an ex-husband of Felicia Schiff-Warburg.

The Sarnoff Family will control RCA-NBC TV for more than 60 years.

Sarnoff was an immensely powerful media giant of the 20th century. He will later serve as a Psychological Warfare specialist during World War II.

A major civil war breaks out in China between the governing Kuomintang (KMT or Chinese nationalist Party) and the Communist Party of China (CPC). The anti-Communist **Chiang Kai Shek** leads the KMT. The Red guerillas are led by **Mao Tse Tung**, who himself is supported by Comintern boss Joe Stalin. This bloody civil war will eventually blend into the Asian theater of World War II vs Japan, and finally end with Communist victory in 1949.

Mao was Stalin's agent in China. Combined, the 2 monsters murdered as many as 100 million people. Right: Chiang Kai Shek

Charles Lindbergh, the 25-year-old son of the Anti-Fed Congressman of the same name, becomes a world hero when he completes the first solo flight across the Atlantic. His plane "The Spirit of St. Louis" departs New York on May 20, arriving to a hero's welcome near Paris on May 21.

In 1938, Hermann Goering, Chief of the German Air Force, will present Lindbergh with a German Medal of Honor. Lindbergh's acceptance of the medal causes an outcry in the United States among critics of "Nazism". Lindbergh's politics mirror those of his father. 'Lucky Lindy" will use his fame to speak out on the issues of the day. In future years, Lindbergh's stature will make him a leader in the "**America First**" movement.

1- Young Lindbergh, an American patriot idolized in America and Europe.
2- Papa Lindbergh, with boy Charles, was hated by the Rothschild bankers.

1928
ZIONIST WILLIAM PALEY TAKES OVER CBS RADIO

William S. Paley *(Paloff)* is the son of Jewish immigrants who came from the Ukraine region of the Czarist Russian Empire. In 1928, the 27-year old businessman secures majority ownership of the CBS radio network *(of which his father Samuel Paloff had been part owner)*. Within the next decade, Paley expands CBS into a national powerhouse with 114 affiliate stations.

During World War II, Paley, like Sarnoff of NBC, will also serve under General Eisenhower as a colonel in the *Psychological Warfare* branch of the Office of War Information. **(8)**

As the King of the CBS radio (and later TV), Paley is without question, one of the most powerful figures of the 20th Century. With David Sarnoff already controlling RCA-NBC, and Paley now in control of CBS, the important pre-TV medium of radio is now mainly under Zionist control.

Like Sarnoff's NBC, Paley's CBS will shape what Americans believe for many years to come. Paley lived until 1990.

1928
STALIN SEIZES THE LAST OF RUSSIA'S FARMS / RESISTERS ARE KILLED

As part of Stalin's first "5 Year Plan", the small farmers of the Soviet Union are forced into a collectivization scheme. The government, not the market, now controls output and sets prices. Land, livestock, and equipment become property of "the people" *(the State)*. Reluctant farmers *(kulaks)* are smeared in the Soviet press as "greedy" "capitalists." Those who continue to resist the state's directives are murdered or imprisoned.

Thousands of private farmers are killed, but the really massive death tolls will occur during the famine of the early 1930's. Like all centrally planned economic schemes, in which "intellectuals" think they know better than the actual farmer, Stalin's collectivization, and other "5-Year Plans", yield only low living standards for the Soviet people.

The bestial Stalin cruelly dispossessed the Kulak farmers. Quote attributed to Stalin: "One death is a tragedy. One million deaths is a statistic." **(9)**

OCTOBER, 1929
THE FEDERAL RESERVE CRASHES THE STOCK MARKET / ENGINEERS 'THE GREAT DEPRESSION'

In the late 1920's, the privately owned U.S. Federal Reserve's policy of "easy money" had made it profitable for investors to borrow money at artificially low interest rates, and then purchase stocks with the money. **Like two con men working a 'mark', the Zionist Fed pumps out credit while the Zionist press hypes the Stock Market "rally".** As surely as night follows day, a massive bubble is inflated.

In 1929, the Fed suddenly hits the brakes on the money supply with a "tight money" policy. When the adjustment to the Fed's bubble occurs, the Stock Market collapses. Investors big and small are ruined. Instead of loosening up the money supply to enable debtors to pay down old debt, the Fed tightens even more. The sudden shortage of currency creates a tidal wave of bankruptcies across the U.S., as debtors cannot get their hands on enough money to pay off old loans. The well connected then swoop in to buy up assets at bargain prices.

The press, the Reds, and the idiot liberals will blame "capitalism" and Republican policies for the coming *worldwide* Great Depression, while deceitfully ignoring the *deliberate* role of Warburg/Rothschild Federal Reserve.

246

1- Every newspaper in America led with the story of the October crash.

2- In later years, future Fed Chairman Greenspan admitted that the Fed actually caused the Great Depression. **(10)** *("Inadvertently" according to him)*

SEPTEMBER, 1930
HITLER'S NSDAP BECOMES 2ND LARGEST PARTY IN GERMANY

The worldwide Great Depression hits debt-heavy Germany especially hard as loans from U.S. banks dry up. The people had already been worn out by the Versailles reparations, the unjust war guilt, the 1920's inflation, and chronic unemployment. There is a real fear among many that a hungry Germany may yet fall to Communism.

As a result, the NSDAP makes its first major electoral breakthrough. Hitler's party wins 6 million votes *(18% of vote)*, increasing its number of seats in the Reichstag *(German parliament)* from 12, to 107. NSDAP is now second only to the 143 seats held by Germany's socialist party, the Social Democrats. The Communist Party also gains 23 seats, raising its Reichstag representation to 77 Reds in the Reichstag, plus any secret members posing as Social Democrats.

On his way up; supporters salute Hitler after the NSDAP's success in the elections. His message is spreading fast, but so are the empty promises of the Communists.

General Leon Degrelle on the education of Adolf Hilter

Belgian SS volunteer General Leon Degrelle with Hitler

"Hitler was self-taught and he made no attempt to hide the fact. The smug conceit of intellectuals, their shiny ideas packaged like so many flashlight batteries, irritated him at times. His own knowledge he had acquired through selective and unremitting study, and he knew far more than thousands of diploma-decorated academics.

I don't think anyone ever read as much as he did. He normally read one book every day, always first reading the conclusion and the index in order to gauge the work's interest for him. He had the power to extract the essence of each book and then store it in his computer-like mind. I have heard him talk about complicated scientific books with faultless precision, even at the height of the war.

His intellectual curiosity was limitless. He was readily familiar with the writings of the most diverse authors, and nothing was too complex for his comprehension. He had a deep knowledge and understanding of Buddha, Confucius and Jesus Christ, as well as Luther, Calvin, and Savonarola; of literary giants such as Dante, Schiller, Shakespeare and Goethe; and analytical writers such as Renan and Gobineau, Chamberlain and Sorel.

248

He trained himself in philosophy by studying Aristotle and Plato. He could quote entire paragraphs of Schopenhauer from memory, and for a long time carried a pocket edition of Schopenhauer with him. Nietzsche taught him much about willpower.

His thirst for knowledge was unquenchable. He spent hundreds of hours studying the works of Tacitus and Mommsen, military strategists such as Clausewitz, and empire builders such as Bismarck. Nothing escaped him: world history or the history of civilizations, the study of the Bible and the Talmud, Thomistic philosophy and all the masterpieces of Homer, Sophocles, Horace, Ovid, Titus Livius and Cicero. He knew Julian the Apostate as if he had been his contemporary.

His knowledge also extended to mechanics. He knew how engines worked; he understood the ballistics of various weapons; and he astonished the best medical scientists with his knowledge of medicine and biology.

The universality of Hitler's knowledge may surprise or displease those unaware of it, but it is nonetheless a historical fact: *Hitler was one of the most cultivated men of this century. Many times more so than Churchill, an intellectual mediocrity; or than Pierre Laval, who had a merely cursory knowledge of history; or than Roosevelt; or Eisenhower, who never got beyond detective novels."* **(11)**
- Leon Degrelle (1993)

1931 – 1939

MONTREAL, TUESDAY, DECEMBER 29, 1931.

,WAY LAUNCHES W DEPARTMENT

n of Communications naugurated by Canadian Pacific

NEIL NAMED CHIEF

Covers Supervision All Lines — Other actions and Retirements Noted

ing with the new year, an-vision will be added to the ints of the Canadian tailway, the Department of ications. This information is announced yesterday by tall, vice-president of the ho department will have on over the company's t, telephone and a radio ting services. ad of the department will Neil, who succeeds John on his retirement. hanges are announced by nt Hall, as follows: T,

SIX MILLION JEWS FACE STARVATION

Bad Conditions in South-Eastern Europe Reported by Rabbi Wise

FEARS CRISIS AT HAND

Chairman of American Joint Distribution Committee Makes Appeal to Canadian Jewry for Help

Six million Jews in Eastern Europe face starvation, and even worse, during the coming winter, if additional funds are not collected by the American Joint Distribution Committee to meet an estimated budget of $2,500,000 unprecedented havoc and misery will rule to the everlasting shame of humanity at large, Rabbi Jonah Wise, of New York, chairman for 1931, told a large gathering of leaders in Montreal Jewish communal life at a luncheon meeting at the Montefiore Club, Guy street, yesterday.

themselves and t responsible for the The Christmas t of Mrs. Rutherford S. T. Blaiklock a Sutherland; with-hosne present incl Annis, president; berton, honorary Mrs. W. A. Gra treasurer. The 60 children between the ages a splendid Chris On Friday they v cial dinner with i pudding.& At thi presented prizes a and obedience du senior and junior donated by Mr. a six dolls for the given by Forbes , great surprise, a ent for each child, Christmas seals a much appreciated ren Hale.

Rotarians' l The first family real Rotary Club day in the Windso wives, sons and d the members of th ular weekly lu Over 200 guests ; the meeting will a instead of 12.45. The speaker wil Douglas, and Mrs. sing several solos. will be broadca CKAC at 1.10 p.m

AWARD OF $ Decision Rende

Yet again, another baseless newspaper claim of 6 million Jews facing death:

DECEMBER 5, 1931
SOVIET JEW KAGANOVICH ORDERS DEMOLITION OF THE CATHEDRAL OF CHRIST THE SAVIOR

The 340 ft. tall **Cathedral of Christ the Savior** is the grandest Orthodox Christian Church in the world. Completed in 1883, it had taken nearly 20 years to build, and 20more to decoratively paint its interior. But after Lenin's death, the Reds choose the location to be the site of the 'Palace of the Soviets'. By order **of Stalin's Jewish minister and brother-in-law, Lazar Kaganovich,** the Cathedral is dynamited and reduced to rubble. Jewish Reds watch and laugh as horrified Christians grieve over the destruction of their religious and cultural icon. Due to poor planning and lack of funds, the Palace of the Soviets never materializes. The site is turned into a swimming pool.

In 1990, the Russian Orthodox Church receives permission, from what is by then a more open Government, to rebuild the Cathedral of Christ the Savior. Though the interior is not as elaborate as the original, the massive new Cathedral is still a very impressive structure.

Christ the Savior Cathedral was dynamited, but Jewish synagogues were untouched. This is the same cathedral (since rebuilt) that will, in 2012, be defiled by the U.S. / CIA -funded feminist band, "Pussy Riot."

MARCH, 1932
THE STRANGE KIDNAPPING & MURDER OF CHARLES LINBERGH'S BABY BOY

Because of his heroism, fame and family history of political activism, the anti-Fed, anti-Globalist, Charles Lindbergh is someone the Globalists need to "keep an eye on". The kidnapping of **Charles Augustus Lindbergh, Jr.**, the first-born son of the great aviator, becomes one of the most highly publicized crimes of the 20th century.

The 20-month-old toddler was abducted from his family home in New Jersey, on the evening of March 1, 1932 and held for ransom. Over two months later, on May 12, 1932, his body is discovered a short distance from the Lindberghs' home. A medical examination determines the cause of death as a massive skull fracture.

A German immigrant named **Bruno Hauptmann** is framed for the crime. In addressing his last words to his spiritual advisor, Rev. James Matthiesen, Hauptmann declares, *"Ich bin absolut unschuldig an den Verbrechen, die man mir zur Last legt"*, which Matthiesen tells Gov. Hoffman means, *"I am absolutely innocent of the crime with which I am burdened."* **(1)**

Was this horrible crime intended as a message to Lindbergh? Some have noted that the murder occurred just before the Jewish observance of Passover *(an event based on the killing of the first-born of ancient Egypt)*, suggesting that the killing may have had ritualistic implications.

The case against the German Hauptmann was full of holes.

1932-1936
LOUIS McFADDEN EXPOSES THE FED...THEN HE DIES

Louis McFadden became the latest enemy of the NWO to die suddenly.

U.S. unemployment tops 23%. The Zio-Globo press blames Hoover, the Republicans, and "unregulated capitalism" for the crisis. There are calls for more government action.

A prominent Congressman who dares to accuse the Fed is the Chairman of the House Banking Committee: **Louis McFadden** (R-PA). McFadden puts the blame directly on the international bankers for fomenting the Russian Revolution, crashing the US economy, and robbing the American people. McFadden pulls no punches:

"(The Fed) was deceitfully and disloyally foisted upon this country by the bankers who came here from Europe and repaid us for our hospitality by undermining our American institutions. Those bankers took money out of this country to finance Japan in a war against Russia. They financed Trotsky's passage from New York to

Russia so that he might assist in the destruction of the Russian Empire. ...What king ever robbed his subjects to such an extent as the Federal Reserve has robbed us?" **(2)**

In 1933, McFadden introduces articles of impeachment for the Secretary of the Treasury, two assistant Secretaries of the Treasury, the entire Board of Governors of the Federal Reserve, and the officers and the directors of its twelve regional banks. In 1936, McFadden dies of a "sudden illness" after dining at a banquet while on a visit to New York.

1932
STALIN & KAGANOVICH ENGINEER ANOTHER FAMINE

The Holodomor *(Ukrainian translation: Killing by hunger)* was a man-made famine occurring mainly, but not exclusively, in the Ukrainian Republic of the Soviet Union during 1932-33. The famine was caused partly by the folly of Stalin's latest economic scheme, and partly due to a deliberate, strategic terror plan engineered by Stalin's powerful Jewish brother-in-law, **Lazar Kaganovich**.

Encyclopedia Britannica estimates 8 million people, 5 million of them Ukrainian, were starved to death by the Stalin-Kaganovich famine. Some estimates run as high as 10 million. The famine-genocide is aimed at stamping out anti-communist resistance as well as starving anti-Red peasants in Belarus, Kazakhstan and Russia.

Despite Soviet denials of the famine and a news blackout in most of the US Zionist/Globalist press, the truth of the Holodomor was indeed known to the West. Unlike Lenin's terror famine of 1921, this time **no outside assistance is permitted into the Soviet Union.** Millions die a slow death and people resort to cannibalism. With this famine, Stalin and his henchmen destroy any remaining resistance to the Red Revolution.

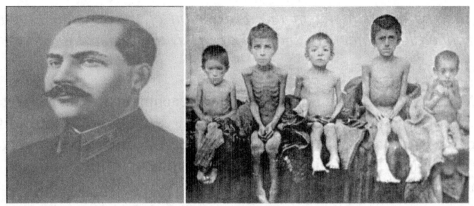

Lazar Kaganovich: "The Butcher of Ukraine" had also blown up the Cathedral of Christ the Savior.

JULY & NOVEMBER, 1932
NSDAP SCORES BIG IN TWO ELECTIONS / BECOMES LARGEST PARTY IN REICHSTAG

German elections in 1932 are held under violent conditions. NSDAP "brown shirts" clash in the streets with Red paramilitary. Hitler's party scores major gains, winning 230 Reichstag seats. It is now the largest political body, but it is still not a majority in the 608 member body.

Political deadlocks trigger another election in November: NSDAP: 196, Social Democrats: 121, Communists: 100, Center Party: 70, and 9 minor parties split 100 seats. Germany's chaotic politics are paralyzed and divided.

The brutal "austerity" policies of Chancellor Heinrich Brüning had shrunk the economy by about 25%, but still did not prevent the German budget deficit from growing. **Unemployment tops 30% as desperate Germans commit suicide by the 10's of 1000's.**

In addition to a Parliamentary Reichstag and a Chancellor, Germany has a President with unique powers. President **Paul von Hindenburg** was a World War I Field Marshall and is a national hero. Politically, he is a non-Party Independent. On the basis of the NSDAP's 196 seats, and in order to end the gridlock, Hitler asks Hindenburg to appoint him as Chancellor. Hindenburg refuses Hitler's request.

1932 Parade: As economic conditions in Germany worsen, NSDAP becomes the largest political party. Hitler now has a platform for addressing the nation.

1933
PRESIDENT HINDENBURG NAMES HITLER AS CHANCELLOR / REDS IMMEDIATELY CALL FOR LABOR STRIKES

After two parliamentary elections in 1933, Germany remains ungovernable as the Socialist and Communist Parties continue to oppose the NSDAP. President Hindenburg is concerned that the Reds will exploit the chaos and attempt another revolution in Germany. Hitler's NSDAP is the only group that can prevent this.

To protect Germany from Communism, Hindenburg relents and allows Hitler to become Chancellor of Germany. Hitler's powers are limited, but the NSDAP now holds the upper hand in what is still a very unstable government.

The Communist Trade Union leaders move quickly to destabilize Hitler, calling for massive strikes. Meanwhile in the U.S., the Zionist Sulzberger-owned New York Times kicks off an anti-Hitler campaign on its front page of January 31, 1933. Zionist Sarnoff's NBC and Zionist Paley's CBS soon follow.

1- Chancellor Hitler shows his respect for Marshal Hindenburg

2- A Communist propaganda poster threatens violence against the Hitler-Hindenburg system.

FEBRUARY, 1933
RED MURDERS THE MAYOR OF CHICAGO AS HE SHAKES HANDS WITH PRESIDENT-ELECT FDR

While shaking hands with President-elect Roosevelt in Miami, Florida, Chicago Mayor **Anton Cermak** is fatally wounded when anarchist **Giuseppe Zangara**, fires multiple shots. In addition to Cermak, Zangara hits four other people, one of whom, a woman, also died of her injuries.

Official history holds that Zangara, who had been an expert marksman in the Italian Army, was really intending to kill Roosevelt but suddenly forgot how to shoot properly – killing Cermak and hitting four others instead. But why would the Reds want to kill the man who was just about to be sworn-in as the reddest President in U.S. history?

A more plausible explanation is that the Red patsy fanatic was put forth for the purpose of "sending a message" to FDR – "obey, or next time it will be you".

On March 20, 1933, after spending only 10 days on Death Row, Zangara is executed in Old Sparky, the electric chair at Florida State Prison.

 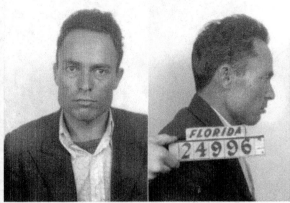

Cermack after the shooting and Red assassin Zangara's mug shots.

Four weeks after Hitler's appointment as Chancellor, angry Reds set the **Reichstag (Parliament)** on fire. Local police catch a Dutch Communist named **Marinus Vander Lubbe** on the premises. He had just arrived in Germany a few weeks ago. The fire was to have been the start of the Red-instigated civil war, aimed at toppling the crumbling Weimar state before Hitler and the NSDAP could establish themselves.

Hindenburg and Hitler act fast. Emergency decrees are issued and Communist leaders are rounded up. The Red Revolution backfires. Instead of plunging Germany into civil war, the Reichstag Fire starts a chain of events that leads to the **The Enabling Act** and Hitler's consolidation of power. NSDAP becomes Germany's only Party as the Weimar Republic is swept away by **The Third Reich**, led by "The Fuehrer" *(leader)*.

Some modern historians promote the theory that Hitler staged the fire himself and then blamed the Reds for it. *There is no evidence at all to support this theory*. It is a baseless claim that ignores both the violent history and the standard destabilization tactics that the Communists are well known for.

The Reichstag fire backfired on the Communists! Above: Brainwashed Red drifter Marinus Vander Lubbe

New York Governor and Globalist puppet **Franklin Delano Roosevelt, (FDR)** defeats President Hoover in a 1932 landslide. Upon taking office in 1933, FDR *(a cousin of Teddy Roosevelt)* moves quickly to remake America into a welfare state. His expensive schemes, known as "**The New Deal**" take shape in "the first 100 days".

FDR uses the economic crisis, which was created by his handlers, as the pretext for this expansion of government power, ignoring the fact that it was the Federal Reserve's artificial manipulation of currency and stocks, *not the free market* that caused the crisis.

The New Deal will be a colossal failure. It's reckless spending, high taxes, and ballooning deficits will only prolong the Depression and lead to even more expensive schemes, exactly what the Globalist Fed bankers want. The debt-driven economic calamity that the U.S. is headed towards today has its roots in FDR's fundamental transformation of the American Republic into a perpetual warfare and welfare state.

1- The grinning phony will surpass the warmongering evil of cousin Teddy.

2- FDR with billionaire backer and unofficial "advisor", Bernard Baruch. At that time, Baruch was the most powerful of the New York Jewish financiers.

MARCH, 1933
HITLER BECOMES FUEHRER AND <u>DEFIES</u> THE NEW WORLD ORDER

Like FDR, Hitler came into true *authoritative* power in March 1933. Like FDR, Hitler inherits an economic disaster. Like FDR, Hitler's "first 100 days" in office are marked by a flurry of determined activity. **But the similarities end there.**

Whereas FDR is implementing all of the Globalists' economic and foreign policy plans, Hitler is openly defying the Globalists. He implements the following policies:

* **Pulls Germany out of the Globalist League of Nations**
* Bans the Communist Party and arrests its leaders
* Replaces the national Marxist Trade Unions with company unions
* Implements the "Strength Through Joy" affordable luxury vacation program
* Establishes NSDAP as Germany's only political Party
* Ends reparations payments from the Versailles Treaty/Dawes Plan
* Takes control of Germany's Reichsbank and issues National currency
* Restricts Jewish ownership of radio and newspapers
* Cuts taxes and provides incentives for mothers to stay home and raise children

* Relaxes the strict "gun control" laws of the previous government
* Rebuilds German infrastructure and initiates the Autobahn Highway system

The Globalists & Marxists have lost control of Germany!

Hitler becomes a living legend as his policies begin to put Germany back on its feet. Meanwhile, a subtle propaganda campaign is launched against him in the West.

MARCH, 1933
INTERNATIONAL JEWRY DECLARES WAR ON GERMANY

Jewish leaders formally issue a "Declaration of War" against Germany. On March 23, 1933, 20,000 Jews protest at New York's City Hall. Rallies and boycotts are directed against German goods. The front page of the March 24, London Daily Express carries the headline: *"Judea Declares War on Germany"*.

Jewish leaders are quoted as calling for "Holy War" against the German people:

"The Jewish wholesaler will quit his house, the banker his stock exchange, the merchant his business and the beggar his humble hut, in order to join the holy war against Hitler's people. ....Germany is now confronted with an international boycott of its trade, its finances, and its industry." **(3)**

On March 27, '33, 40,000 Jews and other assorted Reds gather in Madison Square Garden to protest the new Chancellor. The NY Daily News front page blares: ***"40,000 Roar Protest Here Against Hitler."***

Worldwide Jewish leadership is firing the opening propaganda shots of what, in due time, will escalate into World War II. Hitler responds to the false "atrocity" charges being made against the new Germany, stating on March 28: *"Lies and slander of positively hair-raising perversity are being launched against Germany."* **(4)**

1- 1933 / Daily Express (London): "Judea Declares War on Germany."

2- 1933 / NY Daily New: 40,000 Roar Protest Against Hitler

International Jewry openly declares a sanctions war on Germany.

APRIL, 1933
FDR BANS THE PRIVATE OWNERSHIP OF GOLD / FED STEALS THE GOLD

Citing an "emergency", as all tyrants do, FDR signs **Executive Order 6102** *"forbidding the Hoarding of gold coin, gold bullion, and gold certificates within the continental United States"*. **(5)** Under the false pretext of "economic stabilization", the order criminalizes the possession of monetary gold by any individual, partnership, or corporation.

Americans are required to deliver all but a small amount of gold coin, gold bullion, and gold certificates owned by them **to the privately owned Federal Reserve**, in exchange for $20.67 *(equivalent to $372.75 today)* per troy ounce. Violation of the order is punishable by fine up to $10,000 *(equivalent to $180,334 today)* or up to ten years in prison, or both!

Numerous Americans are arrested and imprisoned for possession of Gold. In those cases, their Gold is seized without compensation.

POSTMASTER: PLEASE POST IN A CONSPICUOUS PLACE.—JAMES A. FARLEY, Postmaster General

UNDER EXECUTIVE ORDER OF THE PRESIDENT

Issued April 5, 1933

all persons are required to deliver

ON OR BEFORE MAY 1, 1933

all **GOLD COIN, GOLD BULLION, AND GOLD CERTIFICATES** now owned by them to a Federal Reserve Bank, branch or agency, or to any member bank of the Federal Reserve System.

Executive Order

FORBIDDING THE HOARDING OF GOLD COIN, GOLD BULLION AND GOLD CERTIFICATES

FDR to America: "Turn your coins in to my friends at the Fed, or go to jail!"

The Washington Post is one of many businesses to go bankrupt during the Great Depression. Owner Ned McLean unloads The Post at a bankruptcy auction. The buyer is Zionist **Federal Reserve Chairman Eugene Meyer** Having just stepped down from the Federal Reserve; Meyer immediately changes The Post's editorial policy, transforming the influential newspaper into a pro-FDR, anti-Germany, and soft-on-Stalin propaganda sheet. In 1940, Meyer will fire the Post's pacifist editor for refusing to endorse U.S. intervention in World War II **(6)**.

The Post will lose money for 20 more years, but Meyer doesn't care. He bought the Post for influence, not profit. The Post will later be handed down to Meyer's daughter, the late **Katherine Meyer-Graham**.

With tension between International Jewry and Germany building, it is <u>ESSENTIAL</u> to note that the four most powerful media sources in America are now ALL under Jewish ownership.

CBS: Paley, NBC: Sarnoff, NY Times: Ochs-Sulzberger, Washington Post: Meyer

A CLEAN SWEEP! When Fed Chairman Eugene Meyer (right) purchased the Washington Post, it gave the Globalist-Zionist moguls a clean sweep of the Big 4 major media giants; and the ability to distort the truth about Hitler and Germany.

FORBIDDEN HISTORY: QUOTE TO REMEMBER

Count Potocki leaving the White House

"Above all, propaganda here (in the U.S.) is entirely in Jewish hands. When bearing public ignorance in mind, their propaganda is so effective that people have no real knowledge of the true state of affairs in Europe. President Roosevelt has been given the power to create huge reserves in armaments for a future war which the Jews are deliberately heading for."
(1934) **(7)**

Count Jerzy Potocki / Polish Ambassador to the U.S.

1930's
THE TYRANNICAL AND STUPID EDICTS OF THE NEW DEAL

Whether they are pro or con, when most people think of the New Deal, massive 'relief' programs and 'make work' schemes come to mind. But the New Deal's dictatorial aspects are often overlooked. The totalitarian and counterproductive, dictates associated with the **National Recovery Act (NRA)** include wage-controls, price-controls, production-controls, as well as mandates governing agriculture and industry.

To manipulate prices upward so that un-payable business loans can be repaid, farmers are ordered to kill livestock as millions go hungry during the Great Depression! In one well known case, a New Jersey tailor named **Jacob Maged** is arrested and convicted for charging *too little* to press suits. Upon his release after 3 days, Maged is forced to increase his prices and display a blue NRA sticker on his shop window. **(8)**

In addition to the NRA, there is the Communist Harry Hopkins' **Works Progress Administration (WPA)** - referred to by its critics as "We Piddle Around". The WPA does build some useful infrastructure, but is, at its core, an expensive and inefficient 'make-work' scheme that becomes the object of many sarcastic stories about digging and filling up holes.

Left: The "criminal" tailor Maged was arrested, fined, forced to raise his prices, and obediently put an NRA sign in his shop window.

Right: New Deal insanity. Killing and wasting cattle is good for the economy?!

NOVEMBER, 1933
FDR GRANTS DIPLOMATIC RECOGNITION TO THE SOVIET UNION (USSR)

Ever since the Reds seized power in Russia, three consecutive U.S. Presidents have refused to recognize the criminal regime. Apart from its genocidal actions towards its own captive people, the Communist International *(Comintern) openly* states that its' goal is to overthrow all "bourgeois" governments, including America's.

FDR ignores these realties and pleases his Globalist masters by reversing this policy. The normalization of relations is a great benefit to the USSR, and will help the Soviets, and international communism, to grow stronger.

As Hitler's Germany continues to be vilified for imaginary offenses; the <u>real</u> crimes of Stalin & Kaganovich are ignored by the media.

1930's cartoon notes the ideological similarities between FDR and Stalin. The two will forge a close relationship during the coming war years.

JUNE 30, 1934
'THE NIGHT OF THE LONG KNIVES' / LEFT WING COUP ATTEMPT IS SUPPRESSED

More than one year into Hitler's rule, Nationalist Marxist and homosexual Ernst Roehm is threatening a 2nd revolution to "redistribute wealth". Roehm commands the massive paramilitary organization known as the SA *(Brownshirts)*, whose members have a reputation for street violence. German military brass despises Roehm and fears his ambition to absorb them into the SA under his own leadership.

Facing an imminent coup attempt from these former allies, Hitler's government carries out '**Operation Hummingbird**'; the purge of Roehm's out-of-control left-wing faction. Many of the coup plotters are executed and hundreds are arrested. The SA now comes under Hitler's command and control as western Jewish newspapers squeal about what they refer to as "**The Night of the Long Knives**".

Coup-plotter Roehm and his 'brownshirts' had their own agenda for Germany.

MAY 12, 1935
THE SUDDEN DEATH OF POLISH MARSHAL PILSUDSKI IS BAD NEWS FOR GERMANY

Polish leader Marshal Jozef Pilsudski had been on good terms with Hitler. Pilsudski had actually congratulated Hitler on winning the 1933 elections, and the **German-Polish Non-Aggression Pact** was signed just 10 months afterwards. Not surprisingly, the Polish Communist Party denounced Pilsudski as a "fascist and a capitalist".

According to the **Non-Aggression Pact**, both countries pledge to resolve their problems through negotiations, not armed conflict. Just before his death, Pilsudski re-emphasized that Poland should maintain neutral relations with Germany.

The popular Marshal will eventually be succeeded by the pompous warmonger, **Marshal Edward Rydz-Smigly**. Pilsudski's death, and Smigly's rise, will prove to be great setbacks for Germany - facts which Hitler will reiterate during the closing weeks of World War II.

1- Hitler attends a Berlin Memorial Service held in honor of Pilsudski, whom he respected greatly.

2- Pilsudski and his Foreign Minister Beck (left) make peace with German Minister for Propaganda & Public Enlightenment, Joseph Goebbels, and German Ambassador to Poland, von Moltke.

AUGUST, 1935
FDR SIGNS THE SOCIAL SECURITY PYRAMID SCHEME INTO LAW

FDR promises the American people that a forced savings plan *("like a shoebox")*, with dollar for dollar employer matching will be there for them in old age. In reality, Social Security TAXES have never funded old age. The sneaky taxes that are collected are used to pay current SS recipients; with any excess used to purchase the government bonds that fund America's out-of-control welfare and warfare state. **There is no "shoe-box" and there never was!**

Every current American senior citizen has therefore been cheated out of what would have been a privately self-funded small fortune at retirement. Just imagine what nearly 50 years of employee-employer forced savings, intelligently diversified and with a reasonable rate of compound growth would have accumulated to in our "shoe-boxes".

Instead, FDR's monstrous pyramid scheme is now busting America's multi-trillion dollar budget and can only be kept afloat by more debt and currency debasement caused by the Fed's printed money. Many Seniors barely survive as younger people already know that FDR's SS will not support them in old age.

1 & 2: The 'shoe-box' is empty! It was a Pyramid Scheme all along.

3- Chile's Social Security system truly is a mostly self-funded private "shoe box", and the people LOVE it!

SEPTEMBER, 1935
THE INVESTIGATION AND ASSASSINATION OF HUEY LONG

Nicknamed "Kingfish", the colorful **Huey Long** served as Louisiana Governor of Louisiana *('28–'32)* and U.S. Senator *('32 -'35)*, He was noted for his honesty and populism. Long had backed FDR, but split with him over FDR's ties to the New York Bankers. Long accuses FDR of being a liar. FDR comes to despise Huey Long, referring to him and General Douglass Macarthur as ***"the two most dangerous men in America"***. To intimidate and discredit him, FDR has Long investigated by the IRS. The Feds fail to find any illegality.

At the height of his fame, Long lashes out at the NWO bankers in his "Barbeque Speech":

"How many men ever went to a barbecue and would let one man take off the table what's intended for nine-tenths of the people to eat? The only way you will be able to feed the balance of the people is to make that man come back and bring back some of that grub he ain't got no business with. How are you going to feed the balance of the people? ***What's Morgan and Baruch and Rockefeller gonna do with all that grub?"*** **(9)**

Long prepares to mount a 1936 challenge to FDR from within the Democrat Party. But on Sept. 8, '35, Dr. Carl Weiss confronts Long at the State Capitol and is said to have fired a bullet into Long's abdomen. Rather than take Weiss alive, bodyguards shoot him 60 times! *(He won't be talking!)* One theory is that Weiss was set up as a patsy to punch Long in the face while a guard actually shoots Long in the back.

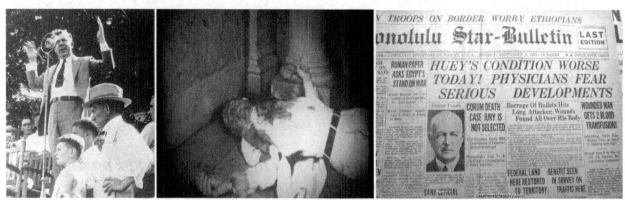

1: Long denounces FDR and the Eastern banking class.

2: Carl Weiss, the patsy "assassin" is needlessly shot to death (ala Lee Harvey Oswald and John Wilkes Booth)

3: Long was actually recovering before his condition "worsened".

1930's
FDR'S ORDERS THE IRS TO ABUSE HIS CRITICS

Like Cousin Teddy, the egomaniac FDR does not respond well to criticism. The tyrant uses the IRS against a host of political rivals and opponents, ranging from populist Sen. Huey Long (D) of Louisiana, United Mine Workers leader John Lewis, Rep. Hamilton Fish (R) of New York, Chicago Tribune publisher Robert "Colonel" McCormick, Philadelphia Inquirer publisher Moses Annenberg *(a fierce opponent of the New Deal)*, and, most notably, former Republican Treasury Secretary Andrew Mellon. **(10)**

FDR's IRS inspectors and prosecutors focused on Mellon's financial records, especially whether deductions for his philanthropic activities amounted to tax evasion. The great philanthropist, who had given so much back to society, strongly denied the accusations. **Even after IRS agents found nothing irregular, FDR's Justice Department pursued the investigation.**

A federal grand jury acquits Mellon of tax fraud in 1934. But the IRS is still pursuing claims against Mellon for at least $3 million in back taxes. Mellon's "tax trial" lasts a grueling 14 months. Possibly as the partial result of the enormous stress that FDR's had imposed him, the 82 year old Mellon dies the next year.

Writes former New York Times reporter David Burnham, author of *A Law Unto Itself: Power, Politics, and the IRS*:

"Although Richard Nixon was notorious for treating the I.R.S. as though it were his private domain, the records show that Franklin Delano Roosevelt may have set the stage for the use of the tax agency for political purposes by most subsequent Presidents," **(11)**

1- Beneath the phony smile, FDR was a cruel bastard who destroyed anyone who opposed him. His abuse may have even killed Richard Mellon.

2- As Treasury Secretary following World War I, Richard Mellon was one of the key architects of President Harding's 1920's debt reduction and National recovery. Mellon's generous philanthropy – with HIS money - amounts to far more than what FDR ever did with public money.

NOVEMBER, 1935
WINSTON CHURCHILL PRAISES HITLER, THEN DROPS A 'POISON PILL'

By November of 1935, it has become clear to the world that the anti-German atrocity stories were baseless. The Jewish boycott effort has failed; Hitler has renounced any claims to the disputed Alsace-Lorraine region *(France)*; and the rapid economic and social recovery of Germany is self-evident. There are

Monarchs, Prime Ministers, politicians, clergymen, artists and poets from across Europe who are publicly singing the praises of 'The Fuehrer'. Even some Americans have come to admire him from afar.

Therefore, in order for the Globalist warmongers to impose their *second* war against Germany, they must reboot their hate campaign *gradually*. Toward that end, Zionist puppet Winston Churchill pens an article for *Strand Magazine*, entitled, **'The Truth About Hitler'**. So as not to sound like the raving, warmongering lunatic that he truly is, Churchill, in order to *appear* "objective", makes a remarkable concession:

"One may dislike Hitler's system and yet admire his patriotic achievement. If our country were defeated, I hope we should find a champion as indomitable to restore our courage and lead us back to our place among the nations." **(12)**

But further down in the article, the "objective" Churchill drops the other shoe by suggesting that Germany may, possibly, yet turn out to be a threat to world peace:

"We cannot tell whether Hitler will be the man who will once again let loose upon the world another war in which civilization will irretrievably succumb, or whether he will go down in history as the man who restored honour and peace of mind to the great Germanic nation and brought them back serene, helpful and strong, to the European family circle.

It is on this mystery of the future that history will pronounce Hitler either as a monster or a hero. *It is this which will determine whether he will rank in Valhalla with Pericles, with Augustus, and with Washington, or welter in the inferno of human scorn with Attila and Tamerlain. It is enough to say that both possibilities are open at the present moment."* **(13)**

The German press and Foreign Ministry are quick to express displeasure with Churchill's under-handed and baseless speculative comparison of Hitler to genocidal Hun and Mongol leaders from antiquity. But Churchill's anti-German hate campaign is just getting started, along with his rise to political influence.

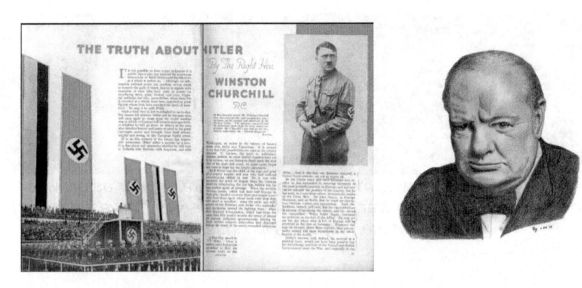

Strand Magazine Nov 1935, Churchill: The Truth about Hitler Page 10-11

Slowly but surely, the ambitious killer of the Lusitania is coming back from the political graveyard he had been banished to.

FEBRUARY 4, 1936
THE MURDER OF WILHELM GUSTLOFF

Wilhelm Gustloff had founded the Swiss branch of the NSDAP in 1932. A Jewish student named **David Frankfurter**, heeding the worldwide call for Jewish "Holy War" against the German people, visits Gustloff's home. Hedwig Gustloff shows the killer into the study, asking him to wait since her husband was on the telephone. When Gustloff comes to meet his unexpected guest, Frankfurter draws his pistol and shoots him 5 times. Hedwig screams and cries hysterically.

Germans and German Swiss are outraged at the murder. Hitler attends Gustloff's funeral and then names a luxury ship, christened by his widow, in Gustloff's honor. The Swiss sentence Frankfurter to 18 years, but he will be pardoned after World War II, before moving to Israel. In 1945, on what would have been Gustloff's 50th birthday, the ship named after him will make history as the greatest sea disaster ever.

Wilhelm Gustloff (left) was murdered by David Frankfurter as his wife watched in horror. After the war, Frankfurter (center & right) was allowed to live out the rest of his life in Israel.

1933-1936
THE MIRACLE OF THE GERMAN RECOVERY

It has been 3 years since Hitler began his program for economic recovery. **It is now the most stunning economic revival in world history. (14)** While the world remains mired in the Great Depression, Germany's once dead economy booms.

Unemployment, which had been over 30% a few years ago, is now under 5%. Productivity is way up, as are wages. By freeing Germany from the heavy taxation of the Weimar Republic, the cruel burden of the Versailles Treaty, and the perpetual interest costs of Weimar's debt-based Central Bank currency, Hitler has unleashed the private economy while using public spending very wisely.

Unlike FDR's wasteful public works programs, Hitler's public works are useful investments, such as the national highway system which Hitler began building in 1933 (**The Autobahn**). Hitler, a great admirer of Henry Ford, sketched the original prototype for the **Volkswagen** *(The People's Wagon)* and suggested to Ferdinand Porsche that, *"It should have the shape of a June bug"*. Hitler wanted every German family to be able to buy a car and take a vacation.

Low taxes, responsible debt, intelligent planning, lean government, sound currency, and a business friendly environment are the secrets of Hitler's economic miracle, and of his **extraordinary popularity** among a grateful German people, including many former liberals who were once Communist voters.

1- Hitler understood the basic principles of automotive engineering. He consulted with Ferdinand Porsche on the manufacture of the Volkswagen; the prototype for which Hitler drew himself (Image # 2)

3 -Henry Ford receives the Grand Cross of the German Eagle from the German consul-general of Cleveland

Along with economic revival, the re-born Germany experiences a cultural and moral rebirth. The NSDAP, whose membership is open to all Germans of sound character, cleans up the pornography and debauchery that thrived under the Weimar State. Classic art makes a comeback, as "modern art" is relegated to its proper status as an object of ridicule. The future is looking bright for Germany. Before the German model can spread to other nations, the dark forces of **The New World Order** must destroy it.

By 1936, support for Hitler in Germany is near universal. Even the formerly pro-Marxist liberals have been won over by his achievements. Photos and films of happy Germans and of Hitler smiling are deliberately censored by the Zionist-Globalist media.

1- Hitler turns first shovel of dirt for the Autobahn project.

2- Overjoyed adoring German crowds greeted Hitler everywhere.

3- Vacation-loving Germans were now the happiest people in Europe.

BEFORE & AFTER

1- The 1970's Broadway play and Hollywood film, 'Cabaret', depicts the depraved "transgender" night life of pre-Hitler Berlin.   2- Hitler's youth groups promoted virtue, discipline and clean living.

Due to the war, Hitler's grand vision (models above) to make Berlin the architectural and cultural wonder of the world would never be realized.

FEBRUARY, 1936
IN AN INTERVIEW WITH LONDON'S 'DAILY MIRROR', HITLER OFFERS FRIENDSHIP TO THE WORLD

"I appeal to reason in international affairs. I want to show that the idea of eternal enmity is wrong. We are not hereditary enemies." - Hitler

FORBIDDEN PHOTOS OF ADOLF HITLER

The images of Hitler shown by the western Yellow Press of his day, as well as the modern day history books and TV documentaries, are careful never to show a smiling Hitler with children, animals, women, or adoring German crowds. This serves to conceal the fact that he had a soft heart and a warm fondness for children and animals; so much so that he was a vegetarian.

FORBIDDEN HISTORY: QUOTE TO REMEMBER

"It is not the Germany of the decade that followed the war- broken, dejected and bowed down with a sense of apprehension and impotence. It is now full of hope and confidence, and of a renewed sense of determination to lead its own life without interference from any influence outside its own frontiers. **One man has accomplished this miracle.** *He is a born leader of men. A magnetic and dynamic personality with a single-minded purpose, a resolute will and a dauntless heart.*

*As to his popularity, there can be no manner of doubt. The old trust him; the young idolize him. It is not the admiration accorded to a popular leader. **It is the worship of a national hero who has saved his country from utter despondence and degradation.....** I have never met a happier people than the Germans."*

-David Lloyd George, Ex-Prime Minister, UK, 9-17-36 (15)

MAY, 1936
IN NEW YORK TIMES, GERMANY IS ACCUSED OF A "*HOLOCAUST*" FIVE YEARS BEFORE THE JEWS WERE EVEN INTERNED!

Europe is at peace and the Jews who have remained in Germany are prospering in the revitalized economy; 75% of them being middle class or higher. Even the legendary Max Warburg, though stripped of his dominance over Germany's Central Bank, chose to stay in Germany until 1938.

A **group of "Christians" fronting for the Chicago and New York Zionists now makes the** ridiculous claim of a "European **Holocaust**". This claim forms the basis of the case for the establishment of a Jewish State in Palestine; which the British had conquered as part of a World War I payoff to the Zionists for their help in dragging the U.S. into the war on Britain's side. Not content with mass immigration to Palestine *(The British Mandate)*, the Zionists, speaking through their "Christian" front men and dupes, now want the British to crack down on the oppressed Arabs and give the Jews an actual nation of their own. The New York Times reported on this bizarre allegation:

*"**WASHINGTON, May 30** - A petition addressed to Prime Minister Stanley Baldwin expressive of the hope that Great Britain will steer a course favoring the establishment of a free Jewish nation in Palestine such as would provide refuge for **millions of persecuted Jews in Eastern Europe and Germany** was presented to Sir Ronald Lindsay, the British Ambassador, today by a Christian delegation representing the Pro-Palestine Federation of America ... The petition, stressed the intolerable sufferings of the **millions of Jews** in "**the European holocaust.**" (16)*

282

Oops! It appears as though some over-eager Zionist went off the script and let the fake 'Holocaust'' cat out of the bag a full 5 years too soon!

AUGUST, 1936
THE BERLIN OLYMPICS / HITLER AND JESSE OWENS

The 1936 Olympics had been awarded to Germany before Hitler became Chancellor. So despite the protests of Jewish groups, it is too late to take the games away. The games showcase the new Germany. Visitors are impressed at the spirit and positive outlook of the German people. Germany wins more medals than any other nation, but black American Jesse Owens is the biggest star of the games.

The German crowd cheers wildly for Owens as he wins 4 Gold Medals as both a sprinter and long jumper. But the Zionist media uses Owens to vilify Hitler. It was reported then, *and repeated endlessly ever since*, that Hitler "snubbed" Owens because he was black, storming out of the stadium in a fit of rage when Owens won his first race. This "snub" makes Hitler seem petty and rude in the eyes of the world. **But the story of the Owens' "snub" is a big lie.**

Owens himself confirms that the "snub" story is a hoax, stating:

"When I passed the Chancellor, he arose, waved his hand at me, and I waved back. I think the writers showed bad taste in criticizing the man of the hour (Hitler) in Germany." **(17)**

Years later, in his autobiography, Owens again clarifies:

"Hitler didn't snub me -it was FDR who snubbed me. The president didn't even send me a telegram." **(18)**

1- The "snub" of Jesse Owens was a false propaganda story.

2- Owens was befriended by German long-jump competitor Luz Long. They became pen pals.

1936 – 1939
THE SPANISH CIVIL WAR / NATIONALISTS vs REDS

Nationalist **General Francisco Franco** leads a rebellion against a democratic socialist government in Spain. The country is deeply divided, with Socialists, Communists, and liberals fighting for the government, and Nationalists, conservatives, and the Catholic Church favoring Franco. The war becomes a proxy war between Nationalism and Globalism. Germany, Portugal and Italy provide military aid to Franco as Stalin sends arms to the Spanish government.

The Comintern sends volunteers to fight for the Spanish regime. American Communists of the **Abraham Lincoln Brigade** arrive to fight alongside the Reds. As usual, Red fighters commit atrocities against civilians, such as setting fire to the wives and children of Nationalist officers after dousing them with petrol. Determined to stamp out Christianity, they rape nuns, torture priests, and set fire to churches with the worshippers locked inside.

The Spanish Civil War finally ends in victory for Franco, but the war between New World Order Globalism and European Nationalism is only just beginning.

1- Hitler helped Franco to defeat Stalin's Communists in Spain

2- Intolerant Spanish Reds "execute" a statue of Jesus.

DECEMBER 10, 1936
THE PRO-HITLER KING OF ENGLAND IS FORCED TO ABDICATE HIS THRONE

England's **King Edward VIII** is an admirer of Adolf Hitler. This creates a dilemma for the Globo-Zionists who wish to instigate a war with Germany. Six months into his reign, there is an assassination attempt against him. **Jerome Bannigan** produces a loaded revolver near the King. After being quickly pounced upon by police and arrested, he claims to have been recruited by "a foreign power".

Weeks later, Eugene Myers' *Washington Post* reports that Edward plans to marry an American woman who has still not divorced her husband. British politicians use the "crisis" to squeeze Edward out, giving him a choice between **Ms. Wallis Simpson**, or abdicating his thrown. As the story goes, it is for love of Ms. Simpson that Edward gives up the throne. The real reason for the silent coup is concealed from the public.

Hitler will later state: *"I am certain through him permanent friendly relations could have been achieved. If he had stayed, everything would have been different. His abdication was a severe loss for us."* **(19)** With Edward gone, the Globalists proceed with plans to wage war on Germany. Edward is replaced by his stuttering, stammering idiot brother -**George VI - ("The King's Speech")**, who will spend the coming war years making 'patriotic' radio speeches.

Many in England defended their King and opposed abdication. After stepping down from the throne of England, Edward and his American bride visit Hitler in 1937.

FEBRUARY, 1937
FDR ATTEMPTS TO PACK THE SUPREME COURT WITH 6 OF HIS STOOGES

FDR proposes the **Judicial Procedures Reform Bill** (AKA the **"court-packing plan"**) to add more justices to the U.S. Supreme Court. Roosevelt's purpose is to obtain favorable rulings regarding New Deal schemes that the court has ruled unconstitutional. The bill will grant FDR the power to appoint an additional "rubber stamp" Justice to the Supreme Court, up to a maximum of six, for every member of the court over the age of 70 *(who FDR openly mocks as "nine old men")*.

FDR's outrageous scheme is so unpopular that many fellow Democrats begin to distance themselves from him. The horrible power grab fails.

Even many of FDR's Democrat supporters and the press were shocked by FDR'S infamous 'Court Packing Scheme'. Cartoonists mocked FDR.

MAY 6, 1937
THE HINDENBURG DISASTER

The **Hindenburg Airship**, named after the man who helped Hitler become Chancellor, is the pride of Germany's fleet. American crowds marvel as the airships passes over New York, saluting them with the German "Sieg Heil". The airships are designed to float using Helium. But after FDR's Jewish Interior Secretary, **Harold Ickes**, slaps a Helium embargo on Germany; the Zeppelins are redesigned to use highly flammable Hydrogen instead.

The moment Hindenburg begins to dock in Lakehurst, NJ, it bursts into flames and crashes, killing 35 of the 97 passengers. "Static electricity" is blamed, **yet Hindenburg had previously endured <u>direct</u> lightning hits!**

The cause of the explosion remains unknown to this day. But the unusual amount of news reel cameras present that day, the Helium embargo, the timing of the mysterious ignition just as the ship is mooring, the hyping of the idiotic "static electricity" theory, and the anti-German hysteria being whipped up by the press, suggest that the Hindenburg disaster was actually an act of sabotage.

Theories range from an onboard suicide-bomber to an incendiary rifle-bullet fired from the nearby woods. The incident shatters confidence in Germany's airships and marks the end of the airship era.

A suspicious blast at the exact moment of mooring destroys Germany's Airship industry. It was Harold Ickes who cut off helium exports to Germany.

JULY, 1937
WAR BREAKS OUT BETWEEN CHINA & JAPAN

The **Japan-China War** starts when the Japanese claim to have been fired on by Chinese troops at the Marco Polo Bridge near modern day Beijing. Tensions escalate and Japan launches an invasion of China, using Japanese bases in Manchuria, as a launching point.

Manchuria is rich in resources and has strategically vital ports on the Sea of Japan. It is located in Northeastern Asia, bordering China, Korea, and also western Russia. Manchuria was once Chinese controlled, then part of the Russian Empire. Japan won Manchuria from Russia in the war of 1905, but Nationalist Chinese view Manchuria as historically Chinese. The Japan-China war blends into the ongoing Chinese Civil War raging between the Chinese Communists and the Chinese Nationalist government. At the same time that Japan is fighting the Chinese nationalists *(led by Chiang Kai Shek)* the Japanese must also fight the guerilla Reds *(led by Stalin's agent Mao Tse Tung)*.

The US, though still officially neutral, clearly favors Chiang Kai Shek over Japan. But Chiang is only a disposable tool for the Globalist's Asian ambitions; a fact that will serve to prolong the Japan-China War. It's Japan vs. China Reds vs. China Nationalists in a 3-way Far Eastern Battle Royale that will shape the course of Asian history.

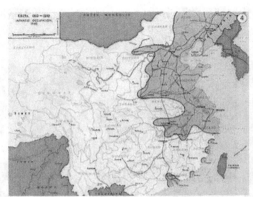 

1- Part of Manchuria (region on right) was won by Japan in the Russo-Japanese war of 1905.

2- FDR & Churchill will later play their boy Chiang (seated left) for a fool and sell him out at the Yalta Conference.

NOVEMBER 25, 1937
GERMANY & JAPAN AGREE TO AN ANTI-COMMUNIST DEFENSE PACT

Germany and Japan agree to the **Anti-Comintern Pact**, a mutual <u>defense</u> Treaty directed at the Soviet controlled Communist International. Italy will join the following year. The pact states:

"recognizing that the aim of the Communist International, known as the Comintern, is to disintegrate and subdue existing States by all the means at its command; convinced that the toleration of interference by the Communist International in the internal affairs of the nations not only endangers their internal peace and social well-being, but is also a menace to the peace of the world desirous of co-operating in the defense against Communist subversive activities." **(20)**

In case of an attack by the Soviet Union against Germany or Japan, the two countries agree to take measures "to safeguard their common interests". Mussolini's Italy will soon join the anti-Comintern and several other nations join later on. **Germany also invites Britain and Poland to join the Anti-Comintern Alliance.** Both nations decline.

German and Japanese officials sign the Anti-Comintern pact.

DECEMBER, 1937
THE IMAGINARY "RAPE" OF NANKING

The alleged **Rape of Nanking** is said to have been committed by the Japanese military in the city of Nanking, then capital of China. China has long claimed that the Japanese massacred 300,000 Chinese people in just six weeks.

But newspaper accounts, photos, documentary films, records and testimonies in those days all suggest that neither a large-scale massacre, nor even a small-scale massacre, ever took place. During the battle for Nanking, every civilian remaining in the city is urged to take refuge in the internationally monitored Safety Zone. This Safety Zone is managed by the International Committee for the Nanking Safety Zone, which is a group of professors, doctors, missionaries and businessmen from Europe and the U.S.. They remain in the city throughout the battle.

On the day that Japanese troops enter Nanking, more than 100 press reporters and photographers enter with them. The press is not only from Japan, but also from Europe and America, including Reuters and AP. However, none of the journalists report the occurrence of a civilian massacre. If the Japanese military had wanted to massacre the citizens of Nanking, it would have been very easily done by simply bombing the very narrow and crowded Nanking Safety Zone.

The most telling indicator is the fact that most of the alleged details of the "massacre" will only surface *after* the unconditional surrender of Japan in 1945. During the war itself, Chinese leader **Chiang Kai-Shek** broadcasts 100's of radio addresses to the Chinese people. But he never mentions that 300,000 people had supposedly been killed! Furthermore, **many of the "massacre" photos which surface later on are clearly fakes. (21)**

Many Chinese are however killed by Chinese Supervisory Units, whose job is to kill Chinese soldiers trying to escape from the battlefield. Many *pro-Japanese* Chinese *(who saw Japan as pro-Asian liberating force)* are also killed by these units, not by the Japanese military.

1- Japanese soldiers distribute food and sweets.

2- After the battle, many Nanking citizens, who abhorred the Chinese military, welcomed the Japanese. The citizens are wearing armbands of the flag of Japan, which were given to all civilians of Nanking to distinguish them from Chinese soldiers hiding in civilian clothing.

As the 'Four Tops' of Motown fame used to sing: *"Now it's the same, old song, with a different ...."*

MARCH 12, 1938
THE ANSCHLUSS / AUSTRIA IS INCORPORATED INTO THE GERMAN REICH

The Anschluss is the *voluntary* incorporation of Austria into the German Reich. The merger with their Germanic brothers is supported by 99% of Austrians and Germans **(22)**, but opposed by the puppet Austrian government instituted by the Allies after World War I.

The Versailles Treaty broke up the Austro-Hungarian Empire and forbid the new nation of Austria from uniting with Germany. But after seeing the great success of Germany, there is no stopping the Austrians desire to unite with their happy brothers and sisters. Without a shot being fired, German forces move in unopposed and are greeted as liberators by the joyous Austrians. As a brotherly gesture towards the Austrians, Hitler invites Austrian troops to march inside of Germany as well.

When Hitler himself comes to visit the land of his youth, he is given a hero's welcome by the frenzied Austrian crowds. Not surprisingly, the western Globo-Zionist media portray the joyful unification as "Germany conquers Austria."

Happy Austrians turn out to welcome Hitler, their hometown boy. Image #4, Hitler lays a wreath at the gravesite of his parents.

Lord Beaverbrook is the top newspaper mogul in Great Britain. His *Daily Express* is the most widely read newspaper in the world. During World War I, he served as UK's Minister of Information.

In a *private letter* written in 1938, Lord Beaverbrook voices concern over Jewish influence leading the UK towards war with Germany. He writes:

"There are 20,000 German Jews in England – in the professions, pursuing research. They all work against an accommodation with Germany." **(23)**

In a subsequent letter he adds:

"The Jews have got a big position in the press here. ... At last I am shaken. The Jews may drive us into war." **(24)**

Lord Beaverbrook was a big name media player. In private letters, he wrote what he would not dare say publicly.

MARCH, 1938
THE MILITARY DICTATORSHIP OF POLAND STRONG-ARMS LITHUANIA AND INVADES CZECH TERRITORY

Poland's **Marshal Rydz-Smigly** issues an ultimatum to the tiny Baltic State of Lithuania. Lithuania had refused to have diplomatic relations with Poland after 1920, protesting the annexation of the Vilnius Region by the new Polish state. The ultimatum demands that Lithuania unconditionally agree to establish diplomatic ties with Poland within 48 hours. The establishment of diplomatic relations would mean a renunciation of Lithuanian claims to the region containing its historic capital, Vilnius.

Tiny Lithuania, preferring peace to war, accepts bully-boy Smigly's ultimatum and conditions. Had Lithuania stood firm, it's quite possible that Stalin would have used the ensuing war as pretext to take the Baltic States *(which he eventually will in 1940)* and start the 2nd Polish-Soviet war. Such is the recklessness of Marshal Rydz-Smigly of Poland. Many in the "democratic" West, including the New York Times, express dismay over Poland's militaristic bullying of Lithuania; a development deemed so dangerous that it causes jitters among Wall Street investors. **(25)**

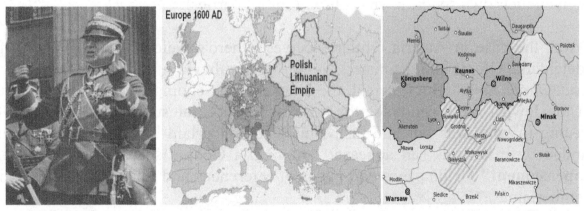

1 & 2- The megalomaniac Smigly dreams of restoring the old Polish Empire from centuries past.

3 – Tiny Lithuania is Poland's first victim of bullying.

SEPTEMBER, 1938
THE MUNICH CONFERENCE / SUDETENLAND IS REUNITED WITH GERMANY

When the Treaty of Versailles dismantled Austria-Hungary, it combined Czechs, Slovaks, Germans and Hungarians into an artificial state called "Czechoslovakia". The German region *(Sudetenland)*, lies south of Germany and has 3.5 million inhabitants. Like the Austrians, The Sudetenlanders also wish to unite with the Reich; but Czechoslovakia's pro-Communist President, **Edvard Benes**, will not allow it. The Sudetenlanders are politically disenfranchised and severely mistreated by the Globalist-owned state of Czechoslovakia. **The role assigned to Benes is to pick a fight with Hitler; a fight which will draw in the UK, France and the USSR.**

To resolve the matter peacefully, Hitler calls for an emergency conference in Munich with England, France, and Italy. The parties agree that the German Sudetenland should rightfully be a part of Germany, and that the Slovaks will have their own state **(Slovak Republic 1939-1945)**. As the artificial Czechoslovakian state is dissolved, Germany establishes autonomous protectorates over what remains **(Bohemia and Moravia)**. Again, **without a shot being fired or a drop of blood being shed,** Germans are welcomed into the Reich while other ethnic groups are given their own states; a win-win-win for all parties!

As was the case in Austria, Hitler receives a hero's welcome upon visiting the Sudetenland. UK Prime Minister **Neville Chamberlain** applauds the deal as *"peace in our time."* But his rival, the drunken cigar chomping Winston Churchill, and the Jewish Press denounce the deal as "Hitler's latest conquest". Simply for agreeing to what was fair and just, Neville Chamberlain has since been unfairly branded by history as "an appeaser". In fact, a Google search of just the term **"appeasement"** yields pages and pages of references and images to poor Neville Chamberlain!

For his part, Benes relocates to Britain and becomes part of Churchill's circle. After the war, he will again serve as President of the Communist-dominated government of a reconstituted Czechoslovakia; using his position to confiscate the property of three million Germans.

Very happy Sudetenland women salute Hitler. Women often wept at the sight of Hitler. In western versions of this photo, the two women on the left are cut out so as to make it seem that the woman on the right is crying tears of sadness.

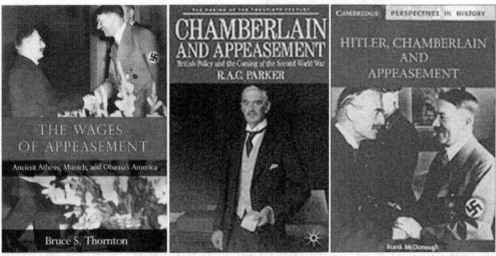

The eternal stupidity of the "Neville Chamberlain appeased Hitler" lie has been enshrined in false history.

Benes with Churchill / Benes with Stalin

The Polish regime continues its aggressive foreign policy by taking advantage of the Sudetenland Crisis and demanding a portion of Zaolzie and some other smaller Czech areas. The Czechs are powerless to stop the forced annexations.

The Polish Army annexes areas with a population of 227,399 people. Again, the "democratic" West shakes its head in dismay, but has to hold its nose and bite its tongue because it was understood that the fool Rydz-Smigly and his gang would be needed for bigger things; namely, picking a fight with Hitler's Germany.

Polish tanks roll into annexed Czech territory. The Czechs join the Lithuanians as the latest victims of Polish bullying. 'Emperor' Smigly will soon set his sights on grabbing territory from German Prussia.

NOVEMBER, 1938
AMERICA TURNS AGAINST FDR / DEMOCRATS LOSE 80 SEATS IN MID-TERM CONGRESSIONAL ELECTIONS

Anger over the failed court-packing scheme coupled with the failure of the New Deal to end the Depression contributes to the Democrats losing 80 Congressional seats in the 1938 mid-term election. FDR is not only losing America, but even many in his Party are turning against his policies; most notably the former New York Governor, Al Smith. Apart from the dictatorial aspects of FDR's regime, the Keynesian economic tax-spend-borrow schemes themselves aren't working.

The Republicans gain 80 House seats, 8 Senate seats, and 11 Governorships. Though it remains one of the worse Congressional election routs in U.S. history, the 1938 anti-FDR , anti-New Deal bloodbath is seldom, if ever, mentioned by Roosveltian court-historians and the media.

No longer "untouchable", FDR's failed schemes had become the butt of many jokes and creative cartoons.

NOVEMBER 9, 1938
KRISTALLNACHT / JEWISH KILLER MURDERS GERMAN DIPLOMAT / ANTI-JEWISH RIOTS ERUPT

Ernst vom Rath is a 29 year old German diplomat stationed in Paris. In a repeat of how Swiss Jew David Frankfurter had asked to speak to Swiss NSDAP head Wilhelm Gustloff before killing him in 1936, a Polish Jew named **Hershel Grynspan** arrives at the German embassy, asking to speak to a member of the diplomatic staff. When vom Rath comes to greet the visitor, Grynspan draws his pistol and murders him in cold blood.

By now, the Germans have had enough of the Jewish inspired boycotts, slanders, warmongering, and *murders* aimed at them. News of the murder triggers rioting, arson, and vandalism directed at Jewish shops and businesses. It is an angry **Hitler who orders the violence to cease immediately and it stops after the first night.**

The night of violence, referred to by Jews as "Kristallnacht" *(Night of the Broken Glass)*, is hyped by the western media. Kristallnacht is still whined about to this

299

day. But the repeated agitation boycotts, and murders which provoked German resentment are never mentioned.

A senseless murder; young Ernst (left) and his killer Hershel Grynspan

1939
H.G. WELLS PUBLISHES 'THE NEW WORLD ORDER'

British writer **H.G. Wells** is best known for classic works like 'The Invisible Man', 'Time Machine', and 'War of the Worlds.' In 1939, Wells, a member of the Globalist Fabian Society, releases a non-fiction book, **The New World Order;** which compliments his earlier work on the same subject, **'The Open Conspiracy'.** Unlike most Globalists, Wells speaks *openly* about his utopian dream. Some excerpts:

"This new and complete Revolution we contemplate can be defined in a very few words. ***It is outright world-socialism;*** *scientifically planned and directed."*...

Countless people will hate the new world order and will die protesting against it. *When we attempt to evaluate its promise, we have to bear in mind the distress of a generation or so of malcontents. ......The term Internationalism has been popularized in recent years to cover an interlocking financial, political,* *and economic world force for the purpose of establishing a* **World Government."** (26)

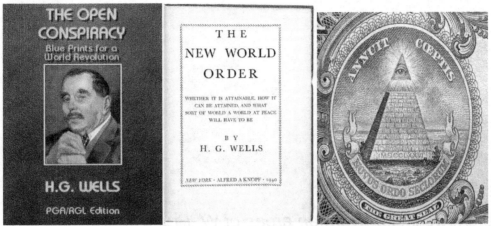

Fabian member Wells: "Countless people will die."

The "free city" of Danzig is 95% German. Along with its surrounding German area of East Prussia, Danzig was isolated from the German mainland by the Versailles Treaty. Formerly German territory now belongs to Poland, cutting right through the Prussian/Pomeranian region of Germany. As had been the case with Germans stranded in Czechoslovakia, the Germans in Poland *(those not brutally expelled in 1919)* are a persecuted minority.

Throughout all of 1939, Hitler tries to solve the problem of the **"Polish Corridor"** peacefully. He proposes that the people living in Danzig and the "corridor" be permitted to vote in a referendum to decide their status. If the region returns to German sovereignty, Poland will be given a 1 mile wide path, running through Germany to the Baltic Sea so that it would not be landlocked.

The Polish military dictatorship of Edward Rydz-Smigly and friends is urged by Britain and, from behind the scenes and across the ocean, Roosevelt, to not make any deals with Germany. (27) When it becomes apparent to Hitler that Poland will not allow a referendum, he then proposes another solution – international control of the formerly German regions. This sensible offer is also ignored. The Globalists intend to use foolish Poland as the match which ignites World War II.

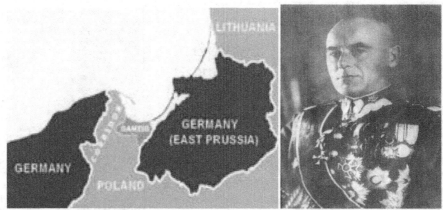

Map shows stolen German areas of W. Prussia, "free" Danzig, and E. Prussia isolated from the rest of Germany. Polish Marshal Rydz-Smigly wants Danzig and all of Prussia.

MAY, 1939
AS GERMANY TURNS TO THE VATICAN FOR PEACE, BRITAIN APPEALS TO STALIN FOR A WAR ALLIANCE

The warmongering faction of Great Britain continues to press for war with Germany. **The war-hawks are openly threatening to dump Neville Chamberlain if he refuses to deliver. (28)** Having failed to ignite the war in Czechoslovakia, the warmonger's "Plan B' is to draw Stalin into a war alliance with Britain and France; and to then use Poland to start a war with Germany. After Poland picks the fight, the western allies will attack Germany from the west as the Soviets advance from the east; an exact replay of how they imposed a two-front war on Germany 25 years ago.

Britain assures Stalin that in case of war, the USSR would not be expected to join until the British and French are in it first. But Stalin is hesitant to join the alliance at this time because he has plans of his own. Hitler is well aware of the plots being cooked up against Germany. **While the British *openly* court Stalin, Germany reaches out to Pope Pius XII – quite a contrast!** The Vatican offers to mediate an international conference between Germany, Poland and the western powers. Germany and Italy are all in, but Britain refuses the Vatican's offer. **(29)**

Excerpts from the May 11, 1939 issue of The New York Times:

British Assurance Given
By Robert P. Post

"The position as it stands now is ....that Russia has been assured that she is not being maneuvered into a position to fight alone and the British are awaiting her reply and any demands she may make to assure that her conditions will be fulfilled.

The note of cautious optimism continued here about the Russian negotiations, the belief being that the two countries are not so far apart as they first appeared to be. **The British are now expected to make certain concessions to the Russian idea of an alliance.**

The negotiations with Russia are having repercussions on the British reaction to **the Pope's conference proposal.** At the present stage the British are reluctant to take part in any such conference with Russia eliminated."

Demand for Soviet Pact Rises
By Sir Arthur Willert
Noted British Journalist

"LONDON, May 10. - The general British reaction on the feasibility of an international conference to smooth out the troubles of Europe is somewhat lukewarm. This applies to reports that the Vatican has put out feelers regarding the possibility of international action for the settlement of the German-Polish problems.

The predominant opinion here is that if a conference were held at this juncture, the Rome-Berlin Axis powers would try to vitiate it by the same intolerable pressure of fear and menace that Chancellor Adolf Hitler so successfully brought to bear on the Munich meeting.

... This view accounts for **the constant sniping at Prime Minister Neville Chamberlain**, from his own supporters in Parliament, as well as from the Opposition parties, on the ground that he is not pushing ahead effectively with the Russian negotiations."

When Adolf Hitler turned to the Pope for peace; "John Bull" turned to Joe Stalin for war!

Contrary to historical distortion, ex-altar boy Hitler enjoyed excellent relations with the Catholic Church, an institution which he viewed as vital to public virtue and world stability.

AUGUST, 1939
JEWISH MAD SCIENTIST ALBERT EINSTEIN ASKS FDR TO BUILD ATOMIC BOMBS

Jewish scientist **Albert Einstein** had left Germany shortly after Hitler came to power. Though dismissed by scientific great Nikola Tesla as a "long haired crank" *(in private letters)*, Einstein had achieved world fame in the press for his "Theory of Relativity", which some researchers now claim was plagiarized from the work of an Italian physicist. **(30)** Einstein is an outspoken advocate of world government and is linked to numerous Communist front groups in Germany.

While Europe is still at peace, Einstein *(at the urging of lesser known Jewish scientists)* writes **a letter to FDR** in which he describes the power of a potential atomic bomb. He falsely insinuates that Germany is already working on such a weapon, and urges FDR to fund research into building atomic bombs. Though not stated so directly in the letter, it is clear that **Mr. Einstein hopes to one day murder millions of Germans with this devilish weapon.** The 'Manhattan Project' will eventually grow out of this effort.

Time's "Person of the Century" & Leo Szilard issued a libelous letter to FDR. The genocidal physicist will later write, in 1942:

"Due to their wretched traditions the Germans are such a badly messed-up people *that it will be very difficult to remedy the situation by sensible, not to speak of humane, means. I keep hoping that at the end of the war, with* God's benevolent help; they will largely kill each other off.*"* **(31)**

End of Volume 1

Be sure to bookmark and follow King's popular website: **TomatoBubble.com**

The Mind-Altering Internet Classics of Alternative History, Economics, Philosophy and Current Events

BIBLIOGRAPHY

(For Both Volumes)

Proofs of a Conspiracy, by John Robison / World Revolution, by Nesta Webster / Secret Societies & Subversive Movements, by Nesta Webster / The Hidden Tyranny, by Benjamin Freedman

Hitler's War, by David Irving / Churchill's War by David Irving / Hitler: Born at Versailles Leon DeGrelle / Mein Side of the Story, by M S King & Hitler

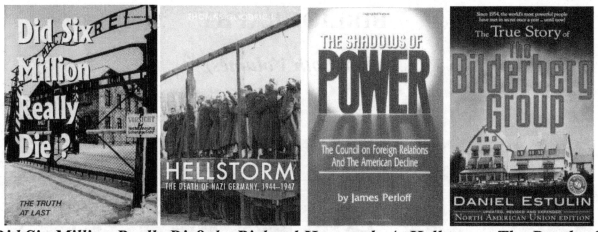

Did Six Million Really Die?, by Richard Harwood / Hellstorm: The Death of Nazi Germany / The Shadows of Power, by James Perloff / The True Story of the Bilderberg Group, by Daniel Estulin

The Fight for America, by Joseph McCarthy / America's Retreat from Victory, by Joseph McCarthy / Blacklisted by History, by M Stanton Evans / The Rockefeller File, by Gary Allen

The Politician, by Robert Welch   /   The Creature from Jekyll Island, by G Edward Griffin   /   Final Judgment, by Michael Collins Piper   /   Stranger than Fiction, by Albert D. Pastore

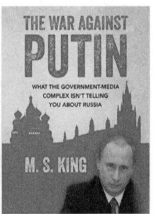

9/11 Synthetic Terror, by Webster Griffin Tarpley   / Obama: The Postmodern Coup, by Webster Griffin Tarpley   /   Darkness at Dawn, by David Satter   / The War Against Putin, by M S King   /

310

FOOTNOTES

The innovative use of Internet Search terms in lieu of the traditional format for footnotes allows the researcher to instantaneously link to numerous sources instead of just one. The reader is encouraged to explore the footnote searches in depth. Not only will one find that the research, events and quotes presented in this book are accurate, but the searches will also open up new avenues of exploration.

1763 - 1820

1- Internet Search Term: rothschild richest family world history

2- Internet Search Term: fortune magazine Rothschild a founding father international finance

3- Internet Search Term: sons of liberty boston massacre

4- Internet Search Term: declaration of independence

5- Internet Search Term: haym salomon

6- Internet Search Term: haym salomon wanted nothing for himself but something for his people

7- Internet Search Term: alexander hamilton jewish school

8- Internet Search Term: jefferson banking establishments are more dangerous armies

9- Internet Search Term: john adams impatient artful indefatigable and unprincipled intriguer

10- Internet Search Term: washington farewell address

11- Internet Search Term: Robison proofs conspiracy an association has been formed

12- Internet Search Term: abbe barruel

13- Internet Search Term: washington not my intention to doubt that doctrines of the illuminati

14- Internet Search Term: napoleon deist

15- Internet Search Term: napoleon when a government is dependent upon bankers for money

16- Internet Search Term: boisrong-tonnere we should have the skin of a white man

17- Internet Search Term: massacre haiti 1804

18- Internet Search Term: napoleon battle austerlitz is the finest of all I have fought

19- Internet Search Term: berel wein napoleon's outward tolerance and fairness toward jews

20- Internet Search Term: napoleon necessary to reduce destroy, the tendency of jewish people

21- Internet Search Term: i have undertaken to reform the jews

22- Internet Search Term: spencer perceval the evangelical prime minister page 177

23- Internet Search Term: http://www.jewishhistory.org/the-1850s/

24- Internet Search Term: naploleon most terrible of all my battles

25- Internet Search Term: napoleon grand armee typhus russia

26- Internet Search Term: napoleon here i am kill your emperor if you wish

1821 - 1880

1- Internet Search Term: citation needed – andrew jackson you are a den of vipers and theives

2- Internet Search Term: andrew jackson national debt is a national blessing, but rather a curse

3- Internet Search Term: richard lawrence money will be more plenty

4- Internet Search Term: andrew jackson I killed the bank

5- Internet Search Term: sidonia "there is no friendship between the Court of St. Petersburg

6- Internet Search Term: sidonia great intellectual movement in Europe Jews participate

7- Internet Search Term: sidonia the mixed persecuting race disappears

8- Internet Search Term: sidonia so you see my dear coningsby

9- Internet Search Term: queen victoria assassination attempts

10- Internet Search Term: rothschild crimean war

11- Internet Search Term: marx darwin's work suits my purpose

12- Internet Search Term: engels darwin, by the way, whom i'm just reading now

13- Internet Search Term: marx book contains the basis on natural history for our view

14- Internet Search Term: marx darwin's work is most important and suits my purpose

15- Internet Search Term: marx i am amused at darwin into whom ilooked again

16- Internet Search Term: marx in his splendid work darwin did not realize

17- Internet Search Term: we spoke of nothing else for months but darwin

18- Internet Search Term: lincoln provoked fort sumter

19- Internet Search Term: lewis reed radical republicans and allies American Jacobins

20- Internet Search Term: august belmont rothschilds

21- Internet Search Term: erlanger loan confederacy

22- Internet Search Term: new york times a rothschild on the rebel loan

23- Internet Search Term: robert e lee both sides forget that we are all Americans

24- Internet Search Term: davis's pet jew judah benjamin

25- Internet Search Term: judah benjamin brilliance recognized salomon rothschild

26- Internet Search Term: eli evans judah benjamin achieved greater political power any jew

27- Internet Search Term: curran judah philip benjamin must be bracketed with disraeli

28- Internet Search Term: stonewall jackson threatens to resign judah benjamin

29- Internet Search Term: davis's pet jew judah benjamin

30- Internet Search Term: solomon rothschild judah benjamin greatest mind in north America

31- Internet Search Term: casualties battle gettysburg

32- Internet Search Term: copperheads civil war british

33- Internet Search Term: belmont's confederate bonds chicago tribune

34- Internet Search Term: judah benjamin burns papers confederate secret service

35- Internet Search Term: sultana sinking 1865

36- Internet Search Term: robert louden coal torpedo

37- Internet Search Term: william davis pragmatic Secretary State never had intention returning

38- Internet Search Term: judah benjamin escape to the farthest place from the united states

39- Internet Search Term: end of an era john wise judah benjamin last year's nest

40- Internet Search Term: bismarck jews citizenship

41- Internet Search Term: cyprus disraeli congress berlin

42- Internet Search Term: congress of berlin disraeli austria hungary

43- Internet Search Term: disraeli destroy three emperors league / disraeli hatred of Russia

44- Internet Search Term: to clear central asia of muscovites

1881 - 1910

1- Internet Search Term: james garfield whoever controls the volume of money

2- Internet Search Term: emma lazarus give me your tired

3- Internet Search Term: panic 1893 j p morgan agent of rothschild

4- Internet Search Term: hasia diner notes some populists believed that Jews made up a class

5- Internet Search Term: franco russian alliance tolstoy people sudden love

6- Internet Search Term: tolstoy franco russian alliance cannot now present itself

7- Internet Search Term: marie carnot order of st andrew

8- Internet Search Term: it is arguable that spanish-american war perhaps most pointless war

9- Internet Search Term: roosevelt i would regard war with spain from two viewpoints

10- Internet Search Term: bismarck so long as you have this present officer corps

11- Internet Search Term: bismarck damned foolish thing in the balkans

12- Internet Search Term: mckinley pope spanish american war

13- Internet Search Term: buffalo soldiers spanish smerican war

14- Internet Search Term: teddy roosevelt only way to get them to do it was to lead them myself

15- Internet Search Term: teddy roosevelt's request for medal of honor was denied by the army
16- Internet Search Term: teddy roosevelt i am entitled to the medal of honor and I want it

17- Internet Search Term: teddy speak softly big stick

18- Internet Search Term: oppenheimer and rothschild

19- Internet Search Term: phillipine american war casualties

20- Internet Search Term: teddy Roosevelt panama revolution colombia

21- Internet Search Term: von longerke jews furnished the brains

22- Internet Search Term: freud smoked cigars

23- Internet Search Term: robert owen the panic was brought about by a deliberate conspiracy

24- Internet Search Term: schiff 1907 unless we have central bank with control credit resources

25- Internet Search Term: mark twain quotes about teddy roosevelt

26- Internet Search Term: ibid

27- Internet Search Term: ibid

28- Internet Search Term: ibid

29- Internet Search Term: teddy roosevelt safari

30- Internet Search Term: ibid

31- Internet Search Term: mark twain he is hunting wild animals heroically in africa

32- Internet Search Term: commodus was also known for fighting exotic animals

33- Internet Search Term: baruch wilson in tow leading him like poodle

34- Internet Search Term: james warburg united world federalists

35- Internet Search Term: naacp jewish founders

36- Internet Search Term: lloyd george nathan rothschild most powerful man in Britain

37- Internet Search Term: the melting pot teddy roosevelt that's a great play mr Zangwill

38- Internet Search Term: benjamin freedman 1974 speech jacob schiff came back to new York

39- Internet Search Term: teddy roosevelt riding bull moose photo fake

40- Internet Search Term: secret meeting at jekyll island vanderlip quote furtive conspirator

1911 – 1920

1- Internet Search Term: taft progressives pull down temple of freedom
2- Internet Search Term: the speech that saved teddy roosevelt's life assassination attempt 1912
3- Internet Search Term: ibid
4- Internet Search Term: ibid
5- Internet Search Term: ibid

6- Internet Search Term: john schrank letter people of united states in a dream
7- Internet Search Term: lindbergh the aldrich plan is the wall street plan
8- Internet Search Term: adl charter the immediate object of the league
9- Internet Search Term: lindbergh worst legislative crime of the ages
10- Internet Search Term: lindbergh financial system been turned over to federal reserve board

11- Internet Search Term: ynet obama mulls naming jewish economist secretary of treasury

12- Internet Search Term: franz ferdinand don't die darling live for our children

13- Internet Search Term: willy nicki telegrams

14- Internet Search Term: ibid

15- Internet Search Term: manifesto of the 93

16- Internet Search Term: edward mandell house flame of indignation lusitania

17- Internet Search Term: secrets of Lusitania arms find challenges allied claims

18- Internet Search Term: lusitania german embassy publishes warnings in newspapers

19- Internet Search Term: winston churchill juno Lusitania

20- Internet Search Term: benjamin freedman speaks balfour declaration

21- Internet Search Term: Trotsky financed by Schiff wall street

22- Internet Search Term: bernays intelligent manipulation habits and opinions

23- Internet Search Term: balfour declaration

24- Internet Search Term: schiff distribution of propaganda among Russians prisoners-of-war

25- Internet Search Term: david r francis bolshevik leaders here are returned exiles
26- Internet Search Term: wilson speech analyzing german peace utterances

27- Internet Search Term: german factory strikes 1918

28- Internet Search Term: - jewish legion world war 1
29- Internet Search Term: balfour british drop yiddish leaflets germany

30- Internet Search Term: comintern overthrow of the international bourgeoisie

31- Internet Search Term: red terror atrocities

32- Internet Search Term: treaty of versailles   provisions

33- Internet Search Term: german hunger blockade after world war 1
34- Internet Search Term: palmer raids
35- Internet Search Term: churchill zionism vs bolshevism

1921 - 1930

1- Internet Search Term: harding inaugural address seek no part directing destinies of old World
2- Internet Search Term: mussolini fraud comedy blackmail
3- Internet Search Term: harding no autopsy
4- Internet Search Term: wiemar jew confetti
5- Internet Search Term: solzhenitsyn bolshevism committed greatest human slaughter
6- Internet Search Term: lloyd george imperiousness of absolute monarchs
7- Internet Search Term: sarnoff communications psychological warfare
8- Internet Search Term: william paley psychological warfare
9- Internet Search Term: stalin one death tragedy million statistic
10- Internet Search Term: greenspan fed caused great depression
11- Internet Search Term: degrelle enigma hitler

1931 - 1939

1- Internet Search Term: bruno hauptmann I am absolutely innocent
2- Internet Search Term: louis mcfadden fed was deceitfully disloyally foisted upon country
3- Internet Search Term: judea declares war on germany
4- Internet Search Term: hitler lies slander hair raising perversity
5- Internet Search Term: executive order 6102 bans gold fdr
6- Internet Search Term: eugene meyer fires quaker editor
7- Internet Search Term: potocki propaganda here entirely in Jewish hands
8- Internet Search Term: jacob maged tailor arrested new jersey
9- Internet Search Term: huey long what's morgan and baruch and rockefeller
10- Internet Search Term: fdr andrew mellon irs
11- Internet Search Term: david burnham records show that Franklin Delano Roosevelt may
12- Internet Search Term: churchill strand magazine truth about hitler 1935
13- Internet Search Term: ibid
14- Internet Search Term: hitler tackled unemployment revived germany economy
15- Internet Search Term: lloyd george i talked to hitler
16- Internet Search Term: new york times americans appeal for jewish refuge
17- Internet Search Term: jesse owens hitler waved at me
18- Internet Search Term: jesse owens hitler didn't snub me
19- Internet Search Term: hitler edward abdication was a severe loss for us
20- Internet Search Term: anti comintern pact
21- Internet Search Term: rape nanking fake photos
22- Internet Search Term: 99% support anschluss
23- Internet Search Term: beaverbrook 20,000 german jews in england
24- Internet Search Term: beaverbrook i am shaken jews drive us into war
25- Internet Search Term: 1938 polish ultimatum to lithuania
26- Internet Search Term: hg wells countless people hate new world order
27- Internet Search Term: roosevelt's campaign to incite war in Europe polish documents
28- Internet Search Term: new york times may 11 1939 arthur willet demand for soviet pact rises

29- Internet Search Term: ibid
30- Internet Search Term: einstein plagiarist italian de pretto
31- Internet Search Term: einstein at the end of the war they will largely kill each other off

CPSIA information can be obtained
at www.ICGtesting.com
Printed in the USA
LVOW03s1935250416

485241LV00007B/42/P